T0309064

DEVELOPING THE INTUITIVE EXECUTIVE

USING ANALYTICS AND INTUITION FOR SUCCESS

DEVELOPING THE INTUITIVE EXECUTIVE

USING ANALYTICS AND INTUITION FOR SUCCESS

Edited by Jay Liebowitz

CRC Press
Taylor & Francis Group

Boca Raton and London

First edition published 2023
by CRC Press
6000 Broken Sound Parkway NW, Suite 300, Boca Raton, FL 33487-2742
and by CRC Press
4 Park Square, Milton Park, Abingdon, Oxon, OX14 4RN

CRC Press is an imprint of Taylor & Francis Group, LLC

© 2024 selection and editorial matter, Jay Liebowitz

Reasonable efforts have been made to publish reliable data and information, but the author and publisher cannot assume responsibility for the validity of all materials or the consequences of their use. The authors and publishers have attempted to trace the copyright holders of all material reproduced in this publication and apologize to copyright holders if permission to publish in this form has not been obtained. If any copyright material has not been acknowledged, please write and let us know so we may rectify in any future reprint.

Except as permitted under U.S. Copyright Law, no part of this book may be reprinted, reproduced, transmitted, or utilized in any form by any electronic, mechanical, or other means, now known or hereafter invented, including photocopying, microfilming, and recording, or in any information storage or retrieval system, without written permission from the publishers.

For permission to photocopy or use material electronically from this work, access www.copyright.com or contact the Copyright Clearance Center, Inc. (CCC), 222 Rosewood Drive, Danvers, MA 01923, 978-750-8400. For works that are not available on CCC, please contact mpkbookspermissions@tandf.co.uk

Trademark notice: Product or corporate names may be trademarks or registered trademarks and are used only for identification and explanation without intent to infringe.

Library of Congress Cataloging-in-Publication Data
A catalog record for this title has been requested.

ISBN: 978-1-032-49821-8 (hbk)
ISBN: 978-1-032-49820-1 (pbk)
ISBN: 978-1-032-61718-3 (ebk)

DOI: 10.1201/9781032617183

Typeset in Adobe Garamond Pro, Avenir LT Pro
by DerryField Publishing Services

Trademarks Used in This Book

Amazon is a registered trademark of Amazon Technologies, Inc.
Google is a registered trademark of Google LLC.
L'Oreal is a registered trademark of L'Oreal.
MidJourney is a trademark (pending) of MidJourney, Inc.
Viper is a registered trademark of FCA US LLC.

Contents

List of Figures and Tables

List of Contributors

Itai Adler
Hebrew University of Jerusalem and Hadassah Medical Center, Israel

Cinla Akinci
University of St. Andrews, UK

Radu Atanasiu
Bucharest International School of Management, Romania; and Vrije Universiteit, The Netherlands

Fatih Cetin
Baskent University, Turkey

Daniela Dumitru
Bucharest University of Economic Studies, Romania

Katharina Fellnhofer
Swiss Federal Institute of Technology Zuerich, Switzerland; and Harvard University, US

Gabriela Paula Florea
University of Bucharest, Romania

Leonie Hallo
The University of Adelaide, Australia

Li-Jun Ji
Queen's University, Canada

Svetlana N. Khapova
Vrije Universiteit Amsterdam, The Netherlands

Paul Knott
University of Canterbury, New Zealand

Markus Launer
Ostfalia University of Applied Sciences, Germany

Peter Magnusson
CTF and Karlstad University, Sweden

Mihaela Minciu
Bucharest University of Economic Studies, Romania

Johan Netz
CTF and Karlstad University, Sweden

Tiep Nguyen
International University, Vietnam; and Vietnam National University, Vietnam

Lars Olsson
CTF and Karlstad University, Sweden

Joanna Paliszkiewicz
Warsaw University of Life Scienes, Poland

Eugene Sadler-Smith
University of Surrey, U.K.

Chaudron Carter Short
Temple University Health System and
Temple University Hospital Inc., US

Anttii Sihvonen
Jyväskylä University, Finland

Marta Sinclair
Griffith Business School, Griffith
University, Brisbane, Australia

Alexandre Sukhov
CTF and Karlstad University, Sweden

Richard Szanto
Corvinus University of Budapest,
Hungary

Ioannis Thanos
Athens University of Economics and
Business, Greece

Christian Walsh
University of Canterbury, New
Zealand

Christopher Wickert
Vrije Universiteit Amsterdam, The
Netherlands

Haili Wu
Xi'an Jiaotong-Liverpool University,
China; and University College
London, UK

About the Editor

Dr. Jay Liebowitz has recently served as the inaugural Executive-in-Residence for Public Service at Columbia University's Data Science Institute. He was previously a Visiting Professor in the Stillman School of Business and the MS-Business Analytics Capstone & Co-Program Director (External Relations) at Seton Hall University.

Dr. Liebowitz previously served as the Distinguished Chair of Applied Business and Finance at Harrisburg University of Science and Technology. Before HU, he was the Orkand Endowed Chair of Management and Technology in the Graduate School at the University of Maryland University College (UMUC). He served as a Full Professor in the Carey Business School at Johns Hopkins University.

Dr. Liebowitz was ranked one of the top 10 knowledge management researchers/practitioners out of 11,000 worldwide, and was ranked #2 in KM Strategy worldwide, according to the January 2010 *Journal of Knowledge Management*. At Johns Hopkins University, he was the founding Program Director for the Graduate Certificate in Competitive Intelligence and the Capstone Director of the MS-Information and Telecommunications Systems for Business Program, where he engaged over 30 organizations in industry, government, and not-for-profits in capstone projects.

Prior to joining Hopkins, Dr. Liebowitz was the first Knowledge Management Officer at NASA Goddard Space Flight Center. Before NASA, Dr. Liebowitz was the Robert W. Deutsch Distinguished Professor of Information Systems at the University of Maryland-Baltimore County, Professor of Management Science at George Washington University, and Chair of Artificial Intelligence at the U.S. Army War College.

Dr. Liebowitz is the Founding Editor-in-Chief of *Expert Systems With Applications: An International Journal* (published by Elsevier, ranked as a top-tier journal; Thomson Impact Factor from June 2021 is 8.665). He is a Fulbright Scholar,

IEEE-USA Federal Communications Commission Executive Fellow, and Computer Educator of the Year (International Association for Computer Information Systems).

Dr. Liebowitz has published over 45 books and myriad journal articles on knowledge management, analytics, financial literacy, intelligent systems, and IT management and served as the Editor-in-Chief of *Procedia-CS* (Elsevier). He is also the Series Book Editor of the *Data Analytics Applications* book series (Taylor & Francis) as well as the Series Book Editor of the new *Digital Transformation: Accelerating Organizational Intelligence* book series (World Scientific Publishing).

In October 2011, the International Association for Computer Information Systems named the "Jay Liebowitz Outstanding Student Research Award" for the best student research paper at the IACIS Annual Conference. Dr. Liebowitz was the Fulbright Visiting Research Chair in Business at Queen's University for the Summer 2017 and a Fulbright Specialist at Dalarna University in Sweden in May 2019. He is in the Top 2 percent of the top scientists in the world, according to a 2019 Stanford Study.

As of 2021, he is the Visiting Distinguished Professor at the International School for Social and Business Studies in Slovenia. His recent books are: *Data Analytics and AI* (Taylor & Francis, 2021), *The Business of Pandemics: The COVID-19 Story* (Taylor & Francis, 2021), *A Research Agenda for Knowledge Management and Analytics* (Elgar Publishers, 2021), *Online Learning Analytics* (Taylor & Francis, 2022), *Digital Transformation for the University of the Future* (World Scientific, 2022), and *Cryptocurrency Concepts, Technology, and Applications* (Taylor & Francis, April 2023). He has lectured and consulted worldwide.

Preface

The leading traits of executives often include creativity and innovation. Research shows that intuition can significantly contribute to these areas. Developing intuitive executives and honing one's intuition, coupled with the ability to apply data and evidence to inform decision making, is the focus of this book.

Some researchers call the complement of applying data analytics to intuition as *quantitative intuition, rational intuition,* or *informed intuition.* Certainly, in our data-driven environment, analytics play a key role in executive decision-making. However, we shouldn't discount an executive's many years of experiential learning as part of the equation. Learning from both failures and successes can help fine-tune one's intuitive awareness—what I call *intuition-based decision-making.* Research also shows that many executives don't trust the internal data quality in their organizations, and so they rely on their intuition versus strictly on the data.

I am proud and fortunate to include the work of the leading researchers worldwide in intuition in the management/executive domain. Their chapters present the key issues, trends, concepts, techniques, and opportunities for applying intuition as part of the executive decision-making process.

I am also thankful to my Taylor & Francis colleagues, most notably John Wyzalek and Stephanie Place, for having the foresight to publish books on this topic, as well as publishing a host of other books in my Data Analytics Applications book series. I am also very appreciative to Theron Shreve and Susan Culligan at DerryField Publishing Services for their careful work in the production process.

In addition, I am grateful to my students and colleagues over the many years who have provided some interesting "food for thought" as we discussed the nuances of this topic.

And certainly, without the wonderful support of my family, none of this would be possible.

I have a "feeling" you will enjoy this book!

Jay Liebowitz, D.Sc.
Medford, MA

Chapter 1

The Intuitive Executive Revisited

Cinla Akinci[1] and Eugene Sadler-Smith[2]

[1]University of St. Andrews, UK; [2]University of Surrey, UK

Introduction

Two decades ago, Sadler-Smith and Shefy (2004) published an article in the journal *Academy of Management Executive* (now *Academy of Management Perspectives*) entitled, 'The Intuitive Executive: Understanding and Applying "Gut Feel" in Decision-Making'. Since its publication, The Intuitive Executive has accrued 746 citations. It is the authors' most-cited work, and its popularity shows no signs of waning; its highest number of annual citations was 79 in 2021. In this chapter, we revisit The Intuitive Executive in order to do two things: first, to review briefly the main thrust of its argument; second, to explore selected issues regarding intuition in business and management that Sadler-Smith and Shefy did not discuss but which are relevant to executive intuition in the 21st century.

The Intuitive Executive

The Intuitive Executive was positioned in its Executive Overview as a response to the pre-eminence of rational decision-making models in business management. It aimed to offer '. . . guidelines whereby executives can make more effective and intelligent use of intuition in ways that acknowledge its limitations while maximising its potential in enhancing firm success in complex and fast-moving business environments' (p. 76). Sadler-Smith and Shefy were ambitious enough to define *executive intuition* in the opening words of their article: 'Executive intuition is the skill of focusing on those potentially important but sometimes faint signals that fuel imagination, creativity, and innovation and feed corporate success in globally competitive business environments' (p. 76). This was premature coming, as it did, five pages before their general, and somewhat wordy, definition of intuition itself: '. . . a form of knowing that manifests itself as an awareness of thoughts, feelings, or bodily sense connected to a deeper perception, understanding, and way of making sense of the world that may not be achieved easily or at all by other means' (p. 81).

Subsequently, Dane and Pratt (2007: 40) offered a more concise and theoretically coherent definition which has become the definition of choice for many researchers (including the authors of this chapter): '. . . intuitions are affectively charged judgements that arise through rapid, non-conscious and holistic associations.' Sadler-Smith and Shefy (2004) overlooked Herbert Simon's 1987 definition from the *Academy of Management Executive* in 1987: '. . . intuitions are analyses frozen into habit as the capacity for rapid response through recognition' (p. 63). Instead they referred to a 'management instinct' which is a product of 'experience and analysis *frozen* over time into familiar routines and habitual responses' (p. 82, emphasis added).

As it turns out, Simon's definition is highly germane to a fundamental distinction that Sadler-Smith and Shefy (2004) drew between *intuition-as-expertise* (essentially a brain-based or cognitive form of intuition) and *intuition-as-feeling* (essentially a body-based or sensory form of intuition) (see also Chapter 2 by Fellnhofer, Sinclair and Sadler-Smith in this volume). Since 2004, the concept of intuitive expertise or expert intuition has figured prominently in intuition research. Expert intuition was one of the four types of intuition identified subsequently by Dane and Pratt (2009) and Gore and Sadler-Smith (2011)—namely, *expert* intuition, *moral* intuition, *social* intuition and *creative* intuition.

Convincing and empirically verified accounts are now available of why and how expert intuition enables experienced decision-makers to make fast, accurate decisions in time-pressured and dynamic situations (Kahneman & Klein 2009; Klein 2017). Klein's model of recognition-primed decision-making (RPD) explains how situations generate cues which allow experienced decision-makers to recognise patterns which activate action scripts, which are then used to affect the situation. This is the intuitive part of the RPD process. In terms of dual-process theory, these recognise-and-respond processes emanate from System 1, also referred to as the *experiential system* (Epstein 1994), *the intuitive mind* (Sadler-Smith 2010) and 'Type 1 processes' (Evans 2019).

Klein also draws our attention to the analytical part of the RPD process, which is sometimes overlooked (Klein et al. 2010). In RPD, the viability of the action script is evaluated in a process of mental simulation. Klein likens this to the decision-maker fast-forwarding a DVD in their head to see if the action script will work. If it is judged to be a viable course of action, it is then implemented; if it's not judged to be viable, then the next intuitively generated option is similarly considered. This (i.e., mental simulation) is the analytical (System 2) part of the process (Klein et al. 2010).

Klein's RPD is an important theory of expert intuition and offers a convincing account of what happens when a viable action script comes to the decision-maker's mind. We referred to this as *recognition-based intuition* in our research with police officers who were involved in taking first-response decisions (see Akinci & Sadler-Smith 2020). However, in this research, we were also keen to explore what happens when a decision-maker's intuition (in the form of a 'gut feeling') 'tells' the officer that the situation is somehow not 'right' and further action is required, but no action script is immediately available to them. In this situation, we discovered that experienced police officers deploy what we called *intuition-based inquiry*. Our discovery of intuition-based inquiry provides a credible explanation for what Sadler-Smith and Shefy (2004) referred to as intuition-as-feeling, which in their words serves 'as an early warning' and provides 'feelings-based signals for or against a course of action' (p. 84). This idea resonates with a quote from one of our participants from our 2020 study: 'If something doesn't look [or feel] right then go find out why' (p. 78).

Another aspect of intuition-as-feeling that has been explored since the publication of The Intuitive Executive is the nature of the subjective experience, labelled variously as 'gut feelings', 'hunches', 'vibes', etc. (Epstein et al. 1996). Understanding intuition from the perspective of the intuitor is important in interpreting intuitions and in intuitive sensemaking (Meziani & Cabantous 2020; Sadler-Smith 2023). A novel way of approaching this topic is through the linguistic technique of *de-nominalisation*. In the case of intuition, this means taking the noun *intuition* and *de-nouning* (i.e., de-nominalising) it into the verb *intuit*.

This approach also fits well with Dane and Pratt's idea of distinguishing between the outcome, 'intuition', and the process, 'intuiting' (Dane & Pratt 2007), and with 'process philosophy' (Jeanes & Sadler-Smith 2018). In practice, be that for research or training and development purposes, this entails asking participants the question, 'What happens when you intuit?' In the form of a stem-and-completion task it becomes, 'Please complete the following statement: "When I intuit . . ."'. This technique was used by Sadler-Smith (2016) to get closer to the subjective experience of HR managers, and it is a tried-and-tested technique in educational and training settings as a means by which participants can articulate their subjective experience of intuition and hence begin to make sense of it both individually and collectively. Conceptually, this works well as the first step in an organisational learning and sensemaking process that begins with intuiting and then passes through the other three stages of a 4I model—that is, interpreting, integrating and institutionalising (Crossan et al. 1999) (see Building Collective Intuitions, below).

Many of the recommendations offered in The Intuitive Executive for how to develop executive intuition are, we would hope, as valid today as they were in 2004. They included:

1. Opening up the 'closet' by recognising and acknowledging intuition as an alternative and complement to rational ways of knowing.

2. Not mixing up insight ('seeing' a solution to a problem) and intuition ('sensing' a solution to a problem; see Sadler-Smith 2023), since insight and intuition are fundamentally different and require different sets of conditions to be used effectively in problem-solving and decision-making. This split between intuition and insight was later developed into a three-way distinction between seeing (i.e., insight), solving (i.e., analysis) and sensing (i.e., intuition) (Sadler-Smith 2023).

3. Getting good (i.e., timely and accurate) feedback as part of a 'kind' learning environment for developing better intuitions (Hogarth 2001). A kind learning environment also includes coaching and high-quality practice.

4. Getting a feel for your 'batting average' in order to get a sense for how reliable your hunches are, when they are likely to work and when they are not (see 'high-validity' versus 'low-validity' environments, Kahneman & Klein 2009) and how they can be improved.

5. Playing devil's advocate in order to stress-test your intuitive judgements as part of a reflective and interpretive process (see Crossan et al. 1999). Sadler-Smith and Shefy (2004) concluded that when intuitions are 'understood and managed effectively, they can be a powerful force in complex and fast-moving business environments and can lead to improved executive decision-making capabilities through the development of a finely tuned intuitive intelligence' (p. 89).

We now turn our attention to two aspects of intuition that were absent from The Intuitive Executive but which are especially relevant to the work of executives in a digitised and dynamic 21st-century business environment in which technology and learning are often mooted as sources of competitive advantage: first, the relationship between intuition and artificial intelligence, and second the importance of learning in building collective intuitions.

Intuition and Artificial Intelligence

In intuition research, the history of algorithms outperforming humans goes back to the 1950s, when psychologist Paul Meehl, in his book *Clinical versus Statistical Prediction* (1954), compared how well the subjective predictions of trained clinicians such as physicians, psychologists and counsellors fared when compared with predictions based on simple statistical algorithms. To many people's surprise, Meehl found that the experts' accuracy of prediction—for example, trained counsellors' predictions of college grades—was either matched or exceeded by the algorithm.

In 1997 Gary Kasparov, the reigning world chess champion, was defeated by IBM's Deep Blue. The match was highly publicised and reflected the enormous progress that had been made in the development of artificially intelligent decision-making computers. It is acknowledged widely that chess masters often play intuitively (de Groot 1978). However, the strategy that Deep Blue used to beat Kasparov was fundamentally different from how another human being might have attempted to compete with a grand master. Deep Blue did not beat Kasparov by replicating or mimicking his thinking processes; in Kasparov's own words: 'Instead of a computer that thought and played like a chess champion, with human creativity and intuition, they [the "AI crowd"] got one that played like a machine, systematically evaluating 200 million chess moves on the chess board per second and winning with brute number-crunching force.'*

If a computer ever becomes capable of out-intuiting a human, it is likely that the rules that the computer relies on will be fundamentally different to those used by humans. It will surely involve a very different mode of cognition to that which evolved in the human organism over many hundreds of millennia for the purposes of adaptation and survival (Sadler-Smith 2023).

It is not surprising that some in the technology industry have predicted the emergence of a fourth generation of AI that can analyse data and express a 'gut feeling' when something is wrong, something does not work, or something does not make sense based on 'intuition-based learning' (Softtek 2021; Tao & He 2009). It is claimed that this fourth-generation AI mirrors human intuitions by making deductions and inferences, which has been referred to variously as 'artificial intuition' (Softtek 2021; Tao & He 2009) and 'intuitive AI' (Conti 2017). These assertions raise questions about the claims being made and the potentially different understandings of the term 'intuition' in vendor versus behavioural science circles (Paydas Turan, Dörfler, & Sadler-Smith 2023).

---

* https://www.kasparov.com/a-brutal-intelligence-ai-chess-and-the-human-mind-deep-thinking-review-june-29-2017/

Moreover, it is important that intuition researchers and executives are aware of developments in this fast-moving area of the AI industry and engage in critical debates with vendors to ascertain the following: first, the extent to which what is currently on offer is in fact 'intuitive'; and second, what the prospects are for the development of an artificial intuition perhaps as *the* ultimate form of AI (Sadler-Smith 2023).

At the time of writing, much has been said in the media about the potential of 'generative AI'—that is, AI that uses unsupervised learning algorithms to create new content such as text, still or moving images, audio, etc. (Rouse 2022). GPT (short for generative pre-trained transformer) is a generative AI model created by the Microsoft-backed AI company OpenAI, which is able to generate human-like text and is seen as a breakthrough because it seems to 'understand' context better than previous approaches. GPTs are trained on large data sets and can be adapted to a wide variety of downstream tasks, including translating text and speech in near real-time, opening meetings and classrooms to diverse and hearing-impaired attendees, understanding chains of genes in DNA and amino acids in proteins to accelerate drug design, detect trends and anomalies to prevent fraud and so on (Merritt 2022).

OpenAI's ChatGPT, released in November 2022, uses a generative AI approach and transformer modelling techniques. It is based on a large language model (LLM) trained on millions of data points, including large chunks of text from books, articles, etc. ChatGPT is capable of producing 'convincing and coherent replies to questions by predicting the next plausible word in a sequence of words' (Criddle & Staton 2022). Paydas Turan, Dörfler and Sadler-Smith (2023) directly evaluated ChatGPT's 'opinion' of the possibility for artificial intuition by asking it, 'Are you [ChatGPT] intuitive?' It replied:

> As an artificial intelligence, I do not possess the ability to experience or make use of intuition in the same way that humans do. I am programmed to process and analyse information using logical and systematic methods, and to provide responses based on my knowledge and understanding of the given inputs. While I may be able to provide insights and recommendations based on my extensive database of information and my ability to process and analyse that information, I do not have the ability to experience gut feelings or make intuitive judgements in the way that humans do.

In *Mind over Machine: The Power of Human Intuition and Expertise in the Era of the Computer* (1986), philosopher Hubert Dreyfus and his engineer and applied mathematician brother Stuart Dreyfus (who together developed the highly influential Skill Acquisition Model [SAM], the highest level of which is intuitive expertise) were of the view that 'Computers as reasoning machines can't match human intuition and expertise' (p. *xvii*). The computers of the

1980s were certainly no match for human intuition; it is highly debatable whether they are able to do so in 2023, despite the claims of some vendors.

Whether this will always be the case is an open question, and making any predictions about the progress of technology in the information age is a hostage to fortune. Perhaps the acid test of whether a computer will ever be able to out-intuit a human depends on if they can be programmed and trained to match and surpass human beings' unique abilities to synthesise and sense in addition to the computer's prodigious capabilities to analyse and solve (Sadler-Smith 2023). The best of both worlds is a *hybrid intelligence,* in which human synthesising and sensing are combined with algorithmic analysing and solving (Paydas Turan & Sadler-Smith 2023) as part of a 'human-machine team' (HMT).*

Building Collective Intuitions

Despite the various developments on the topic, including explanations for the underlying cognitive and affective mechanisms of intuitive judgement (Hodgkinson et al. 2008), suggesting different types of intuition (Dane & Pratt 2009; Gore & Sadler-Smith 2011) and exploring its role in organisational performance (e.g., Khatri & Ng 2000; Sadler-Smith 2004), intuition research has yet to fully engage with the notion of collective intuition. Whilst it is acknowledged that intuiting is an individual-level process—that is, the phenomenon is a personal and highly subjective experience—in organisational settings, intuitions inevitably are articulated and interpreted collectively in team decision-making.

In prior work a number of scholars have highlighted the importance of collective intuition; however, research on the topic is still scarce and fragmented, lacking a fully developed understanding of the construct in organisational decision-making. For instance, Eisenhardt (1989; 1999) and colleagues (Eisenhardt & Martin 2000) argued that intuitions shared among senior managers are of great value to decision-making and may contribute to faster and more accurate reactions and facilitate collective learning processes (Sadler-Smith 2008).

Accordingly, experienced executives consciously attempt to build a collective intuition that allows them to move quickly and accurately in markets as opportunities arise. One feature that distinguishes effective top management teams (TMTs) from less successful ones is that the latter fail to build collective intuition. In a related study, Seifert and Hadida (2009) showed that reliance on more than one individual judgement may increase the predictive power of intuition.

---

* https://www.army.mod.uk/news-and-events/news/2022/03/army-launches-human -machine-teaming/

Our paper (Akinci and Sadler-Smith 2019) entitled, 'Collective intuition: Implications for Improved Decision Making and Organisational Learning', published in the *British Journal of Management,* makes a novel contribution for advancing research on this topic. It does so first by conceptualising and offering a definition of collective intuition, and second by shifting intuition research forward from an almost exclusive reliance on the individual level of analysis to the study of intuition at the collective level. In light of our findings, we conceptualised collective intuition as 'independently formed judgement based on domain-specific knowledge, experience and cognitive ability, shared and interpreted collectively' (p. 573). On this point we should clarify that collective intuitions are different to group intuitions in that the former presume that the same information is gleaned independently by several group members, whereas the latter refer to individual intuitions of group members related to the same question or problem that can be integrated into a collective insight or solution (Sinclair & Hamilton 2014).

Collective intuitions are powerful, difficult-to-imitate and valuable organisational cognitive resources (cf. the resource-based view of the firm, Barney 1991), as relayed to us in our research into decision-making processes within police senior management teams (Akinci & Sadler-Smith 2019). Participants drew advice and experience from other people (i.e., experts) to validate their own intuitive judgement rather than from sources of explicit information. In this respect, we observed that collective reflecting and sensemaking were both imperative for building shared meaning and understanding (Weick 1995, 2001) and integral to the development of collective intuitions.

Our conceptualisation of collective intuition extends the sensemaking and intuition literature (Meziani & Cabantous 2020)—which as noted has tended to focus on intuitive judgement principally at the individual level—into the organisational domain. Our research shed light on the collective factors which inform how groups of individuals (in TMTs) under conditions of equivocality and uncertainty construct interpretations and arrive at a course of action. In organisational settings, it is crucial that the role of experience in these processes must be conceptualised not merely as an individual-level phenomenon but collectively as well.

Sadler-Smith (2008) addressed an important question by asking, 'How might individuals' capability to make intuitive judgements be built (feed-in), surfaced, and shared so that they may contribute to the development of shared mental models (feed-forward and feedback) and even perhaps a collective intuition?' (p. 497). The cognitive perspective suggests that team members interact through communication, coordination and other processes and behaviours, and in doing so transform a collection of individual knowledge into team knowledge, resulting in effective team cognition that ultimately guides action. This is also referred to as 'dominant logic', 'shared schema' (Prahalad & Bettis 1986) or 'collective mind' (Weick & Roberts 1993) and develops as a result of the experiences and social interactions of top managers and is expressed as learned, problem-solving behaviours (Leonard, Beauvais, & Scholl 2005).

Similarly, Kline (2005) suggested that the expert team developed strong shared mental models that caused them to intuitively understand an event in relation to prior events they have experienced together. Collectively understanding the event allows each team member to independently make an intuitive judgement that is the same as his/her teammates. Collective sharing and reflecting on intuitive experiences have implications for learning from past incidents (including mistakes) and developing collective intuitions to improve future decision-making (Akinci & Sadler-Smith 2019). As such, lessons learned from previous experiences ought to be translated and used to make sense of new situations (Elliott & Macpherson 2010).

A key issue in organisational learning is capturing meaning that is experienced collectively, across the organisation, beyond individual insights (Sillence & Shipton 2013). Our evidence, in Akinci and Sadler-Smith (2019), suggests that managers' ability to interpret and make sense of their intuitive judgements individually and collectively is imperative in this respect. Tacitly held intuitions need to become explicit and openly communicated with others in order to be able to interpret, share and use them.

Collective intuitions strengthen the validity of and help to build individual intuitions. Therefore, managers should willingly voice their intuitive judgements in managerial decision-making and encourage their teams to do the same. In this way, a 'kind' as opposed to a 'wicked' environment for the learning of intuitions may be produced (Hogarth 2001). We captured how the intuitive decision-making process may develop and unfold in collective settings (as described below and in Akinci & Sadler-Smith 2019), and thereby built on to the 4I framework (Crossan et al. 1999). Furthermore, we offered a more complete picture of this organisational learning model with the identification of the additional feedforward and feedback loop processes (see Figure 1.1 on next page).

First, we identified an additional process of inquiring alongside the intuiting process, which signifies the use of both intuitive and analytical processes in decision-making. The traditional organisational learning literature posits a significant role for intuiting without due cognisance of the role of deliberating in a human information-processing system that is essentially dual in nature. Informed by dual-process theories (e.g., Epstein 1994) emanating from developments in the psychology of thinking and reasoning (Evans & Stanovich 2013) and social cognition (Lieberman 2007), we illustrated how expert intuition (rooted in domain-specific learning and experience; Salas, Rosen & DiazGranados 2010) and deliberation (i.e., rational, analytical thinking)

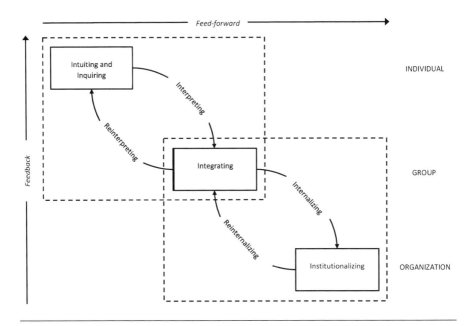

Figure 1.1   Feed-forward and feedback loop processes of organizational learning (*Source:* Akinci & Sadler-Smith [2019]. Adapted from Crossan, Lane & White [1999].)

function jointly in collective decision-making processes and affect decision-making and learning at various levels of the organisation.

Similar to our discovery of 'intuition-based inquiry' (Akinci & Sadler-Smith 2020) and in line with the view of information processing as a dual process, intuiting and inquiring (i.e., deliberating) were evident at the outset of the decision-making processes. The police officers in our study described intuitive knowing as using expertise and gut feeling (System 1); some used the term 'professional judgement' to refer to intuitive judgements arising from their domain-specific learning, knowledge and experiences in policing, consistent with the notion of expertise.

Intuition also appeared as a gut feeling that felt right or wrong, manifesting as a positively or negatively valenced affect. Furthermore, participants also formed judgements by attending to the situation more deliberately (i.e., inquiring) through scanning and analysing (System 2). Scanning involved a deliberate search for knowledge from external or internal sources to monitor the environment for information (which we now consider might include 'weak signals', see Ansoff 1975); while analysing involved longer and more careful consideration of the situation or information, which then fed into and influenced the decision process.

Second, we investigated intuitions in a collective context beyond the individual level of analysis. Collective intuitions figured prominently in group-level decision-making and were relayed to us by participants as instances in which they arrived independently at the same intuitive judgement as their colleagues when confronted jointly by a given problem. These were then captured and shared in senior management team meetings as a source of articulable knowledge and information. Collective intuitions surfaced when senior decision-makers sought the team's judgement to gain a wider perspective and to confirm or refute the credibility of their personal intuitions. In doing so, they utilised their collective expertise in the policing domain. Collectively, intuitions became explicit and were validated through consulting advice from the organisation's experienced and trusted officers and managers.

Third, we identified an additional process of 'internalising' as the learning moves from the group to the organisation level. Our findings indicated that individual and group learning was not always established formally and explicitly within the organisation's systems, structures and procedures (as per the 'institutionalising' process); however, a form of non-formal learning became internalised within the organisation through the knowledge and understanding of the situation. Internalising captured learning through collective practice and co-experience and linked team processes with perceived norms, values and codes of professional conduct within the community of practice, thereby capitalising on the power of collective intuitions that may fail to be developed into more formal learning structures (e.g., systems, procedures, etc.).

Finally, we further elaborated on the Crossan et al. (1999) 4I framework with the identification of the feedback loop processes which were absent in the original model. Our findings revealed that interpreting and internalising manifested as recursive processes across individual, group and organisation levels as an interactive process between cognition and action. We discovered a continuous refinement of the collectively formed intuitions and deliberative reasoning through the process of reinterpreting recurring between the group and individual levels. Reinterpreting allowed senior officers to reconsider and refine their individually and collectively constructed intuitive judgements and assumptions through conversations. Moving between organisation and group levels, reinternalising presented collective learning opportunities for the senior management teams as a result of their shared experiences of organisational success and failure and informed their on-going decision-making. These feedback loop processes help develop collective intuitions, improve the quality of intuitive decision-making and contribute to organisational learning.

Most recently, in a review of team intuition, Samba, Williams and Fuller (2022) identified four forms of intuition that top management teams can use in the course of strategic decision-making. The authors describe TMT intuition in terms of two dimensions: locus of intuition (where the intuition originates—a top manager or the TMT) and integration of intuition (the extent to which managers' psychological contents are integrated into TMT intuition). The four forms are described as follows: (1) *dominant actor intuition* reflects the intuition of one top manager; (2) *shared intuition* is the form of TMT intuition that occurs when the members of a TMT naturally have the same or similar intuitions; (3) *actor-driven collective intuition* also reflects the intuition of one top manager, but the driving actor needs to secure teammates' validation of his or her intuition; (4) *team-driven collective intuition*, also called *collective intuition*, involves the simultaneous relationships among different top managers and different ideas, opinions, and perspectives. It is more than managers producing similar intuitions (as in shared intuition) or deliberating their colleagues' intuitions (as in actor-driven collective intuition). Instead, the authors argue, this form of TMT intuition is fundamentally a product of social interactions that may be reflected in the TMT's strategic decisions.

While it is useful to identify the source of intuitions and how they are used in TMT's strategic decision-making, the real-life examples of strategic and operational decisions taken by police senior management teams in our study (Akinci & Sadler-Smith 2019) suggested a more universal and holistic view and use of collective intuition in team decisions regardless of its source or trajectory. In some cases, we observed conflicting intuitions amongst the members of the senior teams, and in others we encountered the consequences of failed intuitions that were held collectively.

One common conclusion we arrived at in all instances was that the crucial element, as far as the senior team was concerned, appeared to be the outcome of the intuitive decision (i.e., was it an intuitive hit or an intuitive miss? [see Akinci 2014]), regardless of whom the intuition might have come from or whether it was upheld by a single individual or the entire team.

Moving forward in the direction that Samba et al. (2022) offered, intuition research has much to gain from an empirical investigation not only of these different forms of team intuition but also in various contexts of decision-making and organisational settings. Without a doubt, the relevance of this work in general extends beyond the context of strategic decision-making into other settings in which decisions frequently are made under high-risk circumstances.

Summary and Conclusion

From its conception two decades ago, the idea of 'the intuitive executive' was long due a revisit. With the new light cast on the intuitive executive, our revisited and updated version encapsulates three main features.

First, the intuitive executive has an inquiring mind. As we discovered in our studies, inquiring is used alongside intuiting as a sense-making mechanism both at the individual level—that is, intuition-based inquiry (Akinci & Sadler-Smith 2020)—and at the collective level, feeding inquiry into collective decision-making processes (Akinci & Sadler-Smith 2019).

Second, the intuitive executive possesses skills that complement AI for improved decision-making. We agree with the Dreyfus brothers that computers as reasoning machines can't fully match human intuition and expertise. A 'hybrid intelligence' (Paydas Turan & Sadler-Smith 2023) that combines the intuitive judgement that only humans can process by synthesising and sensing with the algorithmic powers of analysing and solving capabilities of computer-generated AI seems to offer the best of two worlds.

Third, the intuitive executive has an important role in developing collective intuitions and contributing to organisational learning. As we have illustrated in the elaboration of the 4I framework (Akinci & Sadler-Smith 2019), senior management teams may pass on their knowledge, learning and experiences by way of interpreting and sharing their intuitions in organisational settings. Doing so helps both develop executive intuition collectively at various levels of the organisation and implement expert intuitions to be leveraged collectively as valuable sources of organisational knowledge and learning, as well as rare and difficult-to-imitate sources of competitive advantage.

As outlined above, there have been several very promising developments in the field, and with many more new opportunities emerging for intuition research, the future of the intuitive executive looks as exciting and as relevant as it was twenty years ago.

References

Akinci, C. (2014). Capturing intuitions in decision making: A case for the critical incident technique. In: M. Sinclair (Ed.), *Handbook of Research Methods on Intuition*, 147–159. Cheltenham, UK: Edward Elgar.

Akinci, C., and Sadler-Smith, E. (2019). Collective intuition: Implications for improved decision making and organizational learning. *British Journal of Management*, 30: 558–577.

Akinci, C., and Sadler-Smith, E. (2020). 'If something doesn't look right, go find out why': How intuitive decision making is accomplished in police first-response. *European Journal of Work and Organizational Psychology*, 29(1): 78–92.

Ansoff, H. I. (1975). Managing strategic surprise by response to weak signals. *California Management Review*, 18(2): 21–33.

Barney, J. (1991). Firm resources and sustained competitive advantage. *Journal of Management*, 17: 99–120.

Conti, M. (2017). 'The incredible inventions of intuitive AI'. TED Talk. https://www.ted.com/speakers/maurice_conti. Accessed 13.06.2022.

Criddle, C., and Staton, B. (2022). AI breakthrough ChatGPT raises alarm over student cheating. *Financial Times*, 18th December 2022. https://www.ft.com/content/2e97b7ce-8223-431e-a61d-1e462b6893c3; Accessed 27.12.2022.

Crossan, M. M., Lane, H. W., and White, R. E. (1999). An organizational learning framework: From intuition to institution. *Academy of Management Review*, 24(3): 522–537.

Dane, E., and Pratt, M. G. (2007). Exploring intuition and its role in managerial decision making. *Academy of Management Review*, 32(1): 33–54.

Dane, E., and Pratt, M. G. (2009). Conceptualizing and measuring intuition: A review of recent trends. In: Hodgkinson, G., and Ford, J. K. (Eds.). *International Review of Industrial and Organizational Psychology*, 24: 1–40. Chichester, UK: Wiley.

de Groot, A. D. (1978). *Thought and Choice in Chess* (2nd ed.). The Hague: Mouton Publishers.

Dreyfus, H. L., and Dreyfus, S. E. (1986). *Mind over Machine: The Power of Human Intuition and Expertise in the Era of the Computer*. New York: The Free Press.

Eisenhardt, K. M. (1989). Making fast strategic decisions in high-velocity environments. *Academy of Management Journal*, 32: 543–576.

Eisenhardt, K. M. (1999). Strategy as strategic decision making. *Sloan Management Review*, Spring: 65–72.

Eisenhardt, K. M., and Martin, J. (2000). Dynamic capabilities: What are they? *Strategic Management Journal*, 21: 1105–1121.

Elliott, D., and Macpherson, A. (2010). Policy and practice: Recursive learning from crisis. *Group & Organization Management*, 35: 572–605.

Epstein, S. (1994). Integration of the cognitive and the psychodynamic unconscious. *American Psychologist*, 49: 709–724.

Epstein, S., Pacini, R., Denes-Raj, V., and Heier, H. (1996). Individual differences in intuitive-experiential and analytical-rational thinking styles. *Journal of Personality and Social Psychology*, 71: 390–405.

Evans, J. St. B. T. (2019). Reflections on reflection: The nature and function of type 2 processes in dual-process theories of reasoning. *Thinking & Reasoning*, 25(4): 383–415.

Evans, J. St. B. T., and Stanovich, K. E. (2013). Dual-process theories of higher cognition advancing the debate. *Perspectives on Psychological Science*, 8: 223–241.

Gore, J., and Sadler-Smith, E. (2011). Unpacking intuition: A process and out-come framework. *Review of General Psychology,* 15(4): 304–316.

Hodgkinson, G. P., Langan-Fox, J., and Sadler-Smith, E. (2008). Intuition: A fundamental bridging construct in the behavioural sciences. *British Journal of Psychology*, 99: 1–27.

Hogarth, R. M. (2001). *Educating Intuition.* Chicago, IL: University of Chicago Press.

Jeanes, E., and Sadler-Smith, E. (2018). *Rethinking intuition: A process perspective.* Paper presented at the 10th International Process Symposium, Halkidiki, June 2018.

Kahneman, D., and Klein, G. (2009). Conditions for intuitive expertise: A failure to disagree. *The American Psychologist*, 64: 515–526.

Khatri, N., and Ng, H. A. (2000). The role of intuition in strategic decision mak-ing. *Human Relations*, 53(1): 57–86.

Klein, G. A. (2017). *Sources of Power: How People Make Decisions.* Cambridge, MA: MIT Press.

Klein, G., Calderwood, R., and Clinton-Cirocco, A. (2010). Rapid decision mak-ing on the fire ground: The original study plus a postscript. *Journal of Cognitive Engineering and Decision-Making*, 4(3):186–209.

Kline, D. A. (2005). Intuitive team decision making. In: H. Montgomery, R. Lip-shitz, and B. Brehmer (Eds.), *How Processionals Make Decisions.* Mahwah, NJ: LEA.

Leonard, N. H., Beauvais, L. L., and Scholl, R. W. (2005). A multi-level model of group cognitive style in strategic decision making. *Journal of Managerial Issues,* 17(1): 119–138.

Lieberman, M. D. (2007). Social cognitive neuroscience: A review of core pro-cesses. *Annual Review of Psychology*, 58: 259–289.

Meehl, P. E. (1954). *Clinical versus Statistical Prediction: A Theoretical Analysis and a Review of the Evidence.* University of Minnesota Press. https://doi.org /10.1037/11281-000

Merritt, R. (2022). What is a transformer model? Nvidia, March 25, 2022. https:// blogs.nvidia.com/blog/2022/03/25/what-is-a-transformer-model/

Meziani, N., and Cabantous, L. (2020). Acting intuition into sense: How film crews make sense with embodied ways of knowing. *Journal of Management Studies*, 57(7):1384–1419.

Paydas Turan, C., Dörfler, V., and Sadler-Smith, E. (2023). The impossibility of artificial intuition. Paper submitted to the AoM Annual Meeting, Boston, August 2023.

Paydas Turan, C., and Sadler-Smith, E. (2023). A dual-process model of hybrid intelligence for improved decision-making in the digital age. Paper submit-ted to the AoM Annual Meeting, Boston, August 2023.

Prahalad, C. K., and Bettis, R. A. (1986). The dominant logic: A new linkage between diversity and performance. *Strategic Management Journal*, 7: 485–501.

Rouse, M. (2022). Generative AI. *Technopedia*. https://www.techopedia.com/definition/34633/generative-ai Accessed 27.12.2022.

Sadler-Smith, E. (2004). Cognitive style and the performance of small and medium sized enterprises. *Organization Studies*, 25: 155–182.

Sadler-Smith, E. (2008). The role of intuition in collective learning and the development of shared meaning. *Advances in Developing Human Resources*, 10(4):494–508.

Sadler-Smith, E. (2010). *The Intuitive Mind*. Chichester, UK: John Wiley & Sons.

Sadler-Smith, E. (2016). What happens when you intuit?: Understanding human resource practitioners' subjective experience of intuition through a novel linguistic method. *Human Relations*, 69(5):1069–1093.

Sadler-Smith, E. (2023). *Intuition in Business*. Oxford: Oxford University Press.

Sadler-Smith, E., and Shefy, E. (2004). The intuitive executive: Understanding and applying 'gut feel' in decision-making. *Academy of Management Perspectives,* 18(4): 76–91.

Salas, E., Rosen, M. A., and DiazGranados, D. (2010). Expertise-based intuition and decision making in organizations. *Journal of Management*, 36: 941–973.

Samba, C., Williams, D. W., and Fuller, R. M. (2022). The forms and use of intuition in top management teams. *The Leadership Quarterly*, 33(3): 101349.

Seifert, M., and Hadida, A. L. (2009). Decision making, expertise and task ambiguity: Predicting success in the music industry. In: G. Solomon (Ed.). *Best Paper Proceedings of the 2009 Academy of Management Meeting:* Academy of Management.

Sillence, J., and Shipton, H. (2013). More than a cognitive experience: Unfamiliarity, invalidation, and emotion in organizational learning. *Journal of Management Inquiry*, 22(3): 342–355.

Simon, H. A. (1987). Making management decisions: The role of intuition and emotion. *Academy of Management Perspectives*, 1(1): 57–64.

Sinclair, M., and Hamilton, A. (2014). Mapping group intuitions. In: M. Sinclair (Ed.), *Handbook of Intuition Research as Practice.* Cheltenham, UK: Edward Elgar, 199–216.

Softtek (2021). Fourth generation of AI arrives. https://softtek.eu/en/tech-magazine-en/artificial-intelligence-en/fourth-generation-of-ai-arrives-artificial-intuition/

Tao, W., and He, P. (2009). *Intuitive learning and artificial intuition networks*. Second International Conference on Education Technology and Training: 297–300. https://ieeexplore.ieee.org/document/5381516

Weick, K. E. (1995). *Sensemaking in Organizations*. Thousand Oaks, CA: Sage.

Weick, K. E. (2001). *Making Sense of the Organization*. Malden, MA: Blackwell Publishing.

Weick, K. E., and Roberts, K. H. (1993). Collective mind in organizations: Heedful interrelating on flight decks. *Administrative Science Quarterly*, 38: 357–381.

Chapter 2

Training Intuition: Challenges and Opportunities

Katharina Fellnhofer,[1,2] Eugene Sadler-Smith,[3] and Marta Sinclair[4]

[1] Chair of Education Systems, Department of Management, Technology and Economics, Swiss Federal Institute of Technology Zuerich (ETH Zuerich), Zurich, Switzerland

[2] Department of Sociology, Harvard University, Cambridge, MA, US

[3] Surrey Business School, University of Surrey, Surrey, UK

[4] Department of Business Strategy and Innovation, Griffith Business School, Griffith University, Brisbane, QLD, Australia

Acknowledgement

This project has received funding from the European Union's Horizon 2020 research and innovation programme under the Marie Skłodowska-Curie grant agreement No 882168.

1. Introduction

There are long-standing academic debates about the value of intuition in problem-solving and decision-making (Sinclair & Ashkanasy 2005). It is widely agreed that intuition can be enhanced over time via learning, experience and practice (Dreyfus & Dreyfus 2006; Hogarth 2001; Klein 2017; Lufityanto et al. 2016; Simon 1987). There appears to be a consensus that intuition can be both a powerful and a perilous tool, depending on the decision-makers themselves and the contexts in which their decisions are taken (Osman 2004; Kahneman & Klein 2009). However, due to conceptual inconsistencies across disciplines as to what constitutes intuition and related methodological issues, such as challenges in measuring intuition and relevant outcomes, precisely *how* to enhance intuition remains open to debate. In light of this, in our review of methods we will also take note of if/how the effectiveness of proposed training methods might be assessed.

The aim of this chapter is to inform this important debate by examining the conceptual work on educating, training and enhancing intuition in laboratory and field settings to identify the most promising methods of intuition development and to suggest future research directions. We identify educational and training methods with a focus on the 'brain' (i.e., the cognitive aspects) and the 'body' (i.e., the affective, interoceptive, sensory, somatic and visceral aspects) that show the most promise and suggest designs for future study that have the greatest potential to move the field forward.

Although there are many different definitions of intuition, for the purpose of this chapter, we categorize those broadly into two streams—the brain- and the body-related approaches for judgement and decision-making (see above). Based on this simple two-fold categorization, we outline a research strategy pointing to the need for new, more integrated approaches to studying and assessing the development of intuition through education and training in both classroom and corporate settings. We identify some of the important methodological and practical breakthroughs needed to enhance intuition in different contexts.

2. The angle and insights

Although several scholars focus on their own specific perspectives—for example, the 'upside' of intuition as in the work of Klein and colleagues (2010) or the 'downside' of intuition as in Kahneman and Tversky's (1972) original heuristics and biases research—in recent decades an acceptance and a reconciliation of this ambiguity has been debated and to some extent resolved (Kahneman & Klein 2009). We argue that in addition to building a repertoire of empirical evidence about how and why intuition works best, we must also investigate how to enhance people's ability and willingness to use it. While conceptual work in this field has come on in leaps and bounds in recent decades, allowing a more nuanced study of intuition's effects on decision-making, problem-solving, forecasting, foreseeing and the like (see Akinci & Sadler-Smith 2012 for a review in management), knowledge of how to enhance intuition through education and training is more limited (e.g., Sadler-Smith & Shefy 2007; Gillin 2020).

As noted above, we will categorize published work into two approaches to enhancing intuition—via the *brain* and via the *body*. In addition to journal publications, we will also review significant new work profiled in edited volumes, handbooks and material presented at intuition conference symposia, including over a decade's worth of presentations at the annual Academy of Management (AoM) meetings in North America.

Although the topic of developing intuition has been widely debated, there is still little in the way of systematic reviews and evidence-based commentaries. Our brain- and body-related approaches find themes and resonances in current developments: as our world becomes more complex, shaken by crises and characterized by uncertainty, time pressure, ambiguity and instability, enhancing intuition is of ever-growing importance (Calabretta et al. 2017); it has been credited with outperforming analytical thinking, specifically when facing complexity or uncertainty (Gigerenzer & Gaissmaier 2011). Moreover, important policy-shaping bodies such as the OECD (2014, 2019a, 2019b, 2021) and World Economic Forum (2022) emphasize that such skills are crucial for decision-making, problem-solving and innovation in an uncertain and fast-moving world.

We reflect also on the concept of *sensory intuitions* as a relatively new stream of research. Intuition manifests in two ways: first, *intuition as expertise* (Sadler-Smith & Shefy 2004), which relates to the cognitive aspects of intuition; we refer to the associated methods as *brain-based*. And second, *intuition as feeling* (Sadler-Smith & Shefy 2004), which relates to the affective, somatic and visceral aspects of the phenomenon; we refer to the associated methods as *body-based*. There is an overall need to clarify terminologies related to brain- and body-based methods. Moreover, it has been suggested that it is possible to distinguish between 'cognitive feelings' (referred to colloquially as *hunches*) versus 'bodily feelings' (referred to colloquially as *gut feelings*), both of which could be grouped under the umbrella term of *interoception* (Sadler-Smith 2016, 1085).

Every person experiences intuition differently—for example, while some people are sensitive to cognitive feelings, others are more sensitive to bodily feelings (Dunn et al. 2010). Thus, we organised the chapter into two sections dedicated to brain-based and body-based methods for developing intuition and identifying methods that show promise for further investigation. In the brain-based section, we approach the question of how to develop better intuitive judgement from the perspective of two contrasting, but ultimately complement-ary, schools of thought. In the body-based section, we expand our conceptual understanding of intuition and its components and focus on its affective and sensory components.

3. Brain-based methods for developing intuition

This section of our chapter approaches the question of how to develop improved intuitive judgement from the perspective of two contrasting, but ultimately com-plementary, schools of thought. The works of two highly esteemed intuition researchers are centre stage: Daniel Kahneman (2002 Nobel Prize laureate and one of the founders of the *heuristics and biases* approach) and Gary Klein (one of the founders of the *naturalistic decision-making* approach). In a widely cited article in *American Psychologist* published in 2009 and entitled Conditions for Intuitive Expertise: A Failure to Disagree, they summarised their contrasting positions thus:

> One of us (GK) has spent much of his career thinking about ways to promote reliance on expert intuition in executive decision making and identifies him-self as a member of the intellectual community of scholars and practitioners who study naturalistic decision making (NDM). The other (DK) has spent much of his career running experiments in which intuitive judgment was commonly found to be flawed; he is identified with the 'heuristics and biases' (HB) approach to the field (Kahneman & Klein 2009, 515).

Klein's approach accentuates the positives of expert intuition in which the 'analyses frozen into habit' referred to by Simon (1987, 63) enable experienced participants to take fast, effective decisions in dynamic and fast-moving environ-ments. Kahneman's approach, on the other hand, accentuates the negatives of the unbridled intuitions which emanate unconsciously from the automatic oper-ations of Type 1 processes (see below).

This upside-versus-downside view offers a balanced approach to improving intuitive decision-making via brain-based methods. The methods are brain-based because they focus on intuitive cognition in terms of:

1. Type 1 processing, also referred to as *System 1* (Kahneman 2011), the *expe-riential system* (Epstein et al. 1996) or the *intuitive mind* (Sadler-Smith 2010), and whose attributes include *contextually dependent, automatic, largely uncon-scious, associative, intuitive, implicit* and *fast* (Stanovich & West 2000).

2. Type 2 processing, also referred to as *System 2* (Kahneman 2011), the *rational system* (Epstein et al. 1996) or the *analytical mind* (Sadler-Smith 2010), and whose attributes include contextually *independent, analytical, rule-based, explicit* and *relatively slow* (Stanovich & West 2000).

In general terms, the intuitive mind evolved to be an efficient *sensing* system, whilst the analytical mind evolved to be an effective *solving* system (Sadler-Smith 2023). Sensing and solving are qualitatively different, adaptive forms of cognition (Sadler-Smith 2023). That said, we acknowledge two points of criticism: first, those voices who have advanced general critiques of dual-process theory both in the context of intuition and more broadly (e.g., Kruglanski & Gigerenzer 2011; Kruglanski & Orehek 2007); second, the idea of a *System 0* as part of a tripartite (rather) than a dual system of information processing (Dreyfus 2014, 17). In what follows, we discuss ways in which the upside of intuition can be accentuated by developing intuitive expertise and its downside diminished by debiasing judgement and decision-making.

3.1 Developing intuitive expertise

Expert intuition is the most widely studied type of intuition. The other commonly considered types are *moral* intuition, *social* intuition, and *creative* intuition (Dane & Pratt 2009; Gore & Sadler-Smith 2011). Expert intuition is sometimes referred to as *intuition as expertise* or *intuitive expertise* (Sadler-Smith & Shefy 2004). The concept of expert intuition was encapsulated in Herbert Simon's definition as '. . . analyses frozen into habit and the capacity for rapid response through recognition' (Simon 1987, 63). Intuition as expertise figures prominently in Klein's *recognition-primed decision* model (RPD) (Klein et al. 2010; Klein 2003) and Dreyfus and Dreyfus's *skill acquisition model* (SAM) (Dreyfus & Dreyfus 2006).

In the RPD a situation generates cues that let the decision-maker recognize patterns which activate action scripts that are then used to affect the situation (Klein 2003). This is the intuitive (System 1) part of the RPD process. An additional step is involved in which the decision-maker mentally simulates whether the action script is likely to work: if their judgement is that it will work, they go ahead; if it will not, they move to the next best option. This is the analytical (System 2) part of the RPD process.

In the SAM (Dreyfus & Dreyfus 2006), decision-makers progress through five developmental stages: novice, advanced beginner, competence, proficiency, expertise. At the expert level decision-makers 'depend almost entirely on intuition and hardly at all on analysis and comparison of alternatives' (Dreyfus 2004, 180). RPD and SAM offer convincing accounts of how intuition works and how intuitive expertise is developed. In RPD and SAM the ability to make fast, accurate intuitive judgements in dynamic and time-pressured situations is built up through learning (both explicit and implicit), coaching and feedback (Dane & Pratt 2007; Dreyfus & Dreyfus 2005; Hogarth 2001, 2010; Simon 1987).

The acquisition of intuitive expertise through learning is consolidated and honed through practice, which helps to build complex domain-relevant schemas (CDRS) (Dane & Pratt 2007), which are the basis of the mental models of "how things work" (Klein 2003, p. 17). Building complex domain-relevant schemas takes time. For example, Ericsson (1998) discovered that even the most gifted performers need approximately ten years (or around 10,000 hours) of intense training and deliberate practice to become an expert.

However, the so-called '10,000-hours rule' is not as simple as it first appears: exhortations to 'practice, practice, practice' imply 'more is better', but this is not necessarily the best way to build intuitive expertise (Goldberg et al. 2014). Practice that is deliberate, stretching and supported by coaching is likely to be more effective than simply repeating the same behaviours that are within current levels of 'competence and comfort'; hence deliberate, high-quality practice entails focusing on the things that you cannot do well (Ericsson et al. 2007, 116). As Ericsson and colleagues noted wryly:

> It may appear that excellence is simply the result of practicing daily for years or even decades. However, living in a cave does not make you a geologist. Not all practice makes perfect. You need a particular kind of practice—deliberate practice—to develop [intuitive] expertise (Ericsson et al. 2007, 118).

Coaching also builds intuitive expertise. Expert coaches can give immediate, accurate and relevant feedback on performance (Hogarth 2001). Coaches who are themselves domain experts (as opposed to generalist coaches such as 'life coaches') are able to focus on important questions such as, 'How complex and uncertain is the environment?', 'How do cues in the environment reliably predict outcomes?' and 'How likely is it that the future will resemble the past?' Coaches can also remind managers that they need to have a healthy scepticism towards, as well as an informed awareness of, the use of intuition in decision-making and problem-solving (Soyer & Hogarth 2021).

Part of a coach's remit should be to help decision-makers to understand where and when intuitive expertise should and should not be used. In theoretical terms, this involves helping decision-makers to distinguish between *high-validity environments* (Kahneman & Klein 2009)—that is, situations in which it is prudent to use intuition because there are stable and reliable relationships between cues and outcomes—and those situations in which it is unwise to use intuitive judgements—that is, *low-validity environments*. As an example of a low-validity environment: making accurate, long-term forecasts of political events fails because 'large-scale historical developments are too complex to be forecast. The task is simply impossible' (Kahneman & Klein 2009, 520).

On the other hand, games such as chess, bridge or poker are high-validity environments because the ability to identify favourable moves or bets improves with learning and practice but does not guarantee that every intuitive move or bet will succeed, given that uncertainty is never absent. The necessary condition for the development of intuitive expertise is adequate opportunity to learn the relevant cue-outcome relationships (Kahneman & Klein 2009) through relevant experience, deliberate practice and optimal feedback. This is best gained under guidance in the flow of working and in simulations.

Feedback plays a key role in developing intuitive expertise. To be optimal, feedback should be accurate, timely and diagnostic; this helps to create a 'kind learning structure' for developing intuitive expertise (Hogarth 2001). 'Wicked learning structures', on the other hand, are characterised by feedback that is inaccurate, delayed and undiagnostic. Wicked learning structures are sub-optimal, not least because decision-makers do not get to find out whether or not their intuitions have been accurate (Hogarth 2001). Receiving sub-optimal feedback in a wicked learning structure is a good way to develop inaccurate intuitions (Sadler-Smith 2023).

One way to create a kind learning structure (in addition to practice and coaching) is to use devil's advocacy (Sadler-Smith & Shefy 2004) to aid the interpreting of intuitions (Crossan et al. 1999) and deliberately testing them before they are implemented. Devil's advocacy is psychologically safe because it challenges the *intuition,* not the *intuitor.* It also melds logic with intuition, thus integrating System 2 and System 1 processes (Hodgkinson & Sadler-Smith 2018). This latter point emphasises the need to educate decision-makers to use both intuition and analysis when taking important decisions (see Simon 1987). Indeed, a skilful integration of both has been at the forefront of recent research (Sinclair 2020).

3.2 Debiasing decision-making

A heuristic is a mental shortcut. Heuristics are usually viewed as a product of System 1 processing and are one of the main sources of systematic, regular, and hence predictable, errors and biases (Kahneman & Tversky 1972). There are a number of different sources of bias—for example, the *representativeness heuristic* (as in the well-known Linda Problem, see Tversky & Kahneman 1983), the *availability heuristic* (as in overestimating the likelihood of being the victim of a terrorist attack), *anchoring and adjustment* (as in starting a negotiation with an excessively high or low opening gambit) and the *affect heuristic* (as in over-estimating the risks and underestimating the benefits of something, such as nuclear power, because it happens to evoke negative feelings) (Gilovich et al. 2002).

The use of heuristics, which are largely unintentional because they are a product of automatic and unconscious processes, makes it more likely that decision-makers will make inaccurate intuitive judgement calls through the operation of unconscious biases—for example, ignoring base rates, adjusting from a too high/low anchor, etc. The use of heuristics should be avoided wherever possible by debiasing (Kahneman et al. 2021). The good news is that intuitive errors and biases are predictable and amenable to correction if the decision-maker is self-aware and has relevant knowledge and skills. The bad news is that doing so is easier said than done.

Kahneman et al. (2021) identified two main approaches to debiasing, which they refer to as debiasing *ex-post* and debiasing *ex-ante*. Debiasing ex-post occurs after a judgement has been arrived at, and hence serves as a corrective action on an initial intuitive estimate. For example, managers typically make intuitive under-estimates of project costs and delivery times because of the *planning fallacy* (Buehler et al. 1994). Intuitive estimates can be de-biased by adding a data-driven correction factor for how long a project will take and how much it will cost (Green & Armstrong 2007). Debiasing ex-post is readily achievable if the potential for error is acknowledged and identified. It is an example of an analytical (System 2) intervention in a default intuitive (System 1) process (see *default intervention* models of dual-processing; Evan 2003, Hodgkinson & Sadler-Smith 2018).

Debiasing ex-ante occurs before the judgement has been made and is potentially a more difficult challenge. Kahneman et al. (2021) suggested two ways in which intuitive judgements can be debiased beforehand:

1. First, training managers so that they understand and can recognise the logical and statistical sources of their biases—for example, by understanding the role that stereotyping plays in the biases associated with the representativeness heuristic (Kahneman & Tversky 1972), managers may become more aware of when they are likely to fall foul of unconscious biases in hiring employees, performance appraisal, promotion decisions, selecting leaders, etc. This is the basis of unconscious bias training, and it is now accepted widely that managers and organizations have a duty to identify it and act to mitigate the causes (Kapur 2015).

2. Second, *boosting* can improve managers' statistical literacy (Kahneman et al. 2021). For example, educating aspiring entrepreneurs about base rates of business venturing failures and the perils of ease-of-availability and recall of high-profile entrepreneurial successes could help aspiring entrepreneurs to ground their assessments accurately and arrive at a realistic assessment of their chances of success (Hogarth & Karelaia 2021).

That said, Kahneman et al. (2021) were not overly optimistic about the chances of fully de-programming an unbridled human brain of its in-built tendencies to commit logical and statistical errors of judgement. This is because even informed judges who can apply statistical reasoning principles to judgements in their professional domain are far from immune from committing the same errors in other non-professional spheres—for example, the chances of winning a lottery (Kahneman et al. 2021, 238). The process of correcting System 1 biases is metacognitive, in that it requires decision-makers to reflect on, understand and adjust their own mental processes.

In his 2001 book *Educating Intuition*, eminent intuition scholar Robin Hogarth proposed what was at that time the radical idea that intuition can be explicitly educated. His argument for the educability of intuition is based on the idea that intuitive expertise is a result of learning, practice and experience, but that these must take place in the right environments. The corollary of this is that experiences, including learning and development, should be organized in such a way that 'people learn the "right" lessons from their interactions with the world' (Hogarth 2010, 348). Brain-based methods for developing intuition involve learning how to accentuate intuition's upside whilst simultaneously diminishing its downside; ultimately this is about recognising the right environments in which intuitions can be exercised productively.

This kind of intuition training, obviously, takes time, and it is therefore difficult to yield immediate results. What short-term courses or corporate workshops can do, though, is to 'lay foundations' for future self-development by increasing managers' self-awareness and introducing them to new toolsets. One of the few long-term attempts, to our best knowledge, was the entrepreneurial education intervention, customized for employees of a financial services firm partaking in a master's program at a South Australian university between 2010 and 2017 (Gillin 2020). Its effectiveness, however, was measured in overall outcomes (for example, changes in entrepreneurial mindset or cognitive style over time) and did not assess the efficacy of specific brain-based methods. Some of these are discussed in the next section.

4. Body-based methods for developing intuition

4.1 Conceptual understanding of intuition and its components

As outlined in the previous section, the first wave of research into the role of intuition in management (e.g., Agor 1984, 1986; Mintzberg 1989; Simon 1987) was focused predominantly on the so-called expert intuition that appears to be mostly of the *intellectual/mental* kind (for the lack of terminology, some researchers used the term *cognitive* to delineate this specific aspect only, see above). To a large extent, that was due to the increased dynamics and unpredictability of the business environment (accelerated since the 1990s) when first practicing managers and then researchers realized that traditional decision-making models became insufficient owing to their mechanistic nature.

Among the initial challenges to be addressed were decision speed, problem ambiguity, environmental uncertainty, availability of adequate information and other situational constraints faced by decision-makers. Instead of a standardized approach, decision-making suddenly became contextual, depending on the nature of the problem and the ensuing decision, the cognitive profile of the enacting person and the situational characteristics of the decision scenario (see Sinclair 2003; Sinclair & Ashkanasy 2002/2003).

Expert intuition fits the bill, as it enabled the decision-maker to draw on the pool of accumulated complex domain-relevant schemas (CDRS) (Dane & Pratt 2007) and reach a quick conclusion without being consciously aware of the underlying information processing. This 'knowing what without knowing how' (Dörfler & Ackermann 2012; Vaughan 1979) has contributed to the initial belief that intuition is something mysterious (since we cannot explain and thus understand it). Also, narrowing the concept down to expertise made it easier to study it using the existing psychometric tools (although relying predominantly on self-report, which presents its own challenges, see Hodgkinson 2023), thus eschewing such ephemeral or difficult-to-understand disciplines as transpersonal psychology or quantum physics. Initially, there was not much input from neurology/brain research either since the technology was still being developed, and most management researchers were not equipped to interpret it correctly.

A corollary of the above was a continuous ambiguity in the understanding of the intuition construct, further accentuated by a limited intuition terminology (Petitmengin 1999; Sinclair & Ashkanasy 2002/2003) and lack of cross-pollination across disciplinary research (Bas et al. 2022). Thus, achieving a speedy decision without knowing how did not offer sufficient theoretical grounds for measurement and training, as it did not elucidate the aspects of intuition that could be measured/trained. Another by-product was the initial emphasis on the 'intellectual' nature when defining intuition, or rather its surfacing into consciousness, in the form of mental images, associations and metaphors (Epstein 1990).

Some of these were later utilized in research design that could be modified for training purposes, such as the Clean Language technique to capture fully formed intuitions by means of metaphors (Cairns-Lee 2020). Other, related, techniques relied heavily on language to assist verbalization, such as elicitation interviews aiding to 'become aware of the usually unnoticed part of a given cognitive process, and to describe it with precision' (Petitmengin 2014, 189), the interview conversation method designed to bring subconscious decision-making into awareness for future learning (Anastasiu et al. 2021) or ventriloquism as a method to 'talk intuitions into existence' (Meziani 2020). There also have been attempts to instil intuition through a strategic application of pausing (Govender et al. 2023).

4.2 Affective components

Surprisingly, despite the emergence of relevant affect/emotion-related research, especially *somatic marker hypothesis* (SMH) (Damasio 1994) and *affective tags* (Slovic et al. 2007), this aspect of intuition was not incorporated into its definition until the mid-2000s; for example, as 'non-sequential information processing mode, which comprises both cognitive and affective elements and results in direct knowing without any use of conscious reasoning' (Sinclair & Ashkanasy 2005, 7) and the seminal definition coined by Dane and Pratt in 2007 as 'affectively charged judgments that arise through rapid, nonconscious, and holistic associations' (p. 40).

This definition, generally accepted by management scholars, is linked explicitly to decision-making that appears to be less infused with affect than problem-solving does (Sinclair 2010). It also aligns predominantly with the notion of expert intuition, known for its speed, contrary to affect-laden creative or moral intuition (see Dörfle & Ackermann 2012; Haidt 2001), where the former usually requires a period of incubation (Goldberg 1983) and the latter is shaped by cultural and social values rather than domain expertise (Haidt 2001). More important, neither definition explains the specific role affect plays in the intuiting process (and thus does not offer grounds to measure its effectiveness or design a specific training). Moreover, affect was initially used as an umbrella term encompassing discrete emotions, generic moods and even non-emotional feelings (Sinclair 2003). This big-picture clustering caused additional problems with measurement and training design.

To dissect this conundrum, we will investigate the role of affect in intuiting (unconscious information processing) and intuition (conscious outcome of the processing) through a process lens in terms of what happens *before*, *during* and *after* we intuit (see Sinclair 2010, for details). In the first stage, different types of affect (i.e., specific discrete emotions vs. generic diffuse mood; stable affective traits and attitudes vs. fleeting affective states) can act as antecedents, either enabling or blocking intuitive processing. For example, women were found to have generally higher affective awareness, which makes them more aware of subtle affective cues, thus facilitating access to intuition (Sinclair 2003, 2020).

On the other hand, their heightened awareness may make them more vulnerable to the effects of temporary negative mood, which can lead to a conscious switch to rational decision-making strategies as a sign of caution (Elsbach & Barr 1999; Sinclair et al. 2010; Sinclair 2020). The relationships seem to be more complicated, prone to moderation and mediation effects, but they bear consequences for intuition training: in general, access to intuition can be enhanced by increasing affective awareness (Sinclair 2020) and by changing *attitude* to *intuition,* so we trust it more and are comfortable voicing it. That requires not only an individual but also an organizational shift, by establishing a supportive environment (Bas et al. 2022), and when that is in place, a mechanism for effective pacing of engagement activities drawing on intuition to prevent burnout (Teerikangas et al. 2020). In terms of specific affect-related training, the research method of dialogical inquiry, developed by Coget (2014), that identifies *intuitive incidents* evoked by discreet emotions of anger or fear with the help of verbal and visual means, looks particularly promising.

The second stage, infusion of affect during the actual information processing, appears to be more challenging from a measurement and training perspective since the process occurs subconsciously and thus is difficult to track. But new developments in neuroimaging may offer some possibilities (Lieberman 2000; Lieberman et al. 2004). Their applicability could be contextual though, as affect infusion may occur differently for creative intuition (Bechara 2004; Sadler-Smith et al. 2008) or, for instance, moral intuition (Haidt 2001; Egorov & Pircher 2020). More research is needed in this respect.

The fundamental question here is whether all non-conscious information processing is indeed intuitive—not in terms of the outcome but of the process itself (Sinclair 2010). In other words, does the process rely on different parts of the brain and/or utilize different neural synapses? If not, expert intuition may be nothing but a super-fast analysis that cannot be registered consciously (Klein 1998). And heuristics, which sometimes have been viewed as a kind or aspect of intuition, may be nothing but low-effort analysis. This speculative conclusion may explain the distinction between mature and immature intuition of Baylor's U-shaped model (Baylor 2001).

Regardless of what future research will bring, how can we utilize the current limited knowledge for intuition training? One answer may lie in *sensing,* if we develop a method for how to detect subtle affective changes in our brain and other parts of the body. Nascent research suggests that intuitive signals may be registered by nerves not only in the brain, but also before they travel to the brain (McGraty et al. 2004; Radin 2011); in the heart; gut/digestive system (Soosalu et al. 2019); and possibly even by the vagus nerve (Tantia 2011).

It is interesting that one of the few studies conducted in this area so far (Soosalu & Henwood 2020) suggests that the only pronounced gender difference lies in the heart region, which is linked to emotions and a stronger intuition proclivity in women (Sinclair 2020). A series of heart-based techniques to evoke a state of psychophysiological coherence that facilitates, among other things, access to intuition has been used by HeartMath Institute for years (Childre & Martin 1999; McGraty et al. 1998; Tiller et al. 1996). According to Tomasino (2011, 256), the training 'can be facilitated by *heart rhythm feedback* technology' (McGraty & Tomasino 2004) that 'enables the psychophysiological coherence state to be objectively monitored and quantified'.

Researchers have also suggested that individual differences may exist in the ability to detect bodily states (interoceptive awareness) associated with intuitions (Dunn et al. 2010).

The third phase, a confirmatory feeling (Sinclair & Ashkanasy 2005) or feeling of rightness (Herbert & Pollatos 2012) that tends to accompany the fully formed intuition as it emerges into consciousness usually acts as reassurance. It helps the decision-maker to distinguish it from wishful thinking by adding an element of certainty. That also could be trainable by assisting decision-makers to increase their self-awareness but also to develop their own *intuition vocabulary,* as the feeling seems to be different for each individual (Petitmengin 1999; Bas et al. 2022; Bas & Dörfler 2023). This feeling, however, is not necessarily affective; it can be physical or visceral, and it also can be registered by different senses, such as a unique taste in the mouth, a specific smell, etc. (Sinclair 2010; Kündig & Sinclair 2012). It points to the importance of training decision-makers how to develop their own intuition vocabulary.

4.3 Sensory components

The sensory (non-affective) component of intuition has not received the attention of management scholars until relatively recently. As the new addition to the concept definition, it is undergoing similar 'teething problems' in terms of terminology, its relationship with other components of the construct and, as a result, measurement and training. On one hand, many scholars use the terms *affective* and *sensory* interchangeably, which creates similar problems to those outlined above. There is also inconsistency in naming the component itself, as suggested in our introduction. It has been labelled *sensory,* which often (but not always) lumps physical and affective into one category. As a result, extreme caution is needed to verify what is meant by the term used in different studies—in order to 'compare apples to apples'.

Another frequently used term is *visceral,* which may refer to all bodily sensations or only to interoception—which some researchers use as a synonym while others limit it to sensations in internal organs (see Dunn et al. 2010).

The inconsistencies may gain more importance in the future if we indeed identify different roles of intuition intercepted by different body regions, as mentioned above. From the big picture perspective, this would give some credence to popular beliefs that the heart is the centre of emotions while the gut is the centre of instinct (see Cappon's conclusion that intuition is an evolved instinct, Cappon 1993, 1994). For training purposes, it would be helpful to draw more attention to sensing and bodily sensations that often have been neglected in Western management education (Bas et al. 2022), then incorporate them into appropriate developmental tools.

For the above reasons, to the best of our knowledge, the only available training was 'imported to management' from such practical disciplines as psychotherapy or body movement for anxiety/stress reduction. The most commonly used method is *focusing* (Gendlin 1962), as a guided technique to identify emotions and/or sensations stored in the body without our awareness and to explore the reason behind the emotion/sensation. This method has been incorporated as a component of some intuition courses (e.g., Sadler-Smith & Shefy 2007); it also has been adopted to train entrepreneurs how to incorporate intuition when making challenging decisions (Yeung & Sinclair 2023). It is interesting that findings suggest that entrepreneurs use a combination of expert and creative intuition (Yeung & Sinclair, in preparation), which will likely influence affect infusion and should be reflected in training design. An important limitation of this method is the minimum required level of affective and sensory awareness (Yeung & Sinclair 2023).

A similar principle underlies body movement or dance therapy, used commonly in the clinical field to treat trauma (Tantia 2014). Some consultants and practitioners have been using such techniques in intuition workshops for years (e.g., Choquette 2005), but to our knowledge, very little research has been conducted on their effectiveness (except for self-reports of participants). Based on anecdotal evidence, this method appears to help participants 'move from the head into the body' so they do not over-rationalize their decisions. This appears to follow the same principle as some studies based on Unconscious Thought Theory (UTT) (Dijksterhuis & Nordgren 2006) that use *distraction tasks* to block the mind from interfering with the intuitive process by keeping it busy with other mental activities.

Technically speaking, if we include the function of all body organs in the category of sensing, certain methods usually associated with intellectual intuition should be also mentioned here. For instance, eye movement that increases peripheral vision was used to study and train intuition in the original wave of research by Cappon (1993, 1994) and is now further developed, thanks to new technology, by Lufityanto (Lufityanto 2020; Lufityanto et al. 2016) and Fellnhofer (Fellnhofer 2023; Fellnhofer & Renold 2022). The application of online design makes this method a prime candidate for accurate measurement and training. It is yet to be determined which aspects of intuition it trains, but it appears that it would be suitable for the development of holistic thinking, registering subconscious information that is coded affectively (Fellnhofer 2023) or increasing the overall number of registered intellectual cues (Sinclair 2010).

A training following a similar line of thought applied to problem finding was tested in Italian primary schools, where children were coached on how to identify possible underlying problems of a task to enhance their intuition (Iannello et al. 2020). There also have been considerations of more direct methods using brain stimulation (Iannello et al. 2014), but even if the technology becomes available, medical and ethical concerns would have to be addressed. More indirectly, some researchers used various deep relaxation techniques to allow decision-makers to access fragments of their subconsciousness and thus intuition, such as yoga nidra (see Merrett 2015, about proprietary training by Stratford for Human Synergistics, and Stratford 2019 for personal communication) or drumming to induce certain brain waves (Sinclair & Hamilton 2014).

A collateral concern is the accurate measurement of the above aspects of intuition. Not only are they difficult to capture, and therefore are usually evaluated in terms of the overall decision outcome, but when assessed by means of self-report, they are sometimes associated with instruments that measure something else. For example, holistic aspects of intuition that appear to be of a more intellectual nature may be erroneously associated with REI (Pacini & Epstein 1999, which assesses mostly affective aspects (Sinclair 2020).

The few reputable intuition courses or programs offered at universities usually combined multiple techniques that, rather than measuring the effectiveness of each specifically, gauged the overall satisfaction and reported benefits of participants, often through self-report (e.g. diary methods, Sadler-Smith & Shefy 2007). Among those that appear to be grounded in solid research are, for example, the intuition training that was offered as part of an MBA module at the University of Plymouth (see: Sadler-Smith & Shefy 2007), a customized Entrepreneurship Master's program for a corporate client at the University of Adelaide (Gillin 2020) or an entrepreneurial training program based on Baldacchino's intuition model, trialled at the University of Malta (Coleiro & Baldacchino, AOM 2022).

5. Conclusion

Intuition is important for decision-making and has the potential to both help and hinder our judgements. There is a clear need to be aware of intuition's powers and perils so that decision-makers can decide if, and when, it is likely to be their friend or their foe. Formal education systems have yet to integrate intuition into school classrooms and corporate training rooms. Although intuition represents a developable skill, for it to be more accepted, practitioners need more and better guidance on how to develop and use it in the workplace and in their personal lives. The challenge is to determine which approaches work best and for whom.

We have identified several brain-based and body-based methods, but we have not explored in any detail those methods which are at the nexus of the brain and the body, such as mindfulness (Sadler-Smith & Shefy 2007). Our work presents the first step on this 'journey' that will hopefully usher intuition into our classrooms (with appropriate caveats). What we have discovered so far is first a lack of theoretical models for how intuition could be developed in educational and training settings, and second a paucity of specific tools and techniques that practitioners could use readily to develop intuition.

Progress in this important aspect of management and leadership development requires the ability to assess the effectiveness of the training tools, but this is currently hampered by the availability of suitable and appropriate measurement. Whilst considerable progress has been made in designing, developing and pilot-testing methods for educating intuition, it also appears that more theoretical and methodological work is needed to support the application of intuition training tools in practical settings.

References

Agor, W. H. (1984). *Intuitive Management: Integrating Left and Right Brain Management Skills.* New York: Prentice Hall Press.

Agor, W. H. (1986). *The Logic of Intuitive Decision Making: A Research-Based Approach for Top Management.* New York: Quorum Books.

Akinci, C., and Sadler-Smith, E. (2012). Intuition in management research: A historical review. *International Journal of Management Reviews,* 14(1): 104–122.

Anastasiu, R., and Wickert, C. (2021). Can we train intuition? Intuition in Organizations Symposium, Academy of Management Annual Meeting, August, virtual.

Bas, A., and Dörfler, V. (2023). Knowing by intuiting. Submitted to Intuition in Organizations Symposium, Academy of Management Annual Meeting, August.

Bas, A., Sinclair, M., and Dörfler, V. (2022). Sensing: The elephant in the room of management learning. *Management Learning,* 1–42.

Baylor, A. L. (2001). A U-shaped model for the development of intuition by level of expertise. *New Ideas in Psychology,* 19(3): 237–244.

Bechara, A. (2004). The role of emotion in decision making: Evidence from neurological patients with orbito-frontal damage. *Brain and Cognition,* 55: 30–40.

Buehler, R., Griffin, D., and Ross, M. (1994). Exploring the 'planning fallacy': Why people underestimate their task completion times. *Journal of Personality and Social Psychology,* 67(3): 366.

Cairns-Lee, H. (2020). Researching intuition through metaphor. In: M. Sinclair (Ed.), *Handbook of Intuition Research as Practice,* 282–292. Cheltenham, UK: Edward Elgar.

Calabretta, G., Gemser, G., and Wijnberg, N. M. (2017). The interplay between intuition and rationality in strategic decision making: A paradox perspective. *Organization Studies,* 38(3–4): 365–401.

Cappon, D. (1993). The anatomy of intuition. *Psychology Today,* 26: 40–91.

Cappon, D. (1994). *Intuition and Management: Research and Applications.* Westport, CT: Quorum Books.

Childre, D., and Martin, H. (1999). *The HeartMath Solution.* San Francisco, CA: Harper.

Choquette, S. (2005). *Trust Your Vibes at Work.* Carlsbad, CA: Hay House.

Coget, J.-F. (2014). Dialogical inquiry: A qualitative method for studying intuition in the field. In: M. Sinclair (Ed.), *Handbook of Intuition Research as Practice,* 176–187. Cheltenham, UK: Edward Elgar.

Coleiro, K., and Baldacchino, L. (2022). A training programme for entrepreneurial intuition. Intuition in Organizations Symposium, Academy of Management Annual Meeting, August, virtual.

Crossan, M. M., Lane, H. W., and White, R. E. (1999). An organizational learning framework: From intuition to institution. *Academy of Management Review,* 24(3): 522–537.

Damasio, A. R. (1994). *Descartes' Error: Emotion, Reason, and the Human Brain.* New York: Putnam.

Dane, E., and Pratt, M. G. (2007). Exploring intuition and its role in managerial decision making. *Academy of Management Review,* 32(1): 33–54.

Dane, E., and Pratt, M. G. (2009). Conceptualizing and measuring intuition: A review of recent trends. In: Hodgkinson, G., and Ford, J. K. (Eds.), *International Review of Industrial and Organizational Psychology,* 24, 1–40. Chichester, UK: Wiley.

Dijksterhuis, A., and Nordgren, L. F. (2006). A theory of unconscious thought. *Perspectives on Psychological Science,* 1(2): 95–109.

Dörfler, V., and Ackermann, F. (2012). Understanding of intuition: The case for two forms of intuition. *Management Learning,* 43(5): 545–564.

Dreyfus, S. E. (2004). The five-stage model of adult skill acquisition. *Bulletin of Science, Technology & Society,* 24(3): 177–181.

Dreyfus, S. E. (2014). System 0: The overlooked explanation of expert intuition. In: M. Sinclair (Ed.), *Handbook of Research Methods on Intuition,* 15–27. Cheltenham, UK: Edward Elgar.

Dreyfus, H. L., and Dreyfus, S. E. (2005). Peripheral vision: Expertise in real world contexts. *Organization Studies,* 26(5): 779–792.

Dunn, B. D., Galton, H. C., Morgan, R., Evans, D., Oliver, C., Meyer, M., . . . & Dalgleish, T. (2010). Listening to your heart: How interoception shapes emotion experience and intuitive decision making. *Psychological Science,* 21(12): 1835–1844.

Egorov, A., and Pircher, A. V. (2020). Moral intuition and moral leader development. In: M. Sinclair (Ed.), *Handbook of Intuition Research as Practice,* 157–166. Cheltenham, UK: Edward Elgar.

Elsbach, K. D., and Barr, P. S. (1999). The effects of mood on individuals' use of structured decision protocols. *Organization Science,* 10: 181–198.

Epstein, S. (1990). Cognitive-experiential theory. In: L. Pervin (Ed.), *Handbook of Personality Theory and Research,* 165–192. New York: Guildford Press.

Epstein, S., Pacini, R., Denes-Raj, V., and Heier, H. (1996). Individual differences in intuitive-experiential and analytical-rational thinking styles. *Journal of Personality and Social Psychology,* 71(2): 390–405.

Ericsson, K. A. (1998). The scientific study of expert levels of performance: General implications for optimal learning and creativity. *High Ability Studies,* 9(1): 75–100.

Evans, J. St. B. T. (2003). In two minds: Dual-process accounts of reasoning. *Trends in Cognitive Sciences,* 7: 454–459.

Fellnhofer, K. (2023). How can intuition measurement inform training? Submitted to Intuition in Organizations Symposium, Academy of Management Annual Meeting, August.

Fellnhofer, K., and Renold, U. (2022). How can we train diverse cognitive skills of tomorrow's managers with new technologies? Academy of Management Annual Meeting, August, virtual.

Foerde, K. (2010). Implicit learning and memory: Psychological and neural aspects. In: S. Della Salla (Ed.), *Encyclopedia of Behavioral Neuroscience,* 84–93.

Gendlin, E. T. (1962). *Experiencing and the Creation of Meaning.* New York: Free Press of Glencoe.

Gigerenzer, G., and Gaissmaier, W. (2011). Heuristic decision making. *Annual Review of Psychology,* 62: 451–482.

Gillin, M. L. M. (2020). Facilitating intuitive decision-making and an entrepreneurial mindset in corporate culture—A case study. In: M. Sinclair (Ed.), *Handbook of Intuition Research as Practice,* 226–240. Cheltenham, UK: Edward Elgar.

Gilovich T., Griffin, D., and Kahneman, D. (2002). *Heuristics and Biases.* Cambridge: Cambridge University Press.

Goldberg, P. (1983). *The Intuitive Edge: Understanding and Developing Intuition.* Los Angeles, CA: Jeremy P. Tarcher.

Goldberg, S. B., Del Re, A. C., Hoyt, W. T., and Davis, J. M. (2014). The secret ingredient in mindfulness interventions? A case for practice quality over quantity. *Journal of Counselling Psychology,* 61(3): 491–497.

Gore, J., and Sadler-Smith, E. (2011). Unpacking intuition: A process and outcome framework. *Review of General Psychology,* 15(4): 304–316.

Govender, C., Williamson, C., and Davis, A. (2023). Can pausing enhance intuition? Submitted to Intuition in Organizations Symposium, Academy of Management Annual Meeting, August.

Green, K. C., and Armstrong, J. S. (2007). Structured analogies for forecasting. *International Journal of Forecasting,* 23(3): 365–376.

Haidt, J. (2001). The emotional dog and its rational tail: A social intuitionist approach to moral judgment. *Psychological Review,* 4: 814–834.

Herbert, B. M., and Pollatos, O. (2012). The body in the mind: On the relationship between interoception and embodiment. *Topics in Cognitive Science,* 4(4): 692–704.

Hodgkinson, G. P. (2023). In praise of experimental methods and behavioral assessments. Submitted to Intuition in Organizations symposium, Academy of Management Annual Meeting, August.

Hodgkinson, G. P., and Sadler-Smith, E. (2018). The dynamics of intuition and analysis in managerial and organizational decision making. *Academy of Management Perspectives,* 32(4): 473–492.

Hogarth, R. M. (2001). *Educating Intuition.* Chicago, IL: Chicago University Press.

Hogarth, R. M., and Karelaia, N. (2012). Entrepreneurial success and failure: Confidence and fallible judgment. *Organization Science,* 23(6): 1733–1747.

Iannello, P., Colombo, B., and Antonietti, A. (2014). Non-invasive brain stimulation techniques in the study of intuition. In: M. Sinclair (Ed.), *Handbook of Intuition Research as Practice,* 130–143. Cheltenham, UK: Edward Elgar.

Iannello, P., Colombo, B., and Germagnoli, S. (2020). Enhancing intuition in problem solving through problem finding. In: M. Sinclair (Ed.), *Handbook of Intuition Research as Practice,* 255–269. Cheltenham, UK: Edward Elgar.

Kahneman, D. (2011). *Thinking, Fast and Slow.* London: Allen Lane.

Kahneman, D., and Klein, G. (2009). Conditions for intuitive expertise: A failure to disagree. *American Psychologist,* 64(6): 515–526.

Kahneman, D., Sibony, O., and Thaler, R. (2021). *Noise.* London: William Collins.

Kahneman, D., and Tversky, A. (1972). Subjective probability: A judgment of representativeness. *Cognitive Psychology,* 3(3): 430–454.

Kapur, N. (2015). Unconscious bias harms patients and staff. *BMJ,* 351.

Klein, G. (1998). *Sources of Power: How People Make Decisions.* MIT Press.

Klein, G. (2003). *Intuition at Work.* New York: Doubleday.

Klein, G., Calderwood, R., and Clinton-Cirocco, A. (2010). Rapid decision making on the fire ground: The original study plus a postscript. *Journal of Cognitive Engineering and Decision Making,* 4(3): 186–209.

Kruglanski, A. W., and Gigerenzer, G. (2011). Intuitive and deliberative judgments are based on common principles. *Psychological Review,* 118: 97–109.

Kruglanski, A. W., and Orehek, E. (2007). Partitioning the domain of social inference: Dual mode and system models and their alternatives. *Annual Review of Psychology,* 58: 291–316.

Kündig, B., and Sinclair, M. (2012). *Intuitive richtig: Wir wissen mehr als wir denken [Intuition: We know more than we think].* Windpferd, Oberstdorf.

Lieberman, M. D. (2000). Intuition: A social cognitive neuroscience approach. *Psychological Bulletin,* 126(1): 109–137.

Lieberman, M. D., Jarcho, J. M., and Satpute, A. B. (2004). Evidence-based and intuition-based self-knowledge: An FMRI study. *Journal of Personality and Social Psychology,* 87(4): 421–435.

Lufityanto, G. (2020). Psychophysical measurement of intuition. In: M. Sinclair (Ed.), *Handbook of Intuition Research as Practice,* 115–127. Cheltenham, UK: Edward Elgar.

Lufityanto, G., Donkin, C., and Pearson, J. (2016). Measuring intuition: Non-conscious emotional information boosts decision accuracy and confidence. *Psychological Science,* 27(5): 622–634.

McGraty, R., Atkinson, M., and Bradley, R. T. (2004). Electrophysiological evidence of intuition: Part 1. The surprising role of the heart. *Journal of Alternative and Complementary Medicine,* 10: 133–143.

McGraty, R., Barrios-Choplin, B., Rozman, D., Atkinson, M., and Watkins, A. D. (1998). The impact of a new emotional self-management program on stress, emotions, heart rate variability, DHEA and cortisol. *Integrative Physiological and Behavioral Science,* 33(2): 151–170.

McGraty, R., and Tomasino, D. (2004). Heart rhythm coherence feedback: A new tool for stress reduction, rehabilitation and performance enhancement. *Proceedings of the First Baltic Forum on Neuronal Regulation and Feedback,* Riga, November 2–5.

Merrett, R. (2015). A neuroscience approach to innovative thinking and problem solving. *CIO Executive,* 12: 59.

Meziani, N. (2020). Talking intuition into existence: The role of ventriloquism figures. In: M. Sinclair (Ed.), *Handbook of Intuition Research as Practice,* 271–292. Cheltenham, UK: Edward Elgar.

Mintzberg, H. (1989). Mintzberg on management: Inside our strange world of organizations. New York: The Free Press.

OECD (2014). Are 15-year-olds good at solving problems? *OECD Education and Skills Today,* April.

OECD (2019a). *PISA 2018 Insights and Interpretations.* Paris, France: OECD Publishing.

OECD (2019b). *Tools and Ethics for Applied Behavioural Insights: The BASIC Toolkit.* Paris, France: OECD Publishing.

OECD (2021). *OECD Skills Outlook 2021: Learning for Life.* Paris, France: OECD Publishing.

Osman, M. (2004). An evaluation of dual-process theories of reasoning. *Psychonomic Bulletin and Review,* 11(6): 988–1010.

Pacini, R., and Epstein, S. (1999). The relationship of rational and experiential information processing styles to personality, basic beliefs, and the ratio-bias phenomena. *Journal of Personality and Social Psychology,* 76: 972–987.

Petitmengin, C. (1999). The intuitive experience. *Journal of Consciousness,* 6: 43–77.

Petitmengin, C. (2014). Researching the microdynamics of intuitive experience. In: M. Sinclair (Ed.), *Handbook of Intuition Research as Practice,* 199–198. Cheltenham, UK: Edward Elgar.

Radin, D. (2011). Intuition and the noetic. In: M. Sinclair (Ed.), *Handbook of Intuition Research as Practice,* 183–196. Cheltenham, UK: Edward Elgar.

Reber, A. S., 1989. Implicit learning and tacit knowledge. *Journal of Experimental Psychology: General,* 118(3): 219–235. https://doi.org/10.1037/0096-3445 .118.3.219

Sadler-Smith, E. (2008). *Inside Intuition.* Routledge/Taylor & Francis Group.

Sadler-Smith, E. (2010). *The Intuitive Mind.* Chichester, UK: John Wiley & Sons

Sadler-Smith, E. (2016). 'What happens when you intuit?': Understanding human resource practitioners' subjective experience of intuition through a novel linguistic method. *Human Relations,* 69(5): 1069–1093.

Sadler-Smith, E. (2023). *Intuition in Business.* Oxford, UK: Oxford University Press.

Sadler-Smith, E., and Shefy, E. (2004). The intuitive executive: Understanding and applying 'gut feel' in decision-making. *Academy of Management Perspectives,* 18(4): 76–91.

Sadler-Smith, E., and Shefy, E. (2007). Developing intuitive awareness in management education. *Academy of Management Learning & Education,* 6(2): 186–205.

Salas, E., Rosen, M. A., and Diaz-Granados, D. (2010). Expertise-based intuition and decision making in organizations. *Journal of Management,* 36(4): 941–973.

Simon, H. A. (1987). Making management decisions: The role of intuition and emotions. *Academy of Management Executive,* 1: 57–64.

Sinclair, M. (2003). 'The use of intuition in managerial decision-making: Determinants and affective moderators'. PhD diss., The University of Queensland.

Sinclair, M. (2010). Misconceptions about intuition. *Psychological Inquiry,* 21(4): 378–386.

Sinclair, M. (2020). Are all intuitions the same? Or does it depend on the factor that triggers them? In: M. Sinclair (Ed.), *Handbook of Intuition Research as Practice,* 139–156. Cheltenham, UK: Edward Elgar.

Sinclair, M., and Ashkanasy, N. M. (2002/2003). Intuitive decision-making among leaders: More than just shooting from the hip. *Mt. Eliza Business Review,* 32–40.

Sinclair, M., and Ashkanasy, N. M. (2005). Intuition: Myth or a decision-making tool? *Management Learning,* 36(3): 353–370.

Sinclair, M., Ashkanasy, N. M., and Chattopadhyay, P. (2010). Affective antecedents of intuitive decision making. *Journal of Management and Organization,* 16(3): 382–398.

Sinclair, M., and Hamilton, A. (2014). Mapping group intuitions. In: M. Sinclair (Ed.), *Handbook of Intuition Research as Practice,* 199–216. Cheltenham, UK: Edward Elgar.

Sinclair, M., Sadler-Smith, E., and Hodgkinson, G. P. (2009) The role of intuition in strategic decision making. In: L. A. Constanzo and R. B. Mackay (Eds.),

Handbook of Research on Strategy and Foresight, 393–417. Cheltenham UK: Edward Elgar.

Slovic, P., Finucane, M. L., Peters, E., and MacGregor, D. G. (2007). The affect heuristic. *European Journal of Operational Research,* 177: 1333–1352.

Soosalu, G., and Henwood, S. (2020). Exploring intuition and decision-making across the 'three brains'. In: M. Sinclair (Ed.), *Handbook of Intuition Research as Practice,* 28–138. Cheltenham, UK: Edward Elgar.

Soosalu, G., Henwood, S., and Deo, A. (2019). *Head, Heart and Gut in Decision-Making: Development of a Multiple Brain Preference Questionnaire* (MBPQ). Thousand Oaks, CA: Sage Open.

Soyer E., and Hogarth, R. M. (2021). *The Myth of Experience.* New York: Public Affairs.

Stanovich, K. E., and West, R. F. (2000). Individual differences in reasoning: Implications for the rationality debate? *Behavioral and Brain Sciences,* 23: 645–726.

Tantia, J. F. (2011). Viva las vagus! The innervation of embodied clinical intuition. *The USA Body Psychotherapy Journal,* Editorial, 10(1): 29–37.

Tantia, J. F. (2014). Is intuition embodied? A phenomenological study of clinical intuition in somatic psychotherapy practice. *Body, Movement and Dance in Psychotherapy,* 9(4): 211–223.

Teerikangas, S., Turunen, M., and Välikangas, L. (2020). Resourcing intuition in practice. In: M. Sinclair (Ed.), *Handbook of Intuition Research as Practice,* 212–225. Cheltenham, UK: Edward Elgar.

Tiller, W. A., McGraty, R., and Atkinson, M. (1996). Cardiac coherence: A new, noninvasive measure of autonomic nervous system order. *Alternative Therapies in Health and Medicine,* 2(1): 52–65.

Tomasino, D. E. (2011). The heart in intuition: Tools for cultivating intuitive intelligence. In: M. Sinclair (Ed.), *Handbook of Intuition Research,* 247–260. Cheltenham, UK: Edward Elgar.

Tversky, A., and Kahneman, D. (1983). Extensional versus intuitive reasoning: The conjunction fallacy in probability judgment. *Psychological Review,* 90(4): 293–315.

Vaughan, F. E. (1979). *Awakening Intuition.* New York: Doubleday.

World Economic Forum (2022). Top 10 work skills of tomorrow how long it takes to learn them. https://www.weforum.org/agenda/2020/10/top-10 -work-skills-of-tomorrow-how-long-it-takes-to-learn-them/

Yeung, N., and Sinclair, M. (2023). Training entrepreneurial intuition—An action research intervention. Submitted to Intuition in Organizations Symposium, Academy of Management Annual Meeting, August.

Yeung, N., and Sinclair, M. (*in preparation*). How expat-preneurs make decisions— The role of intuition.

Chapter 3

Intuition and Analysis: Past, Present, and Future

And the Impact of Artificial Intelligence

Leonie Hallo[1] and Tiep Nguyen[2,3]

[1] The University of Adelaide, Adelaide, South Australia, Australia

[2] School of Civil Engineering and Management, International University, Ho Chi Minh City, Vietnam

[3] Vietnam National University, Ho Chi Minh City, Vietnam

I. Introduction

The last few years have brought unprecedented challenges to society and businesses. The Covid-19 pandemic brought with it very high levels of uncertainty and huge challenges in decision-making for both government and businesses, including remote working, more virtual transactions of all types, and the far greater infiltration of digital technologies. As the pandemic recedes, the results are still with us in terms of changed attitudes and requirements. In line with those changes, managers have learned to respond in an agile way and change their practices to suit the prevailing business conditions.

This is also a great chance for us to think anew about how business decisions are made and the new management approaches needed. Many scholars agree that business managers will need enhanced skills in the face of fast-arising disruptive changes and growing uncertainty while still maintaining ongoing processes. The relationship between business organisations and governments may change as businesses are encouraged to make more holistically based decisions that take account of a wider range of societal values.

Alongside the great disruption caused by the pandemic, the arrival of the digital age and the ubiquitous nature of artificial intelligence (AI) applications create further pressure on managers who must come up with wise decisions that will produce beneficial outcomes. Data analysis has been completely transfigured. We now have huge data assets that can, if successfully employed, bring significant competitive advantage (Tabesh, Mousavidin, & Hasani 2019). The trick is to harness the relevant information and use it for an optimal decision. People now have immediate access to huge amounts of data on their smart phones, and this creates pressures for managers. When everybody can Google® the data they want, this brings empowerment to a far greater range of stakeholders. The status of senior decision-makers is thereby reduced.

In the digital age, we are also facing increasing economic changes due to the interaction of many factors. Unsustainable globalization has been disrupted by various political and supply-chain pressures, promoting distrust between countries. Many suggest that indicators are present which suggest imminent recessions in many countries around the world (Statista 2023). All these factors create greater complexity, and they also lead to shorter decision-making lifecycles.

Due to uncertainty, previous vistas of long-term and medium-term strategies have now been replaced with a need for solely short-term timelines because we cannot predict change with any kind of certainty, and long-held assumptions no longer apply. People therefore need to take a much more flexible approach and have greater familiarity with change management procedures to adapt as needed. While there are many perceived advantages of big data due to highly pressured decision-makers who can access information very easily, it may not be the right information, and this can be a problem.

A survey by McKinsey Digital (2019) indicated that only 20 percent of executives believe that their organisations excel in decision-making, and many say that much of the time spent on decision-making is used ineffectively. Speed is not related to the quality of the decision: indeed, good decision-making should provide decisions high in both quality and speed.

In line with that, this chapter is about *how decisions can be made in the face of pressures for agility, responsibility, and transparency in circumstances of turbulence and greatly enhanced complexity due to a range of factors, including globalisation, digitisation, and growing expectations.* The chapter focuses upon decisions made within the context of business and management. In particular, the chapter talks about two major ways in which people can make decisions—analysis and intuition—and how each can be best employed to optimise choices going forward.

Intuition has a time element embedded in it. As commented by Sinclair (2010, 383): ". . . the environmental scanning and information pool that intuiting utilizes in terms of specific expertise, broad experience, and cursory exposure can be oriented towards past, present, and future." The chapter flips this idea to consider the past, present, and future of the application of intuition and intuiting versus analysis in decision-making.

II. Intuition versus analysis: How are they different?

The definitions of intuition and analysis and the ways in which they relate to each other have long been debated (Okoli & Watt 2018). Intuition is generally perceived as automatic, effortless, unconscious, and rapid, while analysis is viewed as intentional, more effortful, conscious, and slower (Evans 2008). As stated by Sinclair and Ashkanasy (2005, 357), intuition ". . . comprises both cognitive and affective elements and results in direct knowing without any use of conscious reasoning." Intuitive judgements feel right even though they may not be able to be explained (Shapiro & Spence 1997). While people are often highly confident about the result of intuitive thought, the manner in which they arrived at their decision cannot be scrutinised or articulated (Blackman & Sadler-Smith 2009). Intuition has been called "hot" cognition, as opposed to the "cold" cognition embodied by analysis. Intuition is hot because intuitive judgements are often accompanied by affect, such as feelings of relief and warmth (Dane & Pratt 2007).

Analytical thinking, on the other hand, involves breaking down ideas into components, and analytical judgements are made against a framework for determining quality, either internally generated or organisationally declared via organisational values (Zhou, Wang, Bavato, Tasselli, & Wu 2019). Many have argued that analysis represents a superior mode of decision-making and will give a better result.

A significant number of writers disagree strongly with this, believing that intuition may be preferable under certain circumstances (Dane, Rockmann, & Pratt 2012; Julmi 2019). Even the use of the term *non-rational decision-making* suggests a negative bias towards intuition (Cristofaro 2021). However, especially in complex situations, technical solutions based upon rational choice are difficult to apply, and managers may need solutions which go beyond rationality. Under these circumstances, intuition can be very useful, and the solutions provided are often correct (Simon 1986). Many writers, including recent authors, sing the praises of intuition, especially in today's highly complex, uncertain, and risky contexts in which wise decision-making at a more strategic level is needed (Dias, Iizuka, & Rossetto 2021; Intezari & Pauleen 2018; Keller & Sadler-Smith 2019).

In fact, many processes in decision-making take place outside of awareness and conscious thinking, deriving instead from deeper levels. Uncertainty and risk are closely linked. Control and the ability to anticipate are illusory. Experts don't decide by weighing up the pros and cons of each option but rather by evaluating, often on a process of recognition based upon experience and the predictive capabilities through integrating environmental cues. Pattern matching is a very quick process sometimes called "gut feeling". Experts can make rapid holistic decisions about the qualities of ideas and analyse them for value-adding potential (Sukhov et al. 2021). They can then elaborate higher-quality ideas through sensemaking, often based upon bodily sensations, including energy flows, breathing changes, feelings in the gut or heart, et cetera; intuition is a highly personal experience (Craycroft 2022).

What is the role of each style in our current complex world of decision-making? How are those roles likely to change as our whole world transforms rapidly in the future? Given that everything has changed so monumentally, it is time to re-examine the role of each. The argument for the relative value of these two major styles has been rejuvenated by the growth in digital data and tools. It has been argued that theory has not kept up with the change in information contexts that businesses now face (Van Knippenberg, Dahlander, Haas, & George 2015). Certainly, we have access to a huge amount of data of varying quality and relevance. Mobile technology is now widespread. But how well are these data curated to fit given purposes? Some people are inclined to be entranced by data, leading to limited perception. It is difficult now for all managers to be conversant with the kinds of analysis and results produced by artificial intelligence (AI). Doubtless these analytical processes have huge advantages under certain circumstances, but they do need to be tailored to fit the situation at hand. It is also the case that in many situations where decisions need to be made, there is a paucity of relevant data or case studies to draw upon.

III. Intuition and analysis: Past, present, and future

III.1 Intuition and analysis in the past

Philosophical viewpoints

Discussion of these two complementary methods of decision-making goes back many centuries. Intuition has been an important concept within the discipline of philosophy. Greek philosophers distinguished between two ways of acquiring knowledge: a holistic direct way of knowing and an analytical reductionist process. Plato asserted that intuition was the way in which people could understand the abstract world of ideas, the supreme state of mind, whereas analysis was the way in which people can understand the physical world, and a lesser way of knowing, in which we start with unquestioned assumptions and argue deductively from them.

This process falls short of the perfect knowledge represented by intuition. Struck (2016) wrote about intuition in classical antiquity as a way to better understand the world and the self, asserting that both the Greeks and the Romans viewed divination as, ". . . an inexplicable means of acquiring knowledge based firmly in both the natural and divine worlds" (p. 187). This is what we now call intuition. Platonic philosophy has had an enduring significance on our understandings of intuition. In philosophical intuitionism, intuition is holistic, non-propositional, and nonrepresentational, whilst analysis is reductionist, propositional, and representational (Henden 2004).

French philosopher Henry-Louis Bergson argued that intuition and analysis are not complementary components, but are quite different ways of understanding the world. This approach highlighted the importance of intuition and direct experience: intuition is a simple act that enables us to understand a reality absolutely rather than relatively, of placing ourselves within an object "instead of adopting points of view toward it" (Bergson 1946, 190)—a way of apprehending ultimate truth (Shklar 1958). Only intuition can help us to grasp the essence of an object or thing directly and immediately, bypassing logical processes. While analysis separates things and reduces them, providing us with only relative knowledge, intuition alone can grasp the essence of something in its totality; we need to free the mind from logic, reason, and science and circumvent the "shield" of the rational mind.

Intuition and analysis have also been explored in several religious and theological domains. The idea that intuition cannot be grasped through the senses or intellect is, for example, a feature of many Eastern philosophies, including Confucianism, where intuition is seen as a way of accessing the Tao, or ultimate reality, while analysis is more focused upon the world of appearances. Confucius emphasised the importance of moral development to achieve wisdom through study, reflection, and practice. Wang (2003) introduced the idea of *systems intuition* to describe the core of a systems-thinking style present in ancient Chinese works from several thousand years ago. Similarly, Zen Buddhism views intuition as one of the deepest functions of the mind, allowing us to perceive reality directly through moving beyond the intellect (Kondo 1952). Intuition and analysis are complementary tools for spiritual development, but intuition is the foundation for refining our understanding and can be improved through practice and training to perceive the whole picture.

The Vedic tradition within Hinduism views intuition as a way of connecting with the divine, compared with analysis, which helps us to understand the physical world (Raina 2015). In this philosophy, meditation is suggested as a way of developing intuition, coupled with studying scriptures and using reasoning to make good decisions. Both are necessary for spiritual development; but again, intuition is the foundation. Similarly in Sufism, the mystical tradition of Islam, intuition is a way of connecting with God and understanding his will (Deikman 1977). Intuition can bypass the rational mind and give us a deeper understanding. Analysis should be guided by intuition, according to this tradition.

Within the many different versions of Christianity, intuition enables us to come to a knowledge of God and is often interpreted as a form of spiritual discernment that allows people to connect with God and receive guidance through his quiet voice ". . . when all else is stilled" (Gorton 2018, 190). Logic has its role in interpreting scripture (Hales 2004).

The world of philosophy has contributed greatly to our understanding of intuition, and there are many consistencies between ancient Greek philosophy and Western and Eastern understandings. In general, intuition within philosophy is seen as a way of acquiring knowledge that is non-inferential and subjective, and to this extent, it is incontestable.

Understandings from psychology and organisational studies

Within psychology, there have been many debates about the superiority of intuition or analysis, and these continue. One major contribution is the concept of *dual-process thinking,* which dominated discussions on this topic for many years in the late 1900s (Evans & Stanovich 2013; Hodgkinson & Sadler-Smith 2018), in which one system is used for conscious deliberating and the other for non-conscious intuiting. There have long been arguments about the superiority of one type of thinking over the other. In the early days, analysis was viewed as necessarily superior, and all intuitive decisions should be checked through the filter of analysis. The superiority of the analytical approach has been widely supported (Benbasat & Dexter 1979).

Alternatively, it has been suggested that the two processes operate in parallel, with conflict resolved through negotiation. Others suggest that intuition is superior, especially under conditions of complexity and a lack of complete information. Whether intuition and analysis can operate at the same time is still an open question, with the more dominant view being that people switch between the two modes. Authors have also investigated whether intuiting is indeed non-conscious, or whether we can set up the conditions in a conscious way to encourage intuition to arrive.

One reason that intuition is viewed as being inferior is that intuitive understandings seem to arrive quickly and with little effort. This fits well with the view of people as cognitive misers, making the minimal effort necessary to get the job done and often operating on automatic in the face of information overload. The work of Kahneman (Kahneman, Slovic, Slovic, & Tversky 1982; Tversky and Kahneman 1974) introduced the idea of *heuristics* or *rules of thumb* as a way of dealing with our information-rich world; such rules may introduce biases and errors. More recent research in the business and management field has expanded this limiting interpretation of intuition beyond heuristics and biases (Akinci & Sadler-Smith 2009).

Intuition has been categorised in various ways. One major understanding of intuition is *expert intuition* or *intuitive expertise*. Experienced people can assess environmental cues, recognise patterns, devise a range of appropriate actions, and choose one via mental simulation (Dane & Pratt 2007). Generally, decision-makers who use this approach are highly confident and may experience a sense of relief on making their decision (Khatri & Ng 2000). Expert intuition has been well explored in the literature (Dörfler & Eden 2014). Experts need less information than novices do because they can recognise what is relevant and consider important cues first (Gigerenzer 2022). In some ways, this type of decision-making seems rather like analysis. Many articles report solely on this kind of intuition. There is much research indicating that executives do in fact use intuition (Agor 1986), especially of this pattern-matching kind. Several studies have investigated experience-based intuition in crisis management—for example, Okoli, Weller, and Watt (2016) and Akinci (2014). Recognising when to rely upon intuition is itself quite important (Hodgkinson & Healey 2011).

The useful unifying framework of Sinclair (2011) suggests other types of intuition. *Intuitive creation* is the sudden unexpected arrival of a solution, sometimes called "insight": a new understanding of a problem, often accompanied by a solution. This is less about pattern recognition and more about connecting ideas in novel ways, along the line of our understanding of creativity. It is not effortless because there has generally been a period of incubation before ideas become organised. There may well be a positive emotional experience along with the arrival of the new idea (Shen, Yuan, Liu, & Luo 2016). Affect may also be both an antecedent to and a result of intuition: people can be more successful with intuition if they are in a positive mood (Bolte, Goschke, & Kuhl 2003; Velcu-Laitinen 2022) and may experience positive feelings as a result of using their intuition. Some relate this kind of intuition or holistic understanding to the divine or the spiritual (Taylor 2022).

A theme which commenced in the early 2000s examined optimal ways of combining intuition and analysis, suggesting that contrasting the two styles of management is probably not the best way to go, because they both have their place and can be used in combination: therefore, assisting managers to use both would be advantageous. Generally, it is thought that answers arrive first via intuition and are then confirmed or changed through the analytical system. This sequence could be very helpful under conditions of stress and time constraints (Sinclair, Sadler-Smith, & Hodgkinson 2009). Liebowitz (Liebowitz, 2019; Liebowitz et al. 2019) introduced the concept of *informed intuitants* who can combine analytics with intuition when faced with a difficult business decision: they use a complementary set of intuitive and analytical skills including problem-solving, issue diagnosis, insight generation, data synthesis, problem framing, collaboration, creativity, and others. Woiceshyn (2009) suggested the concept of *spiralling,* in which a series of iterative passed through intuition and analysis will give the best result. Thus, zooming in using expert intuition will uncover feasible alternatives, and then analysis can be used to rank options to provide a tentative choice, followed by a final decision. Recognition of both styles is a positive move.

III.2 Intuition and analysis at the present time

The involvement of data science and metacognition

In the years from 2019 onwards, we have seen widespread societal and technological changes along with a greater desire for involvement by stakeholders. The pandemic itself produced sweeping changes, of course. The role of intuition considered against the background of enhanced data science presents an interesting new question. Big data are now developed to a very high level and ubiquitously applied in many areas of life, including organisational strategy making. The exponential increase in business data and analytics gives managers greater efficiency in collecting and analysing information (Erevelles, Fukawa, & Swayne 2016).

The availability of real-time information in a highly dynamic environment and the ability to access it quickly bring leverage potential. Customers also have access to mobile technologies and can access data in real time. Perhaps there is too much information for people to handle comfortably (Giudice da Silva Cezar & Maçada 2021). This significant change in the decision-making scenario has prompted a re-energising of the discussion about the value of intuition versus analysis. Earlier debates considered circumstances in which there was a lack of data and of sufficiently powerful analytical tools (Van Knippenberg et al. 2015). Now the situation has changed completely.

Bullini Orlandi and Pierce (2020) picked up this question in the context of mobile technologies, concluding that intuition still has a central role, although, within highly dynamic environments, analytical approaches are also necessary. As they say, business analytics provides useful new tools for decision-making to handle the overabundance of information. People make decisions on the move in real time, and managers must deal with this highly dynamic market and react quickly. In this totally transformed context, the comparison argument is also transformed. Mobile technologies have been the focus of many studies in the health arena (Haddad, Souza, & Cecatti 2019). Information overload, control, and worker stress have also been investigated in this context (Tams, Ahuja, Thatcher, & Grover 2020).

The investigation of *metacognition* also brings a new approach to the understanding of intuition and analysis. Metacognition is thinking about our own thinking (Carruthers 2021). Luoma and Martela (2021), for example, considered the strategy of reframing—that is, deliberately rethinking decision-making strategies, noting (Luoma & Martela 2021, 102065), "How much time and effort should I dedicate to this decision? Should I just go with the first intuitive option to save resources for more important decisions? Should I analyse the options using conscious reasoning? Or is this a decision of such gravity . . . that it is best to let the decision incubate for a few days?"

The work of Ackerman, Yom-Tov, and Torgovitsky (2020) investigates self-regulation of effort in relation to success probability in cognitive tasks and the impact of confidence—ideas that are relevant to appreciation of analysis in our current very busy world. We monitor the progress of our problem-solving activities in the background, and we regulate our time and effort. Feelings of certainty may be based upon heuristics, including gut feeling and beliefs, which may not be reliable. If we are confident, we will act, but less confidence may lead to hesitation and changing direction.

This is more likely in an uncertain context. When we achieve a feeling of rightness about a decision, we stop. We can also identify when we have made a mistake. If a problem is too hard, we may give up or seek help. Similarly, Scheiter, Ackerman, and Hoogerheide (2020) assert that people may invest more effort when the task is important or because they like a challenge, or less effort because the task seems easy or perhaps impossible, and they give up. Assessment of success probability will be involved in the regulation of mental effort; however, self-assessments of effort may be biased. In this research, we can see nuanced appreciations of the interactions between analysis and intuition.

Paradox theory approaches

Paradox theory has been used to explore how intuition and analysis can be used together. The way in which analysis and intuition relate to each other can be viewed as a paradox (Keller & Sadler-Smith 2019)—that is, they contain the two essential elements of contradiction yet interdependence (Smith & Lewis 2011). Paradox has been defined as, "persistent contradiction between interdependent elements" (Schad, Lewis, Raisch, & Smith 2016, 10).

In some ways this is almost absurd: how to simultaneously consider two conflicting approaches? One way of managing this paradoxical situation is via virtuous cycles of acceptance and resolution and accepting the tension involved as an invitation for the use of a creative lens, expanding one's understanding of both elements, which in the end may bring deeper understanding. Embracing the paradox through separating and bringing together brings strength through recognising the differences of each approach but also integrating them through linkages and iterations backwards and forwards (Keller & Sadler-Smith 2019).

Iterations in sequence are necessary because it is hard for us to keep both ends of the paradox in our brains simultaneously. The use of systems thinking can help us to engage with these different approaches and keep an open mind, seeking synergies (Schad & Smith 2019). Thinking in images instead of words can also be helpful. Miron-Spektor, Ingram, Keller, Smith, and Lewis (2018) produced a model of the paradox mindset in which both accepting and being energised by tensions can help people improve both their performance and innovation success. People holding a paradox mindset feel comfortable with tension, confront that tension, and accept the "both/and" nature of paradox. Tension can produce either virtuous or vicious cycles, depending on the responses of the individual.

Tabesh and Vera (2020) picked up the idea of paradox in the context of crisis decision-making. In a crisis, leaders may have to improvise, and simultaneously attending to both analysis and intuition will reduce discomfort and tension. These authors suggest training in improvisation, which includes paradoxical thinking, balancing rational intuitive and improvisational approaches to decision-making, given that improvisational decision-making is a large part of what managers now must undertake. A paper by Fellnhofer and Sornette (2022) also discussed the intuitive/analytical paradox and the tensions and promise therein, noting that discussions about paradoxes tend to prioritise analysis and underrepresent intuition. The nature of the decision, either simple or complex, relates to the paradoxical situation that intuition will be more accurate in complex and uncertain conditions, whereas analytical thinking is more accurate under simple conditions.

Others-centredness (Byerly, Hill, & Edwards 2022) is a theme in the literature on virtue describing a characteristic that enables people to consider the interests of others and wider well-being as well as their own interests. People who can extend their care beyond themselves to the wider world can make decisions that take into account a more holistic appreciation of an issue and thereby produce a wise, intuitive decision balancing all of the various interests at play (Grossmann et al. 2020). Increased feelings of connectedness are often reported (Yaden, Haidt, Hood Jr, Vago, & Newberg 2017). Dörfler and Stierand (2018) wrote about the notion of *indwelling,* where a person is immersed in the situation to an extent that they can now unleash perspectival metacognition (Kristjánsson, Fowers, Darnell, & Pollard 2021); combined with a strong moral approach, this enables leaders to see opportunities in the future. This approach necessarily involves the reduction of personal ego and balancing various interests.

A study by Hallo and Nguyen (2022) discussed ways in which paradox can be useful in decision-making and problem-solving and proposed developing comfort with inner and outer processes and openness to the unknown. This study explored intuition as a deeper way of understanding within the domain of theories concerning self-transcendence and personal development, as shown in Figure 3.1. Interconnectedness with the fundamental reality of all things has been proposed by many theorists as the ultimate goal of development in life.

Hallo and Nguyen (2022) presented a model of decision-making and problem-solving in which the superficial levels of appreciation—that of the senses and rational thinking—are suited to less complex circumstances. As complexity increases, one can move through the levels of intuition from personal experience through insight to the deepest level of holism, in which the decision-maker may need to zoom out to create a space in which insight can make its appearance. Creative intuition and intuitive foresight can produce a deep form of creative intelligence in which the problem and its surroundings can now be directly experienced as a whole, as well as a combination of constituent parts.

In considering recent examples of governmental decision-making, actions during the time of the pandemic are now being openly challenged by commentators

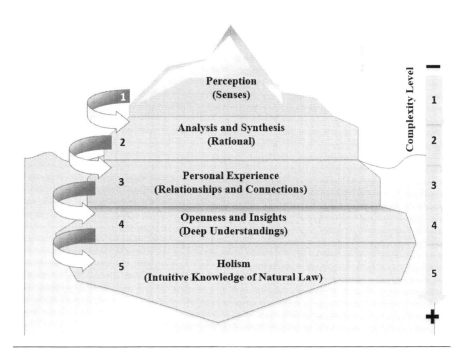

Figure 3.1   The Iceberg Model of decision-making and problem-solving (Adapted from Hallo and Nguyen [2022])

from all sides. There were huge economic and personal costs when authoritarian approaches were unfolded by governments (Kavanagh & Singh 2020). Not all governments took this line, and there were some places in which a more measured response involving individual responsibility was adopted under conditions of informed consent (Nguyen, Hallo, Chileshe, & Nguyen 2023). Many now argue with the stances taken by governments in terms of serious lockdowns and curtailment of individual freedoms (Devine, Gaskell, Jennings, & Stoker 2021). It could be said that wise holistic intuitive decision-making was seriously lacking here.

Another impediment to the appreciation of the potential of invoking holistic intuition is the arrival and popularity of big data, which has created an artificial focus on analytics. People can feel comfortable and supported by superficial data, although they do not really understand the mechanics involved in AI. There is an increased focus now upon attempts to use statistics to produce useful apps or shortcuts. Instead of needing to do research, big data results are available very quickly, but interpretation may be less clear.

Where is the role of intuition in all of this? AI has been used to solve many problems across several domains—for example, the widespread application of smart city design and smart infrastructure to improve the quality of people's lives. The availability of a totally cashless society with all its convenience has changed people's relationship with data. Advances in the involvement of technology across just about all realms of everyday life, including business decision-making, simultanious with shrinking time horizons for decision-making, all have an impact. With increasing complexity, we need to find optimal ways of combining big data and AI with human decision-making to optimise problem-solving in cases of great uncertainty. We can draw on information from big data, but we also need to be aware that the information may be not completely relevant or may be insufficient in the case of complex problems.

III.3 Future opportunities

What will the future of work be like? Will we see factories filled with robots? Will people still work in offices? Will there be major transitions in the workforce? Will we see more high-skilled jobs and fewer low-skilled jobs? Changing demographics, including ageing populations, will have an impact, no doubt. A push towards green economy initiatives will also change the workforce and workplace of the future. The pandemic accelerated trends towards remote working and virtual meetings, and these are here to stay to a greater or lesser extent. We now see an increase in hybrid work arrangements, and many employees are reluctant to go back to the office full-time (Rowley 2023). Hybrid working brings difficulties for managers, requiring very clear roles, goals, and milestones, accompanied by frequent support.

Human resources functions now have access to a great deal more data and can analyse those data to drive performance. We have also seen a huge growth in e-commerce, and all kinds of virtual transactions rose rapidly during Covid-19, including in banking, health, and entertainment. This in turn has promoted growth in certain jobs.

The Role of Artificial Intelligence

This section explores the relative value and combined promise of analysis and intuition with particular reference to AI. Simon (1995, 1) made an early comment on this topic, opining that AI will be able to model ". . . 'ineffable' phenomena such as intuition, insight and inspiration." The very fast adoption of digital technologies was amplified by the pandemic and will accelerate into the future. Scholars have started to investigate the association between intuition and AI. As pointed out by Tabesh (2021), we now exist in a digitally transformed landscape dominated by AI and big data. Not only do we face huge amounts of data, but AI-based processing tools are used to extract the meaning out of many online platforms that need to be sifted and somehow prioritised in order to be optimally useful (Tabesh et al. 2019). Because data collection and analysis have changed so enormously, we also need to re-evaluate how managers make decisions and the potential of intuition.

There seem to be two overarching approaches both in the academic literature and in popular writing: some feel that greedy AI will threaten the ability of people to control their world, reducing the spheres in which human intelligence will operate (Krueger 2022). For example, Gigerenzer (2022) addresses the issue of staying smart in a smart world: will we make decisions on our own, or will AI do it all for us? Gigerenzer expresses surprise at the trust people place in machines. We already know that AI can beat people at chess and that computing power is increasing at a very rapid rate, and the conclusion sometimes seems to be that machines will soon do everything better than people. However, the contexts in which AI is brilliant are well-defined games with fixed rules, not necessarily uncertain and ambiguous situations, because bigger data doesn't necessarily help us. Staying smart in a smart world transformed by digital technology, according to Gigerenzer, means being aware of both the potentials and the risks of digital technologies and algorithms. We need insight and courage to remain smart and stay in charge.

An alternative theme is that the combination of AI and human characteristics offers huge potential and will greatly enhance the ability of people, including leaders, to make wise decisions, taking into account all of the information (Grüning 2022). The complementary use of such processes within organisational decision-making through human-AI symbiosis could extend human cognition, equipping people to better deal with highly complex conditions (Jarrahi 2018; Vincent 2021).

Will we still need intuition? Yes, according to these authors. Enhanced computational capacity has elevated AI across a huge range of domains and industries, and it is here to stay whether we like it or not. AI is still narrow in its competency and lacks many human abilities, such as generalisability, common sense, ethical reasoning, and adaptability (Ganapini et al. 2023). So far, efforts to combine intuition and AI have focused upon the pattern-matching expert intuition kind, in which it is possible for machines to untangle relationships that might be elusive to human decision-makers. However, intuitive synthesis or creative intuition is quite different from AI. Decisions based on this type of intuition are not open to AI because they involve affective components of intuition.

Considered together, both intuition and AI can provide incredible abilities to surface the relationships between variables that are not easily apparent. Uncovering unknown relationships that expert decision makers can tap into can become part of new knowledge and can be used by managers in their future intuiting. Optimistic authors believe that big data and AI analytics can support human intuition and bring enhanced beneficial outcomes in organisations. But there will be limitations. Combining human decision-making and AI could also lead to humans' making mistakes. AI-augmented systems operate quickly, often at speeds that may be difficult for people to fully comprehend (Johnson 2022). Errors can arise when machines interpret human intentions.

The term *artificial intuition* has entered the literature as part of efforts to improve the effectiveness of machines (Diaz-Hernandez & Gonzalez-Villela 2017). This new term means AI acting intuitively (Crowder & Friess 2012), where traditional algorithms could be insufficient in comprehensively understanding the context. Johnny, Trovati, and Ray (2020, 470) defined artificial intuition as, ". . . the ability of a system to assess a problem context and use pattern recognition or properties from the dataset to choose a course of action or aid the decision process in an automatic manner." Research so far has focused on enabling machines to make decisions like the expert decision-making style of intuition.

This is currently a hot topic in the literature (Johanssen & Wang 2021). Commentary has appeared recently highlighting the somewhat over-egging currently occurring in the drive to combine AI with intuition-like characteristics. Johanssen and Wang (2021) explored how artificial intuition is described in various media, including popular journalistic websites. The general argument presented in such publications is that AI could be more autonomous and humanlike than it is currently and could be more effective than human intuition. The authors note that intuition is generally understood as subconscious pattern recognition. Journalistic commentators write about intuition incorrectly as a technicality that can be added to AI to make it more dynamic. However, people generally cannot be taught to be intuitive, and neither can machines, according to these authors. In concluding, they say that artificial intuition is a concept that makes AI seem more efficient, autonomous, and human than it really is.

An interesting conversation now concerns Chat-GPT, a third-generation language prediction model created by Open AI. Is this a real example of the infusion of intuition into AI? Chat-GPT uses natural language processing and produces humanlike responses to questions based upon a massive pool of data trawled from the Internet. Chat-GPT can both understand the intention behind a query and provide relevant information, and it can also create content in various styles. Its arrival has caused panic in the education sector, including in higher education (Mollick & Mollick 2033). However, answers produced in this way are not always accurate or unbiased (Cotton, Cotton, & Shipway 2023; McGee 2023). Aljanabi (2023, 16) cites Chat-GPT as his paper's second author, calling it: "One of the most exciting advancements in the field of artificial intelligence." He (they) write(s) about integration with other AI technologies enabling Chat-GPT to better understand human communication, producing a more intuitive experience for users.

Several other authors have presented papers partly or wholly written by Chat-GPT (King 2022; Bishop 2023; Biswas 2023). There are limitations, however. Hammad (2023) concluded that a non-expert would not be able to write an accurate research paper in the correct sequence using such a program unless they were familiar with the subject matter. Some people are upbeat about developments such as Chat-GPT. A paper by Saghafian (2023) sees no problem in imbuing intuitive expertise into Chat-GPT, drawing upon the concept of the centaur from Greek mythology to describe human-machine collaboration and noting: "Realising that intuition alone can be misleading in understanding and analysing complex systems, and that human-machine collaborations are needed to harness the full power of both advanced analytics and mighty intuition, has led to important ways of supplementing expert's decision-making in the form of *decision support systems*" (Saghafian 2023, 3).

Figure 3.2 describes the limitations of current AI as these relate to task complexity (Hechler, Oberhofer, & Schaeck 2020). While there is a large area in which AI is applicable, relatively simple problems may not require AI, and

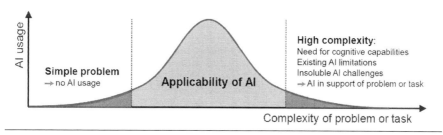

Figure 3.2   When not to use AI (Adapted from Hechler et al. [2020])

highly complex problems need AI to be supported by human intelligence, in keeping with the Iceberg Model presented on page 49.

How can human decision-makers reconcile their own intuitive choices with the information provided by AI? When should human decision-makers override AI? What will be the impact of AI on management decision-making? Will AI take over what managers usually do? How will it impact the products and services being delivered? What will it mean for a business and markets? Will changes in markets mean that some products are no longer needed? If we think about the impact within various domains of business, the impacts may vary, but they will likely be significant.

To ascertain the roles of analysis and intuition into the future, we interviewed ten senior business decision-makers about what they predicted regarding their decision-making context in the next five to ten years; how they saw the interrelationship between analysis and intuition; and how this balance could be optimised for the benefit of everybody, especially given the rise of business analytics.

The questions used in the interview and a summary of the responses are shown in Table 3.1. Implicit in these answers are the importance of focusing on people, the important role of intuition and experience, and the limitations of analysis, especially when making complex decisions about people. These responses are in accord with the Iceberg Model as previously presented in Figure 3.1. AI is one important component in our decision-making in the future; however, when we face complex contexts, we require openness and insight, which lead to holism and intuitive knowledge. This can only be reached through human intelligence that consists of the abilities to learn from experience, adapt to new situations, understand and handle abstract concepts, and use knowledge to manipulate one's environment.

IV. Summary

How can we maximise human potential for decision-making in complex environments through the combination of intuition and analysis? When there is sufficient information and the context is simple, analysis can be very effective. But in many environments in which we need to decide, there is a shortage of relevant information, and this is when intuition can be helpful. Sometimes we have plenty of information, but it is not highly relevant to the current situation and may in fact be quite trivial. On what can you base your decision-making under these circumstances? Instead of focusing only on the availability of limited information, it is important to understand the complexity level of the situation and then identify the information required. Depending on whether the situation is simple, complicated, or complex (Snowden & Boone 2007), decision-makers

Table 3.1 Investigating Intuitive Choices
with Information Provided by AI

List	Questions	Answers
1	Please think about your business in 5 to 10 years' time. What are some of the challenges that may occur?	Challenges in the future include how to deal with great volumes of data at the same time as managing people, the rapid rise of AI and its limitations, and the need to maintain a focus on people.
2	What do you think about the true value of intuition under these circumstances? What do you think about the true value of analysis under these circumstances?	Intuition has a strong role to play in the future; experienced people just know but cannot articulate how they know; we need self-awareness concerning biases; experience-based intuition enables us to reach decisions quickly. Analysis is necessary to understand the foundations and sometimes to justify decisions made, but it is limited and now often of questionable quality, given the rise in the quantity of data available.
3	How do you think people can combine these two styles for more effective decisions, given this vast increase in data analytics that we are currently experiencing and the current trend towards greater and greater complexity?	Most people use both styles, often with analysis first as the foundation, and intuition applied over the top. People spoke about the need to be comfortable with ambiguity; analysis is often not value-free, creative intuition is often based upon experience, and there is so much data now with the rapid rise of AI that we cannot analyse it all.
4	Do you think you will rely more on analysis or more on intuition and why?	Most respondents use intuitive decision-making based upon their previous experience, often having already analysed the situation. Several people expressed discomfort with the data produced by AI that is now being used to make complex decisions concerning people.
5	Do you think this would depend upon the complexity level of the situation? Depend upon the context? Can you please say something more about that?	Disagreements emerged concerning the impact of complexity, with some respondents indicating that complex situations required high levels of analysis, but the majority indicating that intuition was essential in complex systems and especially where people are involved, and that analysis alone was totally inadequate in these circumstances.

can base their decisions on self-perception, analytic information, personal experience, and insight and holism to seek the best solution for their problem.

Big data has a very important role in assisting decision-making when the circumstances are far-reaching, and managers would be foolish not to explore how data analytics and AI can inform their understanding of the current and likely future situation. However, the torrents of data that we receive are not always available in the style and level required to support decision-making, and therefore people need to revert to their experience and examine relevant case studies for reference. In some cases, there are no relevant case studies because the problems we face are completely novel due to the simultaneous conflicts of too many complex factors, and the situation is unprecedented.

Under these circumstances, intuition really comes to the fore, and a creative intuitive approach will be needed to reveal a holistic appreciation leading to a solution based upon practical wisdom. While AI will no doubt evolve to become more robust, flexible, and transferable in the coming decades, there will always be a role for human intuition. Human intelligence will always be central to decision-making in complexity, with AI in a supporting complementary role to conquer future challenges.

References

Ackerman, R., Yom-Tov, E., and Torgovitsky, I. (2020). Using confidence and consensuality to predict time invested in problem solving and in real-life web searching. *Cognition,* 199: 104248.

Agor, W. H. (1986). The logic of intuition: How top executives make important decisions. *Organizational Dynamics,* 14(3): 5–18.

Akinci, C. (2014). Stories of intuition based decisions: Evidence for dual systems of thinking. In: J. Liebowitz (Ed.), *Bursting the Big Bubble.* Auerbach Publications, 57–58.

Akinci, C., and Sadler-Smith, E. (2009). 'Hit or miss?': The role of intuition in decision making. British Academy of Management Conference, University of Brighton, UK.

Aljanabi, M. (2023). ChatGPT: Future directions and open possibilities. *Mesopotamian Journal of CyberSecurity,* 2023: 16–17.

Benbasat, I., and Dexter, A. S. (1979). Value and events approaches to accounting: An experimental evaluation. *Accounting Review,* 735–749.

Bergson, H. (1946). *The Creative Mind.* New York: Philosophical Library.

Bishop, L. (2023). A computer wrote this paper: What ChatGPT means for education, research, and writing. https://ssrn.com/abstract=4338981 or http://dx.doi.org/10.2139/ssrn.4338981

Biswas, S. (2023). ChatGPT and the future of medical writing. *Radiology,* 223312. Radiological Society of North America.

Blackman, D., and Sadler-Smith, E. (2009). The silent and the silenced in organizational knowing and learning. *Management Learning,* 40(5): 569–585.

Bolte, A., Goschke, T., and Kuhl, J. (2003). Emotion and intuition: Effects of positive and negative mood on implicit judgments of semantic coherence. *Psychological Science,* 14(5): 416–421.

Bullini Orlandi, L., and Pierce, P. (2020). Analysis or intuition? Reframing the decision-making styles debate in technological settings. *Management Decision,* 58(1): 129–145. doi:10.1108/MD-10-2017-1030

Byerly, T. R., Hill, P. C., and Edwards, K. J. (2022). Others-centeredness: A uniquely positive tendency to put others first. *Personality and Individual Differences,* 186: 111364.

Carruthers, P. (2021). Explicit nonconceptual metacognition. *Philosophical Studies,* 178: 2337–2356.

Cotton, D. R., Cotton, P. A., and Shipway, J. R. (2023). Chatting and cheating. Ensuring academic integrity in the era of ChatGPT. *Innovations in Education and Teaching International,* 1–12.

Craycroft, K. (2022). "Connecting the mind and body: Using embodied intuition as intelligence." Bachelor's Thesis, University of Jyväskylä.

Cristofaro, M. (2021). *Emotion, cognition, and their marvellous interplay in managerial decision-making.* Newcastle upon Tyne, UK: Cambridge Scholars Publishing.

Crowder, J. A., and Friess, S. (2012). Artificial psychology: The psychology of AI. *People,* 2(3): 4–5.

Dane, E., and Pratt, M. G. (2007). Exploring intuition and its role in managerial decision making. *Academy of Management Review,* 32(1): 33–54.

Dane, E., Rockmann, K. W., and Pratt, M. G. (2012). When should I trust my gut? Linking domain expertise to intuitive decision-making effectiveness. *Organizational Behavior and Human Decision Processes,* 119(2): 187–194.

Deikman, A. J. (1977). Sufism and psychiatry. *The Journal of Nervous and Mental Disease,* 165(5): 318–329.

Devine, D., Gaskell, J., Jennings, W., and Stoker, G. (2021). Trust and the coronavirus pandemic: What are the consequences of and for trust? An early review of the literature. *Political Studies Review,* 19(2): 274–285.

Diaz-Hernandez, O., and Gonzalez-Villela, V. J. (2017). Analysis of human intuition towards artificial intuition synthesis for robotics. *Mechatronics and Applications: An International Journal (MECHATROJ),* 1(1).

Dörfler, V., and Eden, C. (2014). Research on intuition using intuition. In: M. Sinclair (Ed.), *Handbook of Research Methods on Intuition.* Cheltenham, UK: Edward Elgar Publishing, 264–276.

Dörfler, V., and Stierand, M. (2018). Understanding indwelling through studying intuitions of Nobel laureates and top chefs. Paper presented at the 78th Annual Meeting of the Academy of Management, UK.

Erevelles, S., Fukawa, N., and Swayne, L. (2016). Big data consumer analytics and the transformation of marketing. *Journal of Business Research,* 69(2): 897–904.

Evans, J. St. B. T. (2008). Dual-processing accounts of reasoning, judgment, and social cognition. *Annual Review of Psychology,* 59: 255–278.

Evans, J. St. B. T., and Stanovich, K. E. (2013). Dual-process theories of higher cognition: Advancing the debate. *Perspectives on Psychological Science,* 8(3): 223–241.

Fellnhofer, K., and Sornette, D. (2022). Embracing the intuitive-analytical paradox? How intuitive and analytical decision-making drive paradoxes in simple and complex environments. Center for Open Science.

Ganapini, M. B., Campbell, M., Fabiano, F., Horesh, L., Lenchner, J., et al. (2023). Thinking fast and slow in AI: The role of metacognition. Paper presented at the Machine Learning, Optimization, and Data Science: 8th International Workshop, LOD 2022, Certosa di Pontignano, Italy, September 19–22, 2022, Revised Selected Papers, Part II.

Gigerenzer, G. (2022). *How to Stay Smart in a Smart World: Why Human Intelligence Still Beats Algorithms.* Cambridge, MA: MIT Press.

Giudice da Silva Cezar, B., and Maçada, A. C. G. (2021). Data literacy and the cognitive challenges of a data-rich business environment: An analysis of perceived data overload, technostress and their relationship to individual performance. *Aslib Journal of Information Management,* 73(5): 618–638.

Gorton, L. (2018). Divination and human nature: A cognitive history of intuition in classical antiquity. *Ancient Philosophy,* 38(1): 187–190.

Grossmann, I., Weststrate, N. M., Ardelt, M., Brienza, J. P., Dong, M., et al. (2020). The science of wisdom in a polarized world: Knowns and unknowns. *Psychological Inquiry,* 31(2): 103–133.

Grüning, D. J. (2022). Synthesis of human and artificial intelligence: Review of "How to stay smart in a smart world: Why human intelligence still beats algorithms" by Gerd Gigerenzer. In: Wiley Online Library. https://online library.wiley.com/doi/full/10.1002/ffo2.137

Haddad, S. M., Souza, R. T., and Cecatti, J. G. (2019). Mobile technology in health (mHealth) and antenatal care–Searching for apps and available solutions: A systematic review. *International Journal of Medical Informatics,* 127: 1–8.

Hales, S. D. (2004). Intuition, revelation, and relativism. *International Journal of Philosophical Studies,* 12(3): 271–295.

Hallo, L., and Nguyen, T. (2022). Holistic view of intuition and analysis in leadership decision-making and problem-solving. *Administrative Sciences,* 12(1): 4.

Hammad, M. (2023). The impact of artificial intelligence (AI) programs on writing scientific research. *Annals of Biomedical Engineering*, 1–2.

Hechler, E., Oberhofer, M., and Schaeck, T. (2020). Deploying AI in the enterprise. *IT Approaches for Design, DevOps, Governance, Change Management, Blockchain, and Quantum Computing*. Berkeley, CA: Springer Link, Apress.

Henden, G. (2004). *Intuition and Its Role in Strategic Thinking*. Oslo, Norway: Handelshøyskolen BI.

Hodgkinson, G. P., and Healey, M. P. (2011). Psychological foundations of dynamic capabilities: Reflexion and reflection in strategic management. *Strategic Management Journal*, 32(13): 1500–1516.

Hodgkinson, G. P., and Sadler-Smith, E. (2018). The dynamics of intuition and analysis in managerial and organizational decision making. *Academy of Management Perspectives*, 32(4): 473–492.

Intezari, A., and Pauleen, D. J. (2018). Conceptualizing wise management decision-making: A grounded theory approach. *Decision Sciences*, 49(2): 335–400.

Jarrahi, M. H. (2018). Artificial intelligence and the future of work: Human-AI symbiosis in organizational decision making. *Business Horizons*, 61(4): 577–586.

Johanssen, J., and Wang, X. (2021). Artificial intuition in tech journalism on AI: Imagining the human subject. *Human-Machine Communication*, 2: 173–190.

Johnny, O., Trovati, M., and Ray, J. (2020). Towards a computational model of artificial intuition and decision making. Paper presented at the Advances in Intelligent Networking and Collaborative Systems: The 11th International Conference on Intelligent Networking and Collaborative Systems (INCoS-2019).

Johnson, J. (2022). Delegating strategic decision-making to machines: Dr. Strangelove redux? *Journal of Strategic Studies*, 45(3): 439–477.

Julmi, C. (2019). When rational decision-making becomes irrational: A critical assessment and re-conceptualization of intuition effectiveness. *Business Research*, 12(1): 291–314.

Kahneman, D., Slovic, S. P., Slovic, P., and Tversky, A. (1982). *Judgment under Uncertainty: Heuristics and Biases*. Cambridge, UK: Cambridge University Press.

Kavanagh, M. M., and Singh, R. (2020). Democracy, capacity, and coercion in pandemic response: COVID-19 in comparative political perspective. *Journal of Health Politics, Policy and Law*, 45(6): 997–1012.

Keller, J., and Sadler-Smith, E. (2019). Paradoxes and dual processes: A review and synthesis. *International Journal of Management Reviews*, 21(2): 162–184. doi:10.1111/ijmr.12200

Khatri, N., and Ng, H. A. (2000). The role of intuition in strategic decision making. *Human Relations,* 53(1): 57–86.

King, M. R. (2022). The future of AI in medicine: A perspective from a chatbot. *Annals of Biomedical Engineering*, 1–5.

Kondo, A. (1952). Intuition in Zen Buddhism. *American Journal of Psychoanalysis,* 12(1): 10.

Kristjánsson, K., Fowers, B., Darnell, C., and Pollard, D. (2021). Phronesis (practical wisdom) as a type of contextual integrative thinking. *Review of General Psychology,* 25(3): 239–257.

Krueger, J. (2022). Man meets machine: Review of 'How to stay smart in a smart world' by Gerd Gigerenzer. *PsyArXiv.* DOI: 10.31234/osf.io/xk8sw

Liebowitz, J. (2019). *Developing Informed Intuition for Decision-Making.* Boca Raton, FL: Taylor & Francis.

Liebowitz, J., Chan, Y., Jenkin, T., Spicker, D., et al. (2019). If numbers could 'feel': How well do executives trust their intuition? *VINE Journal of Information and Knowledge Management Systems*, 49(4): 531–545.

Luoma, J., and Martela, F. (2021). A dual-processing view of three cognitive strategies in strategic decision making: Intuition, analytic reasoning, and reframing. *Long Range Planning,* 54(3): 102065.

McGee, R. W. (2023). Is Chat GPT biased against conservatives? An empirical study. Working paper, February 14.

McKinsey Digital (2019). *Decision-making in the age of urgency.* https://www.mckinsey.com/capabilities/people-and-organizational-performance/our-insights/decision-making-in-the-age-of-urgency

Miron-Spektor, E., Ingram, A., Keller, J., Smith, W. K., and Lewis, M. W. (2018). Microfoundations of organizational paradox: The problem is how we think about the problem. *Academy of Management Journal,* 61(1): 26–45.

Mollick, E., and Mollick, L. (2033). Why all our classes suddenly became AI classes: Strategies for teaching and learning in a ChatGPT world. *Harvard Business Publishing; Education.*

Nguyen, T., Hallo, L., Chileshe, N., and Nguyen, N. H. (2023). Towards a sustainable integrated management approach to uncertainty surrounding COVID-19. *Systems Research and Behavioral Science,* 1–17.

Okoli, J., and Watt, J. (2018). Crisis decision-making: The overlap between intuitive and analytical strategies. *Management Decision,* 56(5): 1122–1134. doi:10.1108/MD-04-2017-0333

Okoli, J., Weller, G., and Watt, J. (2016). Information processing and intuitive decision-making on the fireground: Towards a model of expert intuition. *Cognition, Technology & Work,* 18(1): 89–103.

Raina, M. (2015). The character of creativity: The Vedic perspective. *The Humanistic Psychologist,* 43(1): 54–69.

Rowley, C. (2023). Back to the future: Post-pandemic work and management. *Personnel Review*, 52(2): 415–424.

Saghafian, S. (2023). The analytics science behind ChatGPT: Human, algorithm, or a human-algorithm centaur? Public impact analytics science blog. https://scholar.harvard.edu/saghafian/blog/analytics-science-behind-chatgpt-human-algorithm-or-human-algorithm-centaur

Schad, J., Lewis, M. W., Raisch, S., and Smith, W. K. (2016). Paradox research in management science: Looking back to move forward. *Academy of Management Annals,* 10(1): 5–64.

Schad, J., and Smith, W. K. (2019). Addressing grand challenges' paradoxes: Leadership skills to manage inconsistencies. *Journal of Leadership Studies,* 12(4): 55–59. doi:10.1002/jls.21609

Scheiter, K., Ackerman, R., and Hoogerheide, V. (2020). Looking at mental effort appraisals through a metacognitive lens: Are they biased? *Educational Psychology Review,* 32: 1003–1027.

Shapiro, S., and Spence, M. T. (1997). Managerial intuition: A conceptual and operational framework. *Business Horizons,* 40(1): 63–69.

Shen, W., Yuan, Y., Liu, C., and Luo, J. (2016). In search of the 'Aha!' experience: Elucidating the emotionality of insight problem-solving. *British Journal of Psychology,* 107(2): 281–298.

Shklar, J. (1958). Bergson and the politics of intuition. *The Review of Politics,* 20(4): 634–656. doi:10.1017/S0034670500034264

Simon, H. (1986). Alternative visions of reality. In: H. Arkes and K. R. Hammond (Eds.), *Judgement and Decision-Making: An Interdisciplinary Reader.* Cambridge, MA: Cambridge University Press.

Simon, H. (1995). Explaining the ineffable: AI on the topics of intuition, insight and inspiration. Paper presented at the Proceedings of the 14th International Joint Conference on Artificial Intelligence, Canada.

Sinclair, M. (2010). Misconceptions about intuition. *Psychological Inquiry,* 21(4): 378–386.

Sinclair, M. (2011). An integrated framework of intuition. *Handbook of Intuition Research*, 3–16.

Sinclair, M., and Ashkanasy, N. M. (2005). Intuition: Myth or a decision-making tool? *Management Learning,* 36(3): 353–370.

Sinclair, M., Sadler-Smith, E., and Hodgkinson, G. P. (2009). The role of intuition in strategic decision making. *Handbook of Research on Strategy and Foresight,* 393–417.

Smith, W. K., and Lewis, M. W. (2011). Toward a theory of paradox: A dynamic equilibrium model of organizing. *Academy of Management Review,* 36(2): 381–403.

Snowden, D. J., and Boone, M. E. (2007). A leader's framework for decision making (Cover story). *Harvard Business Review,* 85(11): 68–76.

Statista (2023). Projected monthly probability of a recession in the United States from January 2022 to January 2024.

Struck, P. T. (2016). Divination and human nature. In: *Divination and Human Nature*. Princeton, NJ: Princeton University Press.

Sukhov, A., Sihvonen, A., Netz, J., Magnusson, P., and Olsson, L. E. (2021). How experts screen ideas: The complex interplay of intuition, analysis and sensemaking. *Journal of Product Innovation Management,* 38(2): 248–270.

Tabesh, P. (2021). Who's making the decisions? How managers can harness artificial intelligence and remain in charge. *Journal of Business Strategy,* 43(6): 373–380.

Tabesh, P., Mousavidin, E., and Hasani, S. (2019). Implementing big data strategies: A managerial perspective. *Business Horizons,* 62(3): 347–358.

Tabesh, P., and Vera, D. M. (2020). Top managers' improvisational decision-making in crisis: A paradox perspective. *Management Decision,* 58(10): 2235–2256.

Tams, S., Ahuja, M., Thatcher, J., and Grover, V. (2020). Worker stress in the age of mobile technology: The combined effects of perceived interruption overload and worker control. *The Journal of Strategic Information Systems,* 29(1): 101595.

Taylor, J. (2022). *Whole Brain Living: The Anatomy of Choice and the Four Characters That Drive Our Life*. Carlsbad, CA: Hay House, Inc.

Tversky, A., and Kahneman, D. (1974). Judgment under uncertainty: Heuristics and biases. *Science,* 185(4157): 1124–1131.

Van Knippenberg, D., Dahlander, L., Haas, M. R., and George, G. (2015). Information, attention, and decision making. *Academy of Management,* 58: 649–657. Briarcliff Manor, NY.

Velcu-Laitinen, O. (2022). Manage your mood to follow your intuition. In: *How to Develop Your Creative Identity at Work: Integrating Personal Creativity Within Your Professional Role*. Springer Lin, Apress, 209–223.

Vincent, V. U. (2021). Integrating intuition and artificial intelligence in organizational decision-making. *Business Horizons,* 64(4): 425–438.

Wang, Z. (2003). Systems intuition: Oriental systems thinking style. *Journal of Systems Science and Systems Engineering,* 12(2): 129–137. doi:10.1007/s11518-006-0125-7

Woiceshyn, J. (2009). Lessons from 'good minds': How CEOs use intuition, analysis and guiding principles to make strategic decisions. *Long Range Planning,* 42(3): 298–319.

Yaden, D., Haidt, J., Hood Jr, R., Vago, D., and Newberg, A. (2017). The varieties of self-transcendent experience. *Review of General Psychology,* 21(2): 143–160.

Zhou, J., Wang, X. M., Bavato, D., Tasselli, S., and Wu, J. (2019). Understanding the receiving side of creativity: A multidisciplinary review and implications for management research. *Journal of Management,* 45(6): 2570–2595.

Chapter 4

Using Temporal Intuition to Navigate New Opportunities

Christian Walsh and Paul Knott

University of Canterbury, Christchurch, New Zealand

Intuition in times of rapid change

In the 21st century, managers and leaders in organisations are being challenged to navigate increasingly volatile, uncertain, complex and ambiguous (VUCA) environments (Baran & Woznyi 2021; Horstmeyer 2020). Along with these VUCA aspects, the rate of change has increased, leading to higher velocity and more dynamic environments (Davis, Eisenhardt, & Bingham 2009; Eisenhardt 1989; Oliver & Roos 2005). In such environments, strategic decision-making becomes time critical and navigating temporal complexity a key issue for managers (Adam 2000; Halbesleben, Novicevic, Harvey, & Buckley 2003; Harvey & Novicevic 2001). Along with increasingly dynamic environments, managers also have vast amounts of data available to them (Shah, Horne, & Capellá 2012). As Oliver and Roos (2005) suggest, "Management teams thus face conflicting demands to make decisions rapidly while evaluating extensive (questionable) information" (p. 889).

The astute use of intuition has long been acknowledged as a key skill that managers and leaders in organisations need to develop and master (Barnard 1938; Hodgkinson, Sadler-Smith, Burke, Claxton, & Sparrow 2009; H. Simon

1987). While 20th-century managers had to use intuition to navigate a lack of data, 21st-century managers and leaders in organisations now often suffer from the opposite problem—namely, too much data and too little time to analyse it all (Shah et al. 2012). It is therefore suggested that they need to use their intuition to actually make sense of data, decide which data is relevant, how best to analyse it, and how to interpret the results of analytics in such a way that will help with the decisions that need to be made (Marder 2015; Shah et al. 2012; Vincent 2021).

Much of the research on intuition in managerial decision-making has been focussed on expert intuition (Dane & Pratt 2007; H. Simon 1987). But more recently it has been acknowledged there are in fact multiple forms of intuition (Dane & Pratt 2009; Gore & Sadler-Smith 2011; Walsh, Collins, & Knott 2022). Of particular interest in navigating high-velocity and dynamic environments is *temporal intuition.* This is a recently identified form of intuition that has particular significance for practicing managers deciding on when the time is right to take specific actions in the process of creating and/or capitalising on a new opportunity. It has been defined as, "a slow-to-form, affectively charged evaluation of timing for prospective action and pace of change based on complex patterns of multiple cues" (Walsh, Collins, et al. 2022, 702). While temporal intuition has been described as a distinct type of intuition, it should be noted that it works in conjunction with expert intuition in particular, but also in *social intuition* and *creative intuition* (Walsh, Collins, et al. 2022; Walsh, Knott, & Collins 2022). We suggest that knowledge and astute use of temporal intuition will help managers better navigate the temporal complexity of new and dynamic environments.

To explore this, we undertook a multi-year study of a number of managers in high-velocity environments as they sought to develop new opportunities. In this chapter, we will first set out the theoretical background, including the different facets of temporal complexity, followed by a detailed description of the research method and cases. We will then discuss the findings from the research cases and show how managers can use temporal intuition to address different aspects of temporal complexity. We conclude with recommendations as to how managers can best utilise the strengths of temporal intuition while also being aware of its weaknesses.

Temporal complexity

Researchers have identified seven key temporal facets that combine to make up the temporal context in organisations, which has been labelled a *timescape.* Each of these facets contribute to the inherently complex nature of navigating the temporal aspects of a novel opportunity (Adam 2000; Halbesleben et al. 2003; Harvey & Novicevic 2001). We will briefly disuss these seven facets, including the significance of each in the context of a new opportunity.

The first facet is *timeframe*. This represents the time horizon for expected or desired events to take place. This is typically measured in linear clock time (e.g., days or weeks), although it can have aspects of seasonality or cyclic time. In terms of new opportunities, this is often reflected in identifiable milestones along a development path. Related to this aspect, *temporal depth* (Bluedorn & Martin 2008) is described as the length of the timeframes that an individual can or does perceive, in both the future and the past. Alongside this temporal focus is the importance that an individual attaches to past, present and future (Bluedorn & Standifer 2006).

The second facet of the timescape is *tempo*. This represents the pace or speed of events in a certain context. Of note, this may or may not be consistent over time. In other words, the pace of change may itself speed up (accelerate) or slow down (decelerate) at different times. In a new opportunity space this may be significant, as different phases of development may operate with a different tempo, and so sensing acceleration or deceleration can signify evolution or regression of progress.

The third facet is *temporality*. This reflects the lifespan of events or processes within the business context. Escalation of commitment and sunk cost fallacy are known biases that mean new opportunities are often given longer lifespans than they may warrant (Staw 1981).

The fourth facet is *synchronisation*. This represents the aligning or misaligning of rhythms and tempos within the timescape. *Entrainment* (Ancona & Chong 1996; Hopp & Greene 2018; Shi & Prescott 2012) describes the synchronisation of two or more organisations' rhythms and is particularly significant when working with other firms on a novel opportunity.

The fifth facet is *sequence*. Patterns may become apparent in the business context that make a particular order of events more or less favourable for the opportunity being pursued. There are often temporal dependencies where one phase or series of actions can only follow another, and they may be closely linked in time.

The sixth facet is *pauses/gaps*. This represents a break in the sequence of events. The number and also duration of each gap can have a large impact on the overall perception of progress. The ability to transition in and out of such pauses/gaps also can have an impact, particularly if momentum is lost.

The seventh facet is *simultaneity*. This represents the degree to which events take place at the same time. In a complex timescape there may be many overlapping actions or phases which may call for additional resources, making it difficult to maintain focus on a set of actions. However, this may be necessary in order to explore multiple options for potential development. Some people have a latent preference for *polychronicity* (Bluedorn & Martin 2008; Bluedorn & Standifer 2006), or working on several tasks simultaneously.

The research

We undertook a multi-year longitudinal research project to examine the types and nature of intuition used by practicing managers when developing new opportunities. We recruited six senior managers from the high-tech sector. This sector was selected based on the relatively rapid rate of change in the environment, which would therefore give us the best chance to see the dynamics unfold, in particular how the individuals used, or didn't use, intuition to navigate the uncertainty. For each mini-case, described in further detail below, we focussed on the individual decision-makers, all of whom were experienced CEOs or founders, and how they progressed the opportunities in front of them. Note the names used here are pseudonyms. To do this, we visited each individual once per quarter for a two-year period, during which time they were exploring and developing a strategic opportunity, or multiple opportunities. To frame the discussions with each individual, we utilised cognitive maps, which are a means of articulating the individual participants' thinking about an issue at the given moment (Huff 1990). This was done to try and avoid post-hoc rationalisation, particularly regarding the use of intuition.

At the first session, we asked the participants to list all the unresolved questions that they had regarding a current opportunity. Following the "Self-Q" method (Bougon, Baird, Komocar, & Ross 1990), we prompted them to think about questions they ask themselves, questions they ask of others, and questions other people ask of them. Participants wrote each question on a sticky note. Then we asked the participants to arrange the questions on a board and draw the causal connections between them, if any. For example, if one question were to be resolved, how would this affect any of the other questions. Through this process an overall structure of the cognitive causal map was created. The map created on the day was photographed and then re-created in PowerPoint to allow for future analysis.

At each subsequent session with the participants, we would first review the previous cognitive map, going through each question on the map in turn and determining whether the participant was at the current time closer to having an answer to that question. We would then discuss the crucial question of why they felt this was the case. What had caused their thinking about the question to change? They would indicate with a small up arrow if they were feeling confident about resolving a particular question, a down arrow if they were less confident about it, or a dash if there was no change. If a question had been resolved, it was struck through, or in some cases the wording changed to suit the current situation. Also, new questions were added to the map as they had become apparent. All the conversations were recorded and subsequently coded and analysed. The alterations to the map which reflected their current thinking were also recorded and codified. Using this method, we could see how their

> **Mini-case 1: Brian**
>
> Brian is the CEO of a well-established high-tech manufacturing operation. Their products are used globally to help control large electrical motors in a range of applications. This is a very specialised, highly technical niche, and while they have a good market share in their niche, they are a smaller player than some of their competitors. They sell predominantly through a distributor network. During the period of our research project, Brian was exploring two key opportunities. One was a promising new geographic market, which would require partnering with a new distributor. The second was the potential for a new product offering that combined some of their technical expertise from multiple disciplines into a single user-friendly package. The entry timing of the new product was a key focus for Brian during the period of our research. "Thinking about where we were, taking on these activities . . . was really because we felt we were ready. Whilst it wasn't quite there, it was a bit of an intuitive act, I suppose, and the next thing for us. What we're doing at the moment is adding distributors, and mapping out our strategic planning requires pretty early-on thought about how we're going to replicate this thing."

thinking about the opportunity had changed over time, and through the analysis of the conversations, we were able to gain insight into what was behind the changing perspective.

Intuition and the facets of temporal complexity in practice

Following detailed analysis of our findings, we were able to see many instances of intuition being used, alongside robust analysis, in the navigation of new opportunity spaces. One of the most significant areas that intuition was commonly used for by the participants in our study was in navigating issues of timing. When we compare these with the facets of temporal complexity (Halbesleben et al. 2003) that we described earlier, we found specific examples of temporal intuition (Walsh, Collins et al. 2022) being used in each facet.

We found our participants frequently used timeframes as a fundamental linear temporal structure (Orlikowski & Yates 2002). In doing so, they used intuition in several key aspects. When setting milestones, a form of timeframe by which certain activities are intended to be achieved, there was often a highly intuitive judgement about how far to stretch the capability of the team. If the milestone was

---

Mini-case 2: Darren

Darren is one of the founders of a niche "wearable healthcare" product. He had been instrumental in growing it into a global business by establishing positive partnerships with clinicians who recommend the product and distributors who supply it. During the period of the research, a new sensor technology was being explored for how it might help with either diagnosis or demonstration of the value proposition and, critically, how it could be commercialised into a complementary offering. Darren was acutely aware of the speed of development and client engagement, but in some cases, there was a necessary slowing down in order to work with particular development partners. "In some ways what it means is it will slow things down, but I think I'm not diss-ing them entirely, in that they will bring some really good robust research to it, obviously some funding, but more important, they can pull things together and apply some pressure to some of these other companies. So it's interesting in terms of time frame and urgency, that is something we are stepping back a wee bit from."

---

set with a too-aggressive timeframe, either with a short time or too much to be done, then it might de-motivate the team if they sense never being able to achieve it in the time available. But this was intuitively balanced with the need for action in order to explore or develop the potential for a new area and the sense of urgency which promoted action. As Gerry (mini-case 4) said, "Sometimes you wonder you are never quite there, but if you force a date on it, you have to [get there]."

Our participants we also very aware of, and sensitive to, issues relating to tempo in the development of the new opportunities. Again, intuition had a significant role in the perception of how fast the opportunity was developing. The participants often referred to expected phases of development or concepts from theories, such as technology adoption (Moore 1999), which gave them some structure to consider how fast they were making progress. As Angus (mini-case 6) said, "We are learning that it is really an early adopter/innovator market, and there is a lot of interest, but people are still not quite sure what it is, how it fits into existing solutions. . . . We are making progress along all these lines, but this project is quite slow, and the sales cycle is somewhat unexpectedly very very slow." This was a particular concern for the start-up–based opportunities because the other aspect of tempo was the speed with which their limited resources were being depleted.

Decisions associated with temporality, or the lifespan of particular initiatives, were also seen in our participant cases. The decision to withdraw from or close down a potential opportunity always had some sense of intuition associated

> **Mini-case 3: Steve**
>
> Steve is a former investor and serial entrepreneur who had taken the reins as CEO of an IP-rich technology start-up. The IP the company was based on had been spun out of the local university and was being applied in the automotive sector. They had secured several rounds of investment, which enabled them to secure several patents and focus on the large-scale market opportunity. The key focus for Steve during the period of our research was establishing the manufacturing processes at the scale needed for the com-mercialisation to be successful. He was always assessing the rate of technical progress the team were able to make and balancing this with their capital requirements. Steve felt that timing was a very important factor when rais-ing capital. "Part of my reason for timing this thing is that we don't want to get caught the last in the line for punch when somebody pulls the bowl."

with it. Bob (mini-case 5) described this following one such instance: "There's certainly no regret about not proceeding with this, so you could say I actually feel very good about not proceeding with it."

Synchronisation was a major consideration in the development of many of our participants' opportunities. This was particularly the case where larger part-ners or customers were involved, as they tended to influence the opportunity timescape. Intuition was required to assess if the participants were synchronised with the partners/customers. Brian referred to this, saying, "You've just got to be around for when they are ready to make the change. Some of the biggest part-ners are, you know, they dictate the time, it's got to be ready in their evolution."

The optimum sequence for developing the opportunities was also a signif-icant aspect of each case. While project management techniques were well deployed in most cases to help with sequencing of developments, there was also an aspect of intuition associated with these decisions. Often this was because the novel opportunity space meant that later steps in the sequence could not be fully defined at the outset. Steve used this analogy to describe the use of intuition that there will be a path forward: "It's a bit like seeing all the stepping stones to get across the river versus not knowing there's a step there but having confidence that you'll find it if you lean forward. But if you wait till all the stones are there, it'll be gone."

Related to issues of sequencing were issues relating to the need to pause or have a gap in the sequence. Generally, the participants would try and maintain momentum and so avoid gaps. However, in some cases, while the opportunity itself was progressing, there were intuitive decisions made about taking pauses

---

Mini-case 4: Gerry

Gerry is the founder and sales director of an established web development and services company. The company had been growing rapidly for a number of years, with Gerry leading the sales activity. As the team had grown, he was starting to back down from the day-to-day sales activity and take a more strategic, long-term focus. As such, during the time of our research, he was exploring several potential new product offerings for the business. "At this level, holistic level, incredibly fluid and agile you know, it's very much, 'Ah, bugger the box and pour the concrete, let's see what happens,' you know, so that's a fascinating sort of culture that we have—you know, let's just try it, let's just see what happens."

---

from the personal involvement. Darren described this as, "just a gut feel that as it gets into a more regimented phase, I need to recognize that I'm not good at that, and therefore we should get other people involved in it."

Simultaneity was one of the major temporal factors concerning our participants. This was reflected in decisions about resourcing and the opportunity costs associated with deploying resources to build capability or execute on an opportunity. While there can be analysis and data associated with existing options, when exploring alternatives, it often came down to intuition. At one point Angus explicitly stated, "One big decision, can we afford to do two things at the one time? My gut feeling, intuition tells me probably not."

Strengths and weaknesses of temporal intuition and recommendations for managers

As with any form of intuition, there are certain situations where the strengths of temporal intuition have utility in practice, and also times where it has weaknesses. As shown in Table 4.1, these strengths and weaknesses can be reflected in the various facets of temporal complexity. We discuss each of these in turn, with the aim of helping practicing managers become more critically aware of these aspects and so be better equipped to use temporal intuition in the most beneficial manner.

In terms of timeframe, as was seen in our research cases, temporal intuition can be a strength when used to assess and create time-based targets that induce a positive sense of urgency that promotes action. Because of the many unknowns in a novel environment, it is not possible to analyse and predict precise milestones. But with the skilled use of temporal intuition, an experienced manager will have a sense of how much progress can be made in a particular

---

Mini-case 5: Bob

Bob is a highly experienced entrepreneur who at the time of our research was considering and then executing the potential acquisition and merger of his domain registration and services company with another company in the same space. "It is at a high level of intuition as to when is the right time to do this, and part of it is our own maturity as an organisation as well. Can we, you know, sometimes one of the ways we kill a weed is by giving it a growth hormone. You know, it grows so rapidly that it kills its resources and dies, and I think there's a lot of, you have to be at a certain stage of maturity in your business, both revenue wise but also people skills wise, before you can undertake acquisitions and not have them actually destroy you. So that's an intuitive thing; well, it's analytical too, but there's a certain sense that yes, we could do this and it wouldn't kill us."

---

timeframe. However, the weakness of temporal intuition in this area is that it can contribute to a sense of over-confidence, which is often seen in new product introductions (Simon & Houghton 2003). To balance this, and depending on the level of uncertainty in the environment, it is therefore recommended that timeframes for milestones be limited to a sub-set of the overall temporal depth of an initiative. If specific milestones are too far into the future, while we may

Table 4.1 Summary of Strengths and Weaknesses of Temporal Intuition across the Facets of Temporal Complexity

	Temporal intuition strengths	Temporal intuition weaknesses
Timeframe	Sense of urgency promotes action	Over-optimism
Tempo	Sense of acceleration/deceleration	Assessing non-linear rates of change
Temporality	Sense potential longevity or dead end	Emotional attachment to ideas
Synchronisation	Sense of entrainment	Speed traps
Sequence	Sense of best order of events/actions	Planning fallacy
Pause/gaps	Sense of momentum or lack of	Letting go control
Simultaneity	Sense of leveraging concurrent events	Masking minor differences in largely similar areas

---

Mini-case 6: Angus

Angus is the co-founder and CEO of a technology startup that was attempting to commercialise the IP they had around chatbot deployment. With a small team of developers and largely self-funded, he was always acutely aware of their burn rate and therefore runway. During the period of our research, he was leading the sales and marketing effort, and he was constantly monitoring which market segments he felt were taking longer than others to educate and convert. "Those are the choices we make every day. How much effort do we put into improving our development environment? OK, if we do it and, broken down by day, can we actually get a return on that in the next couple of weeks? If we don't get a return in the next couple of weeks, if we don't get an ability to do stuff quicker, then we're not doing it. It's almost like you need to dig a trench, and you have spades. And you also want to buy an excavator. Can you afford to buy an excavator? No. Can you build an excavator? Yes we can, but you will have to stop digging the trench."

---

feel confident, too many variables may change and alter the plan, rendering distant milestones either irrelevant or, worse, de-motivating. Defining small steps on the path to a larger goal is more likely to be motivating than large, distant hurdles (Heath & Heath 2011).

In terms of tempo, temporal intuition can be a strength when used to gain a sense of acceleration or deceleration in a particular market or capability development. As seen in our research cases, this was used to provide a sense of acceleration—or alternatively, a struggle to gain momentum. Often this is well in advance of any hard data that can be used to analyse the changing environment. However, the limitation of intuition in this context is that we are inherently limited in our perception and evaluation of non-linear dynamics and rates of change (De Langhe, Puntoni, & Larrick 2017). This is a particular issue for new opportunities in which many of the dynamics, such as adoption rates, network effects and compounding costs, all tend to have non-linear patterns. It is therefore recommended that managers be alert to any changes in pace or tempo and create regular reviews where speed of change is examined. At such sessions there should always be an examination of any non-linear rates of change.

In terms of temporality, temporal intuition can be a strength when used to sense longevity, or lack thereof, of an initiative. As seen in our research, experienced managers get a sense of when it is time to shut down an initiative or pass on an opportunity. Emotional attachment to ideas and escalation of commitment (Staw 1981) are known biases and weaknesses associated with intuition in this area. It is therefore recommended that managers hold deliberate discussions about the longevity of initiatives from the outset.

In terms of synchronisation, temporal intuition can be a strength when used to assess how well in phase the organisation is with other stakeholders. This relies on a sense of *cyclic* time as opposed to *linear clock* time (Crossan, Cunha, Vera, & Cunha 2005). In our research the participant organisations tended to be smaller than some of their large customers, and so they had to adjust their timing to match that of the other organisations who dominate the timing of cycles in the environment—a dynamic referred to as *entrainment* (Ancona & Chong 1996; Hopp & Greene 2018; Shi & Prescott 2012). However, managers also need to be aware of, and avoid, speed traps (Perlow, Okhuysen, & Repenning 2002). This is a weakness of intuition where the perception is that ever-increasing speed of decision cycles is required, whereas in fact sometimes slowing down in order to achieve entrainment may actually be more beneficial. We recommend, therefore, that managers pay attention to the cyclic nature of an opportunity—in particular, the cycle times and phases of larger partners or customers.

In terms of sequence, temporal intuition can be a strength when used to provide a sense of order and structure to actions. In many cases, as we saw in our research, the necessary order of events is not clear for a new opportunity, but by promoting action, the path unfolds as progress is made. As with establishing appropriate timeframes, as discussed above, this is often a motivating factor to promote collective action. The weakness of intuition in this area is the *planning fallacy* (Buehler, Griffin, & Ross 2002). This is where we tend to be over-optimistic when predicting the sequence of events and the time involved in each in order to deliver on a project. This is particularly true when we are looking at it from the inside, as opposed to an outsiders' view. Therefore, we recommend that managers always use an independent view to help assess the reality of a planned sequence of events in a new opportunity space.

In terms of pausing or gaps in the sequence, temporal intuition can be a strength when assessing whether momentum is being created or lost. This in turn can inform whether an initiative should be paused or not. We saw in our research cases that sometimes the decision was made to pause an initiative because momentum had stalled and the timing was not perceived as favourable. But by doing so, the initiative was then able to be quickly re-started at a later time when conditions changed. Another form of pause that we witnessed was where individuals felt they were not best suited to remaining involved and so took time away from a project for some period. However, a weakness of intuition here is that individuals often feel an emotional connection to an initiative, which makes it difficult for them to effectively let go, particularly where this involves ceding control to other parties. We recommend then that when assessing progress, pauses are always presented as an option. We also recommend that as initiatives enter different phases, team makeup for each phase is re-assessed.

In terms of simultaneity, temporal intuition can be a strength when used to align activities where there is a sense of being able to initiate multiple actions concurrently within an organisation. An example of this may be development processes or activities that can happen in parallel. This can help combine resources and save time in the overall process. However, a weakness of this is that sometimes the overall focus on small distinct characteristics within each process may be lost if there is much in common across different parallel activities. But the minor differences may actually be significant to the overall initiative. We recommend, therefore, that when simultaneous actions are undertaken, findings and results from multiple activities are examined not only for common outcomes, but also for variation.

Conclusion

Managers in modern organisations face a complex and ever-changing timescape. This is particularly true when creating and developing new opportunities. In this chapter we have described the use of temporal intuition as seen in our research cases as managers were navigating and making decisions relating to timeframes, tempo, temporality, synchronisation, sequence, pauses and simultaneity. We have described the strengths and weaknesses of temporal intuition in each of these areas and, we hope, provided some guidance for practicing managers to make the most of their own temporal intuition.

References

Adam, B. (2000). The temporal gaze: The challenge for social theory in the context of GM food. *The British Journal of Sociology,* 51(1): 125–142. doi: 10.1111/j.1468-4446.2000.00125.x

Ancona, D. G., and Chong, C.-L. (1996). Entrainment: Pace, cycle, and rhythm in organizational behavior. In: B. M. Staw and L. L. Cummings (Eds.), *Research in Organizational Behaviour,* 251–284. Greenwich: JAI Press Inc.

Baran, B. E., and Woznyi, H. M. (2021). Managing VUCA: The human dynamics of agility. *Organizational Dynamics,* 50. doi: 10.1016/j.orgdyn.2020.100787

Barnard, C. I. (1938). *The Functions of the Executive.* Cambridge, MA: Harvard University Press.

Bluedorn, A. C., and Martin, G. (2008). The time frames of entrepreneurs. *Journal of Business Venturing,* 23(1): 1–20. doi: 10.1016/j.jbusvent.2006.05.005

Bluedorn, A. C., and Standifer, R. L. (2006). Time and the temporal imagination. *Academy of Management Learning & Education,* 5(2): 196–206. doi: 10.5465/AMLE.2006.21253784

Bougon, M., Baird, N., Komocar, J., and Ross, W. (1990). Identifying strategic loops: The Self-Q Interviews. In: A. S. Huff (Ed.), *Mapping Strategic Thought*, 327–354. Chichester, UK: John Wiley & Sons.

Buehler, R., Griffin, D. W., and Ross, M. (2002). Inside the planning fallacy: The causes and consequences of optimistic time predictions. In: T. Gilovich, D. W. Griffin, and D. Kahneman (Eds.), *Heuristics and Biases: The Psychology of Intuitive Judgement*. Cambridge, UK: Cambridge University Press.

Crossan, M., Cunha, M. P. E., Vera, D., and Cunha, J. (2005). Time and organizational improvisation. *The Academy of Management Review*, 30(1): 129–145.

Dane, E., and Pratt, M. G. (2007). Exploring intuition and its role in managerial decision making. *The Academy of Management Review*, 32(1): 33.

Dane, E., and Pratt, M. G. (2009). Conceptualizing and measuring intuition: A review of recent trends. In: G. Hodgkinson and J. Ford (Eds.), *International Review of Industrial and Organizational Psychology*. Chichester, UK: Wiley, 24: 1–40.

Davis, J. P., Eisenhardt, K. M., and Bingham, C. B. (2009). Optimal structure, market dynamism, and the strategy of simple rules. *Administrative Science Quarterly*, 54(3): 413–452. doi: 10.2189/asqu.2009.54.3.413

De Langhe, B., Puntoni, S., and Larrick, R. (2017). Linear thinking in a nonlinear world. *Harvard Business Review* (May–June): 2–11.

Eisenhardt, K. M. (1989). Making fast strategic decisions in high-velocity environments. *The Academy of Management Journal*, 32(3): 543–576.

Gore, J., and Sadler-Smith, E. (2011). Unpacking intuition: A process and outcome framework. *Review of General Psychology*, 15(4): 304–316.

Halbesleben, J. R. B., Novicevic, M. M., Harvey, M. G., and Buckley, M. R. (2003). Awareness of temporal complexity in leadership of creativity and innovation: A competency-based model. *The Leadership Quarterly*, 14(4): 433–454. doi: 10.1016/S1048–9843(03)00046–8

Harvey, M., and Novicevic, M. M. (2001). The impact of hypercompetitive "timescapes" on the development of a global mindset. *Management Decision*, 39(6): 448–460. doi: 10.1108/EUM0000000005563

Heath, C., and Heath, D. (2011). *Switch: How to Change Things When Change Is Hard*. London: Random House Business.

Hodgkinson, G. P., Sadler-Smith, E., Burke, L. A., Claxton, G., and Sparrow, P. R. (2009). Intuition in organizations: Implications for strategic management. *Long Range Planning*, 42(3): 277–297.

Hopp, C., and Greene, F. J. (2018). In pursuit of time: Business plan sequencing, duration and intraentrainment effects on new venture viability. *Journal of Management Studies*, 55(2): 320–351.

Horstmeyer, A. (2020). The generative role of curiosity in soft skills development for contemporary VUCA environments. *Journal of Organizational Change Management*, 33(5): 737–751. doi: 10.1108/JOCM-08-2019-0250

Huff, A. S. (1990). Mapping strategic thought. In: A. S. Huff (Ed.), *Mapping Strategic Thought,* 1–49. Chichester, UK: John Wiley & Sons.

Marder, E. (2015). Understanding brains: Details, intuition, and big data. *PLoS Biology,* 13(5).

Moore, G. (1999). *Crossing the Chasm: Marketing and Selling High-Tech Products to Mainstream Customers.* New York: HarperBusiness.

Oliver, D., and Roos, J. (2005). Decision-making in high-velocity environments: The importance of guiding principles. *Organization Studies,* 26(6): 889–913. doi: 10.1177/0170840605054609

Orlikowski, W. J., and Yates, J. (2002). It's about time: Temporal structuring in organizations. *Organization Science,* 13(6): 684–700.

Perlow, L. A., Okhuysen, G. A., and Repenning, N. P. (2002). The speed trap: Exploring the relationship between decision making and temporal context. *The Academy of Management Journal,* 45(5): 931–955.

Shah, S., Horne, A., and Capellá, J. (2012). Good data won't guarantee good decisions. *Harvard Business Review,* 90(4): 23–25.

Shi, W., and Prescott, J. E. (2012). Rhythm and entrainment of acquisition and alliance initiatives and firm performance: A temporal perspective. *Organization Studies,* 33(10): 1281–1310.

Simon, H. A. (1987). Making management decisions: The role of intuition and emotions. *Academy of Management Executive,* 1: 57–64.

Simon, M., and Houghton, S. M. (2003). The relationship between overconfidence and the introduction of risky products: Evidence from a field study. *Academy of Management Journal,* 46(2): 139–149. doi: 10.2307/30040610

Staw, B. M. (1981). The escalation of commitment to a course of action. *The Academy of Management Review,* 6(4): 577–587.

Vincent, V. U. (2021). Integrating intuition and artificial intelligence in organizational decision-making. *Business Horizons,* 64(4): 425–438. doi: 10.1016/j.bushor.2021.02.008

Walsh, C., Collins, J., and Knott, P. (2022). The four types of intuition managers need to know. *Business Horizons,* 65: 697–708. doi: 10.1016/j.bushor.2021.12.003

Walsh, C., Knott, P., and Collins, J. (2022). Playing chess or painting pictures? Unpacking entrepreneurial intuition. *Journal of Small Business Strategy,* 32(2): 115–127. doi: 10.53703/001c.31082

Chapter 5

Who's Afraid of Intuition in Medicine?

Itai Adler

Hebrew University of Jerusalem and Hadassah Medical Center

1. Introduction

Surprisingly, and perhaps counter-intuitively, intuition is frequently used in medicine. Alongside *rational* decision-making in medicine, which is explained and clarified, there is also *intuitive* decision-making,* to which I was exposed during my clinical studies in medical school. Physicians, experts, and interns use intuition in a routinely accepted manner: "I think this is an exacerbation of his heart condition"; "Based on my experience, it's better to operate sooner"; "My gut tells me that five days of antibiotics should be sufficient." Also in medical textbooks, such as *Harrison's Principles of Internal Medicine* (Jameson et al. 2018), intuitive decision-making is mentioned as an acceptable approach, alongside the

---

* For the purpose of the current discussion, I will use a negative definition of intuition—namely, it is a decision-making method that is considered reliable by the decision-maker, although it cannot be explained in terms of a factual basis. Further on, I will offer additional definitions.

"analytical" approach. The text even mentions that intuitive decision-making is characteristic of experts who are experienced and confident.

Medicine is typically thought of as a scientific field or a practice-based science, and therefore, it seems appropriate that decision-making should be rational, well-grounded, and explained. It is possible that intuition is better suited to basic research and can be applied at the stage of hypothesizing; however, when faced with scientific laws, there seems to be no room for intuition (Adler 2022). What would we say to an engineer who chose to use a smaller amount of concrete to build a bridge based on his or her sense of intuition? Hence, the issue I mean to explore in this chapter is the status and justification of intuition-based practice in medicine.*

---

* The tendency to use intuition refers to a generalized problem and is applicable to specific cases. When a specific case is compared to a general rule, the physician must determine whether the case corresponds to that rule and investigate what can happen when the case does not fully correspond to the general rule. On a lack of correspondence between the case and the general rule, Aristotle suggested that the principle of *epieikeia* be applied, according to which one must hypothesize how the legislator would treat this specific case. While this is appropriate in the field of law, the solution cannot be applied in the field of medicine.

Kant (1998) proffered a different solution, claiming that the ability to correctly apply a general rule to a specific case requires the "power of judgment." Medical schools can teach physicians the general rules, but according to Kant, the power of judgment cannot be taught in a school setting because it is innate.

Hence, medical schools can teach the general rules, but if the physician lacks the specific [judgment] ability to apply the rules correctly, nothing can be done about this. The physician could improve the ability to apply rules using a variety of cases and examples, but without the power of judgment, this practice will not be sufficient.

Wittgenstein approached this issue from a different perspective, by addressing the distinction between "seeing" and "seeing as." In the second part of his *Philosophical Investigations,* Wittgenstein (2009) referred to Jastrow's illusion of a duck-rabbit drawing: if the viewer looks at this horizontally, a rabbit is perceived, and if it is viewed vertically, the viewer sees the drawing as a duck. Wittgenstein discussed the difference between the various perspectives and asked whether what has changed was the seeing or the interpretation of what was seen. As he claimed, the drawing does not instruct to the viewer how to approach it, and consequently, the viewer must look at the object from multiple perspectives to understand it. Thus, as to the application of a rule to a specific case, Wittgenstein claimed that a specific case in and of itself does not provide information about whether it corresponds to the rule—in other words, whether it is a case of a duck or a rabbit.

In the same manner, we were taught to view things in a particular way, according to specific categories. The particular case itself does not contain any hints that can help the viewer categorize it one way or another. Wittgenstein's insight indicates the gap

The concept of intuition has a long and drawn-out history in philosophy. In addition to philosophical research, there has been a broad-ranging discussion in the professional psychological literature about the concept of intuition and other related concepts. I review several major definitions here:

A. **Intuition as recognition.** This approach is widely used in psychology and has been well researched in this field (Simon 1992; Kahneman & Klein 2009). According to this approach, experts have a great deal of information stored in their brains but do not always have access to this information. In certain situations, an expert finds a clue in the environment that triggers the information stored in the brain, which is then used to solve the problem at hand. Klein (1998) gave an example of nurses in the neonatal department who intuitively were able to identify a serious infection in premature newborns, even before receiving the lab test results.

B. **Intuition as tacit knowledge.** Some researchers linked intuition to tacit knowledge, that alongside information that can be described and referred to, there is also concealed knowledge and information that is non-explicit. Polanyi (2009) found it difficult to define this knowledge precisely and, consequently, defined it in negative terms—that is, as knowledge that exists but cannot be verbalized and which is acquired in a manner that differs from the regular path of knowledge acquisition. Gascoigne and Thornton (2014) suggested the notion of "reading the patient." This idea describes both tacit and explicit knowledge that the physician can acquire by examining the patient, even if this knowledge cannot be expressed verbally.

C. **Intuition as a belief or the reason for a belief.** A concept often used in philosophical discourse considers intuition as a belief (Lewis 1983) or something that led to a belief (Williamson 2007; Sosa 1998). The two phenomena are similar in that they lack a rational justification yet are a source of significant authority. Moreover, there appears to be a connection between the two phenomena, given that one who holds a certain intuition often (although not always) believes in it. The advantage of this approach is that it does not introduce new terminology.

---

between the specific case and the application of the rule, demonstrating the need for additional principles and signs by which to interpret the specific case and whether it corresponds to a particular category. Thus Wittgenstein's observation emphasizes the principle that is undoubtedly appropriate in the field of medicine—namely, that each case should be examined separately, and even when a case can be associated with a particular category, it manifests differently in each patient.

D. **Intuition is sui generis.** Intuition is a sui generis epistemic phenomenon, or a unique type of perception (Chudnoff 2014; Bengson 2015; Koksvik 2011). According to this approach, intuition is a specific way of proving a claim.

All of these definitions refer to a basic element of intuition—namely, that it is used in specific cases or, in the words of Wittgenstein (1976):

> What do we know about intuition? What idea have we of it? It's presumably supposed to be a sort of seeing, recognition at a single glance; I wouldn't know what more to say. "So you do after all know what is!" Roughly in the same way as I know what it means "to see a body from all sides at once". I don't want to say that one cannot apply this expression to some process or other, for some good reason or other—but do I, therefore, know what it means? (p. 419)

Wittgenstein compared intuition to seeing a body from all its sides at once. We may try to understand it, but we cannot describe it beyond saying that it is a particular perception. Wittgenstein suggested that intuition belongs to one's private language and, in this sense, has no meaning and, as such, cannot be relied upon, as he demonstrated in the following example (which is related to the world of medicine):

> It is just as if somebody claimed to have knowledge of human anatomy by intuition; and we say: "We don't doubt it; but if you want to be a doctor, you must pass all the examinations like anybody else." (ibid.)

In a similar vein, a physician claiming that a diagnosis is based on intuition would still need to explain and justify the diagnosis, beyond the issue of its accuracy. At best, intuition can indicate the speaker's cognitive state, but it is not an indication of truth.

I believe that the description up until this point has clarified the epistemological complexity of using intuition. To further explore the phenomenon, I used three different but complementary approaches:

First, I conducted an empirical investigation to determine if intuition is used in medicine and how those who claim to do so understand this phenomenon. To this end, I conducted a qualitative study based on interviews with physicians. At a later stage, I wanted to understand the position of "official medicine" regarding the use of intuition and investigated the predominant methodology used in medicine nowadays—evidence-based medicine—and its attitude to intuition. Finally, I turned to philosophical research and offered a model that I believe can justify the *use* of intuition in medicine without contradicting the *rules* of medicine. The following sections are presented in the order described here.

2. Intuition in medicine—A view from the field

Despite the wide use of intuition in medicine, the phenomenon has yet to be sufficiently studied. Although Stolper et al. (2013) investigated the reliability of intuition and proposed a tool for examining this aspect, they did not investigate the phenomenon itself. Woolley and Kostopoulou (2013) conducted a qualitative study about the experience of intuition among practitioners of family medicine, focusing on the decision-making process.

In accordance with the phenomenological approach (Smith 2008), semi-structured interviews (Edwards & Holland 2013) were held with 13 expert physicians, among them novice and veteran practitioners, men and women. The study was approved by the institutional ethics committee, and the findings described herein use only pseudonyms.

2.1 The frequency with which intuition is used in medicine

The interviewees stated that intuition is used frequently in medicine—in fact, on a daily basis: "I think I use it almost every day" (Zvi). Others claimed that their decisions are based on intuition: "I believe that most medical decisions are intuitive" (Amir). In addition to the issue of its frequency, the interviewees noted that intuition is essential in medicine: "I know that it is a characteristic of this profession, part of its foundation. It's not an issue, as far as I'm concerned . . . It's just an integral part of the profession" (Eden). Some noted that the connection between medicine and intuition is so strong that they could not discern intuition-based decision-making from other kinds: "I think intuition can be found in many things we do, but I do not think there can be a distinction between cases determined without the use of intuition and others made with the use of intuition" (Isaac).

The interviewees were asked about the essence of intuition, and some found it difficult to explain: "I think defining intuition is just like defining love—it can't be defined, and that's exactly the point. Intuition is something that you understand from your gut" (Dan). In this example, Dan opted to describe the experience of intuition rather than explain it. Others described intuition in terms of the world of senses. Irit, for example, described it as using the sense of sight: "I walked into the examination room and something was off. The patient wasn't doing well. I didn't know what it was. I walked out and just said 'something is wrong.'" Hadas, on the other hand, referred to intuition in terms of the sense of smell: "We used to joke that he had the best intuition of all the hospital staff because he had the largest nose."

These descriptions coincide with the approach of Woolley and Kostopoulou (2013), who identified three types of intuition: *gut feeling, recognition,* and *insight type.* However, the finding that intuition was likened to a sensation, as revealed through the interviews I conducted, was an aspect that was not found in the study by Woolley and Kostopoulou (2013). In other words, intuition does not necessarily create new insights, but like the basic senses of sight and smell, it can reveal that something is "wrong," although the physician might not yet understand what it is.

2.2 The link between intuition, knowledge, experience, and authority

According to the interviewees, medical intuition is occasionally associated with rational sources and perhaps is even based on them. Unlike in other contexts, medical intuition is related to both medical knowledge and objective findings about the patient, resulting from observations, lab tests, etc. Sometimes the intuition relies on objective knowledge and findings, and sometimes it "clashes" with them.

Rebecca, one of the interviewees, described the link between intuition and medical knowledge in two ways: on the one hand, it refers to knowledge that is not logically stored in the physician's brain; on the other hand, intuition is grounded in knowledge that manifests differently: "It's all knowledge; perhaps for some specific physicians, the knowledge may be organized in an irrational fashion, but it exists."

Other interviewees linked intuition with experience. Dan emphasized that intuition, in his view, is not cerebral, but based on experience—specifically, on the many patients the physician has examined in the past. Having accumulated this experience over many years hones the physician's intuition: "You have to have something to base your intuition on; the considerations [that influence your decision-making] may come from your gut, but this gut has already experienced such considerations."

Experience enables intuition, and that is why relatively novice physicians lack intuition: "You can't have intuition without experience; a student has no intuition" (Edna). Furthermore, physicians with less experience are wary of using this tool and are required to justify their decisions: "So the less experienced you are, the more you must rely on quantifiable things, and, as you gain experience, in my opinion, there's more room to say something like 'my sense tells me that . . .'" (Margalit).

Interviewees also noted a connection between intuition and authority. Those who are perceived to have authority often use intuition to demonstrate their status: "If someone wants to show that he's a leading expert in a particular field and therefore is untouchable, then he or she might say, 'Yes, it's a kind of intuition'" (Isaac).

2.3 The need for intuition in medicine

According to the interviewees' descriptions, it appears that physicians are forced to rely on intuition because they are called upon to provide a solution to a patient's problem: "In principle, the physician is expected to provide answers, and in my opinion, that is why oftentimes physicians must use intuition, because leaving the patient without an answer is considered inappropriate" (Amir). This approach is complicated: on the one hand, the physician is the patient's last resort, especially regarding fatal decisions. "When you are a person's last resort and there is nothing else, you have to find it within yourself to help others" (Isaac). On the other hand, the physician does not always have answers: "Look, I have to do what's best for my patient, that is the oath I took, but in most cases, I won't find information to tell me what is best" (Eden).

The combination of a situation of uncertainty along with the obligation to exercise medical responsibility creates the need to use intuition. The physician is called upon to use all of the resources available to provide treatment, and if the medical knowledge is not sufficient, then the physician must use other skills—and one of them is intuition.

Once I understood that intuition has a role to play in medicine and that its use is inherent to medical treatment, I turned my attention to discovering the attitude conveyed by official medical organizations regarding the use of intuition in medicine.

3. Evidence-based medicine and intuition

Evidence-based medicine is one of the most influential approaches in the world of medicine today. Zimerman (2011) claimed that the importance of this approach, which originated from the school of medicine of McMaster University in Canada in the 1980s and '90s, should not be exaggerated. The practices and methodology recommended according to this approach are considered by many to be an ideal towards which physicians must aim. Medical schools and clinical departments include the EBM approach and its principles in the training and preparation of medical professionals. Thus, for example, in my medical studies during the second decade of the current millennium, the only course offered on medical methodology focused on EBM. Here, I present the ideas of the originators of the approach, mainly David Sackett and Gordon Guyatt, who were considered its representatives.

3.1 The principles of EBM

In November 1992, an article titled Evidence-Based Medicine: A New Approach to Teaching the Practice of Medicine was published in the *Journal of the American Medical Association* (*JAMA*). The article was authored by 31 physicians who referred to themselves as the Evidence-Based Medicine Working Group (1992). Although this was not the first published article that used the term EBM, it was the first to discuss it as a philosophy. The article opens with the following statement:

> A new paradigm for medical practice is emerging. Evidence-based medicine de-emphasizes intuition, unsystematic clinical experience, and pathophysio-logic rationale as sufficient grounds for clinical decision-making and stresses the examination of evidence from clinical research. (p. 2040)

This opening does not explain the essence of the approach, which turned into a movement, but rather describes what it opposes—namely, the value of intuition, unsystematic clinical experience, and biologically-based therapies. Instead, the authors place value on clinical research. The group members suggested that intuition, experience, and biologically-based treatments could be replaced (perhaps only partially) by clinical research. As noted, medicine is an applied science, wherein theoretical knowledge is based on biology, and the application of this knowledge is based on experience and intuition. Clinical research was supposed to replace both of these components (i.e., theoretical knowledge and its application).

The EBM movement demands that physicians reexamine the existing theoretical medical knowledge and reconsider its appropriateness for a given patient. To investigate the quality of existing medical knowledge, the physician must have knowledge of epidemiology and statistics and be able to understand whether the articles published in the professional literature meet the demands of epidemiology. Furthermore, it should be noted that the above-mentioned article does not explain how to determine whether the existing knowledge is (or is not) a good fit for a particular patient; in other words, it does not address the application of the theory. Only in a later article (Guyatt et al. 1994) is the issue of applying knowledge to specific cases and patients addressed. I will review this information after presenting the basic assumptions of EBM.

> Clinical experience and the development of clinical instincts (particularly with respect to diagnosis) are a crucial and necessary part of becoming a competent physician. Many aspects of clinical practice cannot, or will not, ever be adequately tested. Clinical experience and its lessons are particularly important in these situations. (ibid.)

A comparison between this quote and the opening sentence of the earlier article suggests a contradiction regarding the importance of a veteran physician's experience, making it unclear when or whether experience should play a role in medical practice. Furthermore, despite the earlier call for a shift of paradigms, the same article also refers to traditional medical competencies, including knowledge of pathophysiology, the development of clinical judgment, and sensitivity to the patient. Also concerning the issue of authority, which should be minimized by the reliance on clinical research, there is an emphasis on developing a critical approach (p. 2421). The following is a summary of how various skills, new and traditional, are viewed in the article.

3.1.1 Users' Guides to Medical Literature

Following the publication of the above-mentioned article, *JAMA* members began publishing Users' Guides to Medical Literature, a series of articles that offered practical tools to help physicians make decisions based on EBM principles. The second part of the second article in this series (Guyatt et al. 1994) deals, as its subtitle indicates, with the following question: "What were the results and will they help me in caring for my patients?"

Epidemiological research, as the category suggests, examines a particular issue in a predefined population with certain characteristics (e.g., age, sex, preexisting conditions, etc.) driven by the assumption that, at the very least, the findings of the study will be relevant and applicable to a population with similar characteristics. Hence, the authors suggest examining the inclusion and exclusion criteria used in the studies:

Can the Results Be Applied to My Patient Care?

> The first issue to address is how confident you are that you can apply the results to a particular patient or patients in your practice. If the patient would have been enrolled in the study had she been there—that is, she meets all the inclusion criteria, and doesn't violate any of the exclusion criteria—there is little question that the results are applicable. (Guyatt et al. 1994, p. 59)

In other words, although the study did not include the physician's specific patient, if the patient fits the inclusion and exclusion criteria and would be willing to accept the experimental treatment, then it is likely to be effective for that patient. However, if the physician's patient does not meet the inclusion and exclusion criteria used to define the population of the clinical study, the authors suggest using judgment:

> If this is not the case, and she would not have been eligible for the study, judgment is required. The study result probably applies even if, for example, she was 2 years too old for the study, had a more severe disease, had previously been treated with a competing therapy, or had a comorbid condition. (ibid.)

Later on, the authors recommend ignoring the inclusion and exclusion criteria used in the study:

> A better approach than rigidly applying the study's inclusion and exclusion criteria is to ask whether there is some compelling reason why the results should not be applied to the patient. A compelling reason usually won't be found, and most often you can generalize the results to your patient with confidence. (ibid.)

In other words, all of these examples demonstrate the presence of an additional factor in the EBM theory—namely, the use of judgment. Hence it is likely that experience, expertise, clinical knowledge, and perhaps even intuition—aspects that were downplayed at the beginning of the first article—are inherent to the practice of medical judgment.

3.1.2 Clarification and integration—1996

A few years after the publication of the initial manifesto, criticisms of the movement began to be heard. In January 1996, an article written by Sackett et al. (1996) was published in the *British Medical Association Journal* (*BMJ*), titled Evidence-Based Medicine: What It Is and What It Isn't. The subtitle of the article reads "It's about integrating individual clinical expertise and the best external evidence."

This notion is further elaborated, as they call for the integration of personal expertise—the clinical judgment acquired through experience and expertise—and external medical knowledge based on epidemiological studies. They noted that expertise is especially significant and relevant in the realm of diagnostics, where experience can lead to a more accurate diagnosis. In general, this distinction is similar to that between subjective and objective knowledge. The authors refer to the way the knowledge was acquired, noting that subjective knowledge is grounded in personal experience and practice. Moreover, it appears that *personal* knowledge cannot be verbalized or communicated, whereas *external* knowledge is verbalized, published, and communicated to others.

Tonelli (1998) suggested that if the "integration" mentioned in Sacket et al. (1996) remains vague, then the state of medicine before and after the introduction of EBM remains similar. All physicians aim to use knowledge for the benefit of their patients, and the suggested paradigmatic change is insignificant—at best, a honing of the traditional clinical process.

In summary, even according to the principles of EBM, which initially and superficially objected to the use of intuition, the use of personal skills—and intuition among them—cannot be ignored.

4. A proposed justification for the use of intuition in medicine

To propose a justification for the use of intuition in medicine, I would like to demonstrate the structure and functioning of medicine. To this end, I will use Wittgenstein's model of the structure of mathematics and consider its application in the field of medicine, using the interpretational approach of Steiner (2009).

4.1 The mathematical model

In 1939, Wittgenstein delivered a series of lectures about the elements of mathematics (Wittgenstein & Diamond 1976), in the course of which he presented a model which he claimed is the foundation of mathematics. According to this model, mathematics was created in two stages:

> Suppose we in this room are inventing arithmetic. We have a technique of counting, but there is so far no arithmetic. Suppose that I now make the following experiment—I give Levy multiplication. We have invented multiplication up to 100; that is, we've written down things like 81 × 63 but have never yet written down things like 123 × 489. I say to him, "You know what you've done so far. Now do the same sort of thing for these two numbers." I assume he does what we usually do. This is an experiment—and one which we may later adopt as a calculation. (p. 95)

In this description, the first stage is experimental: when there are no rules for multiplying three-digit numbers, the experimenter is asked to follow the rules used with double-digit numbers, based on the assumption that this may render a calculation. After this experiment is conducted several times, the second, normative stage begins.

> What does that mean? Well, suppose that 90 per cent do it all one way. I say, "This is now going to be the right result." The experiment was to show what the most natural way is—which way most of them go. Now everybody is taught to do it—and now there is a right and wrong. Before there was not. (ibid.)

If all of the experimenters agree on a specific outcome, then this outcome will be considered the normative rule that all will follow. Wittgenstein further elaborates:

> If it is a calculation, we adopt it as a calculation—that is, we make a rule out of it. We make the description of it the description of a norm—we say, "This is what we are going to compare things with." (ibid., p. 98)

This second stage, then, comprises what Steiner (2009) refers to as "empirical regularities"—that is, the approach chosen by most people who had no guidelines to rely on. The solidification of empirical regularities creates a normative and binding rule, and from here on this is taught as the proper way to solve the mathematical problem. Steiner (2009) emphasized that stating that a certain action is right or wrong is of major significance, as it provides a scale for assessing other actions, and thus it becomes a unifying principle in society, which relies on this binding rule.

It should be noted that, although the rule is based on an empirical regularity, it is not identical to it; rather, an additional stage is involved. At first, there was a realm with only empirical regularity, wherein this behavior had not yet been normalized or solidified into a formal rule.

4.2 Applying the model to medicine

Medical books are full of lists of symptoms and diseases, explaining how they can be diagnosed and options for treatment based on the diagnosis and prognosis. What is the origin of these diagnoses? How were they created? In my opinion, the process was similar to that described in Wittgenstein's mathematical model. Physicians reviewed cases with certain symptoms and eventually noticed a certain regularity among these cases, and thus decided to give a name to a collection of symptoms in order to find a proper treatment. Additional diagnoses of the same collection of symptoms were published, and thus a rule was established that this is the proper term to use to refer to this collection of symptoms. Nowadays, this is given a formal status, when a diagnosis for a particular disease is added to lists endorsed by prominent health organizations—for example, in the International Statistical Classification of Diseases and Related Health Problems (ICD).

Let's take, for example, the forming of the definition for Parkinson's disease. Dr. Parkinson observed six cases of patients (some of whom he saw in passing, in the street) who presented with the following symptoms (albeit not all at once): tremor at rest, abnormal gait, abnormal posture, and muscle weakness. In an article published in 1817 (Parkinson 2002), he named the phenomenon *paralysis agitans.* However, this was not widely published or accepted (Louis 1997). It should be noted that beyond a description of the disease and its prognosis, Dr. Parkinson did not suggest either a biological model or any other form of treatment. It was only in the 1950s that the biological mechanism of the disease was discovered by Carlsson. As this example demonstrates, what defined Parkinson's disease was a collection of symptoms and Dr. Parkinson's ability to identify the phenomenon as an empirical regularity. Only later did the empirical regularity solidify into a binding diagnostic rule.

It should be noted that, just as Wittgenstein's model demonstrates that mathematics is a human creation, the same is true of medicine. Although in medicine the cases are based on scientific or biological phenomena, the solidification of a definition of a disease into a diagnostic rule is a human act, as shown in the example of Parkinson's disease, which was identified years before the biological mechanism and treatment options were found. It should be further noted that the process that describes the identification of a particular disease also pertains to the finding and identification of a given treatment. A medical case presents and a new treatment is found (either incidentally or through a controlled study), and after empirical regulation is proven, then the treatment becomes the norm in the case of this particular disease.

4.3 A medical lacuna

If, as demonstrated, Wittgenstein's model can be applied to medicine, medical situations may arise that have not yet been identified as an empirical regularity (just as Levy did not know how to multiply three-digit numbers, there are medical conditions for which there are no medical rules as of yet). The most significant difference between medicine and mathematics has to do with time. The creation of mathematics was mostly done in the past, and the two discernible stages have already taken place. In medicine, there are constantly new cases that lead to new rules being formalized and old rules being changed. It is well known that the medical literature is updated on a daily basis, and diagnostic and treatment guidelines are frequently altered.

For each patient, the physician must consider which diagnosis best corresponds to that case. The medical books contain lists of diseases and ways to diagnose them, and the physician must ask him or herself which best fits the current case and which treatment would be most effective. To this end, the physician conducts a differential diagnosis, which is to say, several possibilities are considered with the goal of eliminating as many as possible, based on test results, imaging, and other examinations.

In some cases, the diagnosis is simple. Let's consider the case of a broken arm: the physician can see where it is broken and offer a course of treatment. However, what about cases in which no diagnosis is a perfect match to the collection of symptoms presented? For example, this can occur when a patient has several preexisting conditions, and the exacerbation of any of them could explain the current presentation of symptoms. In such cases, the physician must determine, based on professional judgment, which diagnosis is likely to be the major cause and treat that one. There are also cases in which all possibilities have been eliminated and no explanation of the symptoms can be found, as well as cases in which the selected treatment is not effective. In other words, these are cases that cannot be solved by applying any of the existing diagnostic rules of medicine.

Returning to the framework of Wittgenstein's model, it can be said that each medical case could potentially create a new rule or change existing rules related to either diagnosis or treatment. In many instances, the medical rules are "thin," because they are based on several cases from which essential rules were derived and abstracted. However, this process of abstraction can mean that certain patient characteristics, which may have been significant or pertinent, were disregarded.

Let's take the example of treating pneumonia, which typically involves administering antibiotics for a few days. Yet many of the patients hospitalized in the internal medicine ward due to pneumonia also have other preexisting conditions which need to be taken into account. Pneumonia in a patient with diabetes can present differently. The physician treating the patient with diabetes and pneumonia would claim that the rules for treating pneumonia do not apply to this patient and, thus, a medical lacuna is revealed.

Following Wittgenstein's model, medicine is based on abstract rules for treating actual patients. Thus, the physician's task is to use the rules that have been derived and abstracted to treat the existing patient. This is an odd state of affairs: first, there were actual cases, which were abstracted to define "disease X," which in turn were formalized into a diagnostic rule, and now physicians must use the abstract rule to diagnose and treat actual patients. The move from actual concrete cases to abstraction and back to actual cases creates a lacuna, which the physician must address by applying professional judgment, and this also includes intuition. In this sense, physicians are called upon to reconsider the rules of medicine, taking them back to the first stage of the model, in which there were no clear rules. Compared to mathematics, in which the two stages are separate and sequential, in medicine, the two stages occur simultaneously.

In this context, intuition does not coincide with any specific rule, given that none of the existing rules is applicable to this specific case; hence, the physician is left to exercise judgment, based on intuition, experience, or a known biological mechanism. Accordingly, there is no need for a binding definition of intuition (in fact, sometimes it can feel like anything between a shot in the dark and an educated guess). In this sense, the epistemological threshold of intuition is rather low because of the lacuna in the existing rules; consequently, the issue of intuition's trustworthiness becomes less relevant.

4.4 The boundaries of intuition

Are there no boundaries to intuition? Can a physician do whatever he or she intuits? I believe that there are boundaries, and to prove this, I return to the mathematical model introduced by Wittgenstein. As noted, when faced with a mathematical problem he did not know how to solve, Levy had to do two things:

A. Continue using the method with which he was familiar.

B. Ensure that the outcome conformed to a standard that could hold up as a future rule.

Likewise, the physician must consider whether the suggested diagnosis or treatment could become a future rule.

Another aspect that serves as a boundary to intuition, which was raised by interviewees during the discussion about intuition, was *expertise*: what is the connection between expertise and the use of intuition? According to the proposed model, there is a connection between the two aspects:

A. An experienced expert can tell whether a particular case does not correspond to the current rules and whether there is a need to revert to the earlier, pre-rule stage.

B. The expert is better able to assess what might function as a new rule or would be accepted as an alteration of an existing rule.

5. Summary

This inquiry began by examining medicine in the field to explore how physicians—those who actively use intuition—perceive this use. The interviewees recognized that medical intuition is used but found it difficult to define. Their commitment to providing a solution to patients, combined with the absence of reliable medical information pertaining to a specific patient or case, creates a complex, nearly impossible situation. Despite relying on rational thought, the physician must recruit other abilities and skills that are not rational, such as intuition, in order to attain the overall goal of addressing patients' needs and providing treatment. These findings emphasize that medical intuition comes into play because of the prioritization of addressing patients' needs, which in turn means that the scientific rationale is set aside or deprioritized.

My next step was to examine the approach to intuition as expressed by the founders of the EBM movement. In 1992, they proposed a revolutionary approach that seemed to oppose the use of personal judgment in decision-making. However, a careful review of their writings revealed that EBM does not eliminate the use of such means.

Furthermore, Sackett et al. (1996) indicated that, not only was the use of personal judgment and decision-making not eliminated, it was granted "official recognition." Hence, EBM does not eliminate the use of intuition, personal experience, or basic biological scientific research, based on the understanding that in particular cases, they are essential for providing a proper diagnosis and treatment.

Thus, it appears that the same principle that was identified in the first part of the study (i.e., through the personal interviews) was repeated in the section about the EBM approach. More specifically, when the need to provide a diagnostic solution and treatment clashes with the reliance on scientific knowledge and methods, the need to treat is prioritized. The physician's role is first and foremost to cure; the means and tools by which to achieve this are medical and scientific knowledge, yet the reliance on these resources becomes secondary compared to the overall mission.

Finally, my last step was to demonstrate how the goal of curing is combined with the scientific approach. I offered the model borrowed from Wittgenstein's philosophy of mathematics (1976), according to which this field was created in two stages. The first is experimental and lacks any known rules, hence the task is carried out using preexisting methods. In the second stage, the experiments that proved successful lead to the formulation of binding rules.

As I see it, the same process can be used to describe the development of the field of medicine; however, in medicine, the two stages occur simultaneously. The use of intuition comes into play in the first stage, where there are no existing medical rules. The physician turns to intuition after concluding that there is no existing rule that can provide a solution to the case at hand. In medicine, as the interviews revealed, encounters with such medical lacunae are frequent and daily, and therefore, there is a need to revert to the earlier stage and use intuition to find a viable solution for the patient.

In this sense, current medicine is a unique science, which offers rules and principles for treating medical conditions but addresses an abstract patient. However, the physician, who must find a solution for the patient, is required to make adjustments to suit the particular patient's needs. In other words, the physician creates a medical solution tailored to the particular patient's condition.

Acknowledgments

This chapter is partially based on my doctoral thesis (Adler 2022) awarded by the program on the history and philosophy of science and medicine at the Hebrew University of Jerusalem. I wish to thank my advisers, Dr. Dror Atniel, Dr. Adi Finkelstein, and Prof. Yemima Ben-Menachem. Prof. Ben-Menachem was kind enough to review this chapter and offer her insightful comments, for which I'm extremely thankful. This chapter is dedicated to my wife, Natalie, who is always there for me.

References

Adler, I. (2022). "Intuition in Medcine: An Empirical, Historical and Philosophical View." [PhD Diss. The Hebrew University of Jerusalem.]

Adler, I. (2022). The medical gap: Intuition in medicine. *Med Health Care Philos.,* 25(3): 361–369. doi: 10.1007/s11019-022-10081-4

Bengson, J. (2015). The intellectual given. *Mind,* 124 (July): 707–760. https://doi.org/10.1093/mind/fzv029.

Chudnoff, E. (2014). The rational roles of intuition. In: A. R. Booth and D. Rowbottom (Eds.), *Intuitions.* Oxford: Oxford University Press, 1–44. https://doi.org/10.1093/acprof

Gascoigne, N., and Thornton, T. (2014). *Tacit Knowledge.* London: Routledge.

Guyatt, G. H., et al. (1994). 'Users' guides to the medical literature: II. How to use an article about therapy or prevention; B. What were the results and will they help me in caring for my patients? *JAMA,* 271(1): 59–63.

Edwards, R., and Holland, J. (2013). What forms can qualitative interviews take? In: *What Is Qualitative Interviewing?* 1st ed. *The 'What is?' Research Methods Series,* 29–42. London: Bloomsbury Academic

Evidence-Based Medicine Working Group (1992). Evidence-based medicine. A new approach to teaching the practice of medicine. *Journal of the American Medical Association,* 268(17): 2420-2425. doi: 10.1001/jama.1992.03490170092032

Jameson, J. L., Kasper, D. L., Fauci, A. S., et al. (2018). *Harrison's Principles of Internal Medicine, 20e. Principles of Internal Medicine.* 20th ed. New York: McGraw-Hill Education.

Kahneman, D., and Klein, G. (2009). Conditions for intuitive expertise: A failure to disagree. *The American Psychologist,* 64: 515–526.

Kant, I. (1998). *Critique of Pure Reason.* P. Guyer and A. W. Wood (Eds). Cambridge University Press.

Klein, G. (1998). *Sources of Power: How People Make Decisions.* Cambridge, MA: MIT Press.

Koksvik, O. (2011). "Intuition." Doctoral diss. The Australian National University.

Lewis, D. (1983). *Philosophical Papers,* Vol. I. Oxford University Press. https://doi.org/10.1093/0195032047.001.0001

Louis, E. D. (1997). The shaking palsy, the first forty-five years: A journey through the British literature. *Movement Disorders,* 12(6): 1068–1072.

Parkinson, J. (2002/1817). An essay on the shaking palsy. *The Journal of Neuropsychiatry and Clinical Neurosciences,* 14(2): 223–236.

Polanyi, M. (2009). *The Tacit Dimension.* Chicago, IL: University of Chicago Press.

Sackett, D. L., Rosenberg, W., Gray, J., Haynes, R., and Richardson, W. (1996). Evidence based medicine: What it is and what it isn't. *BMJ,* 312: 7023.

Simon, H. A. (1992). What is an explanation of behavior? *Psychological Science,* 3(3): 150–161. https://doi.org/10.1111/j.1467-9280.1992.tb00017.x

Sosa, E. (1998). Minimal intuition. In: M. DePaul and W. Ramsey (Eds.), *Rethinking Intuition,* 257–269. Rowman & Littlefield.

Steiner, M. (2009). Empirical regularities in Wittgenstein's philosophy of mathematics. *Philosophia Mathematica,* 17(1): 1–34.

Stolper, E., et al. (2011). Gut feelings as a third track in general practitioners' diagnostic reasoning. *Journal of General Internal Medicine,* 26(2): 197–203.

Tonelli, M. R. (1998). The philosophical limits of evidence-based medicine. *Academic Medicine,* 1234–1240.

Williamson, T. (2007). *The Philosophy of Philosophy.* Malden, MA: Blackwell Pub.

Wittgenstein, L. (1976). Cause and effect: Intuitive awareness. *Philosophia,* 6(3–4): 409–425. https://doi.org/10.1007/BF02379281

Wittgenstein, L. (2009). *Philosophical Investigations.* 4th ed. P. M. S. Hacker and J. Schulte (Eds.). Chichester, Malden, Oxford: Wiley-Blackwell.

Wittgenstein, L., and Diamond, C. (1976). *Wittgenstein's Lectures on the Foundations of Mathematics.* Ithaca, NY: Cornell University Press.

Woolley, A., and Kostopoulou, O. (2013). Clinical intuition in family medicine: More than first impressions. *Annals of Family Medicine,* 11(1): 60–66.

Zimerman, A. L. (2011). "Evidence-Based Medicine: The History of a Recent Medical Revolution." (PhD Diss., Bar-Ilan University.)

Chapter 6

Turning Intuition into Managerial Simple Rules

Radu Atanasiu,[1] Christopher Wickert,[2] and Svetlana N. Khapova[3]

[1] Bucharest International School of Management, Romania, and Vrije Universiteit, Amsterdam, The Netherlands

[2] Vrije Universiteit Amsterdam, The Netherlands

[3] Vrije Universiteit Amsterdam, The Netherlands

Introduction

Despite its ambivalent image in organizations, intuition is (secretly or openly) used by most managers to decide on a vast spectrum of situations. Management scholars have, consequently, focused their studies on *managerial intuition* (Simon 1987) and found it to be a valuable decision-making tool (Sinclair & Ashkanasy 2005; Patterson et al. 2012). However, only a few evidence-based methods aim to sharpen managers' intuition and to turn it into a purposefully trained and purposefully applied decision aid. Among existing approaches are recognizing and turning the wicked environments in which we educate our intuition into kind ones (Hogarth 2001), continuously testing and self-benchmarking intuitive judgements (Sadler-Smith & Shefy 2004), mixing intuitive with analytical members in teams (Hodgkinson et al. 2009), and developing intuitive awareness as part of business school curricula (Sadler-Smith & Shefy 2007). Yet, the repertoire of approaches is limited.

This chapter aims to address this limitation and proposes *simple rules heuristics as natural* vehicles to encode, use, test, refine, store, and share managerial knowledge that arises intuitively. Simple rules can be defined as the sub-type of managerial heuristics which are *learned, specific,* and *purposeful* (Bingham & Eisenhardt 2014), as opposed to the *innate, universal, and unintentional* heuristics such as anchoring or availability (Tversky & Kahneman 1974). They are often expressed as catchphrases, such as, 'Every internal team should be small enough that it can be fed with two pizzas' (Hern 2018), and are observed to benefit decision-making (Bingham & Eisenhardt 2014), strategizing (Bingham et al. 2007), and organizing (Eriksson & Kadefors 2017).

Based on the exploration of the natural process which turns intuition into a simple rule, we end this chapter by proposing two methods in which managers and teams can purposefully train their intuition. The first method helps individual managers acknowledge and clarify their past intuitive judgements and articulate them into simple rules. The second method helps teams make sense of negative aspects of their projects and encode their insights into simple rules. Together, these methods help turn intuition and insight into explicit and shareable knowledge and, also, increase the intuitive awareness of managers and teams.

In developing our approach, we draw on extant concepts and frameworks from the literatures on managerial heuristics (Bingham & Eisenhardt 2014; Gigerenzer & Gaissmeier 2011), managerial intuition (Dane & Pratt 2007; Sadler-Smith & Shefy 2007), insight (Dane 2020; Luo & Niki 2003), organizational learning (Crossan et al. 1999, 2011), sensemaking (Weick et al. 2005), and dual processing (Basel & Brühl 2013; Evans & Stanovich 2013), as well as on qualitative data collected in four waves from two samples totaling 63 top and senior managers, data which also served as sources for our previous studies (Atanasiu et al. 2022; Atanasiu et al. 2023 [*under review*]).

With this chapter we make several contributions. We build on extant research which tackles the relationship between intuition and managerial heuristics (Basel & Brühl 2013; Sadler-Smith 2019) by outlining the role of intuition in the creation of these managerial tools, and we offer practitioners methods which use this understanding to purposefully replicate the process. We begin this chapter by defining what simple rules heuristics are. We then describe how managers naturally capture, test, store, and share their intuitions by turning them into simple rules. We conclude this chapter by discussing how managerial intuition can be trained to purposefully produce simple rules.

What are simple rules heuristics?

Despite not being prominent in a manager's daily vocabulary, simple rules heuristics are important managerial tools which are ubiquitous in their daily activity. In this section, we introduce and illustrate this concept, which is central to our subsequent argumentation. Simple rules heuristics are the sub-type of managerial heuristics which are studied by the homonym research stream (Bingham & Eisenhardt 2014). Unlike universal, unintentional, and innate heuristics, associated with biases such as anchoring or availability (Tversky & Kahneman 1974), simple rules are idiosyncratic—specific to their users (Bingham & Eisenhardt 2014), used consciously (Bingham & Eisenhardt 2014), and learned from direct experience (Bingham & Haleblian 2012) to encode, within their proverb-like formulation (Atanasiu 2021; Eriksson & Kadefors 2017), tacit experience into explicit and shareable knowledge (Bingham et al. 2007). In this chapter we follow the example of the proponents of the simple-rules stream of research (e.g., Bingham & Eisenhardt 2011) and use, interchangeably, the terms *simple rules heuristics,* (just) *simple rules,* and (just) *heuristics.*

Extant literature describes simple rules as important tools for deciding, strategizing, and organizing. For *deciding*, classical economics prescribes complex, analytical algorithms that use all the information available (von Neumann & Morgenstern 1953). However, under bounded rationality (Simon 1947), time constraints, complex business environments, and uncertainty, managers forego the use of all available information and of complex analyses and prefer to make decisions guided by simple rules heuristics: "Decision-making in organizations typically involves heuristics because the conditions for rational models rarely hold in an uncertain world" (Gigerenzer & Gaissmeier 2011, 474).

> For instance, Harry Markowitz received the 1990 Nobel Prize in Economics for his Modern Portfolio Theory, which uses complex mathematical algorithms to allocate funds across several vehicles when investing. However, when he retired, the economist ignored his own Nobel-winning optimization method and relied instead on a heuristic: he allocated the same sum to all funds, a heuristic called $1/N$ (Gigerenzer 2008). Later, his choice was empirically validated: DeMiguel et al. (2009) evaluated 14 models of diversification and found that none consistently performs better than the $1/N$ rule.

For *strategizing*, classical economics favors deliberate strategies (Mintzberg & Waters 1985) and strategizing-by-thinking (Eisenhardt & Bingham 2017), which consists of planning ahead based on carefully calculated models and scenarios. However, under conditions of volatility, uncertainty, complexity, and ambiguity, managers prefer emergent strategies (Mintzberg & Waters 1985) and strategizing-by-doing (Eisenhardt & Bingham 2017), guided by adaptive, simple rules heuristics, which are 'the essence of strategy, especially in unpredictable markets where opportunities are often numerous, fast-moving, and uncertain' (Bingham & Eisenhardt 2014, 1698).

> As an illustration, Jack Welch, whom *Fortune* named "The Manager of the Century" in 1999, began his mandate as the CEO of General Electric by reorganizing the conglomerate towards consolidation and aggressive simplification. When choosing which business directions to pursue and which to divest from, Welch did not use the available financial and market data to calculate expected values and build scenarios; instead, he relied on a simple rule: 'Only keep businesses that are (or can be) number one or number two in their industries.'

For *organizing*, rigid systems and formal procedures have increasingly given way to adaptive and learning organizations (Senge 1994). However, what do organizations learn? When they learn, managers and organizations learn simple rules heuristics (Bingham & Eisenhardt 2011; Bingham & Haleblian 2012) that encode tacit experience into explicit (Bingham et al. 2007), well-articulated catchphrases (Eriksson & Kadefors 2017), which guide alignment (Sull & Eisenhardt 2012), coordination (Bingham & Eisenhardt 2014), communication (Eriksson & Kadefors 2017), and monitoring (Pieper et al. 2015).

> For example, to design the internal structure of the organization, Amazon® uses a simple, proverb-like rule, the famous *two-pizza rule*: 'Every internal team in Amazon must be small enough so that it can be fed with two pizzas' (Hern 2018).

Most research on simple rules heuristics is conducted at firm level. Before reaching the collective level, however, they are created and used by an individual manager (Guercini et al. 2015) and only afterwards shared to teams and organizations (Bingham et al. 2019). While exploring the under-researched process of how individual managers distill their experience into simple rules heuristics, a key discovery was the prominent role intuition plays in this process. The next sections describe our new understanding of how intuition is captured into, tested through, and shared as simple rules heuristics.

How do managers capture intuition into simple rules?

They simply come to you. You bump into them. They come. (respondent)

Intuition is the main topic of this book, and surely the reader already has a complex image of the concept. For the purposes of our argument, we favor the definition Dane and Pratt (2007) synthesized from extant conceptualizations:

'Intuitions are affectively charged judgments that arise through rapid, nonconscious, and holistic associations' (p. 40). In this chapter, we also use the term *insight,* which can be defined as, 'the reorientation of one's thinking, including breaking of the unwarranted fixation and forming of novel (. . .) associations' (Luo & Niki 2003, 316). Sadler-Smith and Shefy (2007) outline important differences between insight and intuition—namely, that with intuition, the subject is certain on a certain solution or course of action but cannot always explain why. Based on the understanding of our respondents, in this chapter we use *insight* and *intuition* in a partially overlapping manner, with insight being the sudden understanding of a problem and intuition the non-conscious mental process that precedes, sparks, and sometimes refines the insight and which guides the manager towards choosing between two different explanations and approaches.

The link between heuristics and intuition has been researched, with Basel and Brühl (2013) proposing that, "first, heuristics are spontaneously initiated by System 1 and then later adopted by System 2, as they are a seen as a deliberate strategy" (p. 751). Our research offers empirical support for this proposition, showing how managers use intuition for learning simple rules heuristics from negative situations, a mix of intuition and reflection for articulating them, and then reflection for testing, refining, and adapting these lessons. This sequence will be described as follows: the intuitive and intuitive-reflective phases (insight and articulation) are the focus of the current section—capturing intuition into simple rules—while the purely reflective phase (testing, refining, adapting) is the topic of the next section—testing intuition through simple rules.

Managers create simple rules heuristics by making sense of unexpected failures (Atanasiu 2021; Atanasiu et al. 2022; Bingham & Haleblian 2012). Normally, a sensemaking process consists in scanning for pre-existing heuristics (Schildt et al. 2020, 249) to explain and solve a puzzle. In the absence of such pre-existing heuristics, a manager struggles to create new ones through a complex cognitive interplay of intuition and reflection, accompanied by a rollercoaster of feelings. The first part of the process—the insight and its articulation—is described by the managers we interviewed as rather intuitive: 'They didn't come to me after an internal one-hour debate in my head; they waited, smoldered inside, and, at some point, took shape.'

Insight. An unexpected failure generates dissonance between reality and a manager's expectations. This uncomfortable tension—'It appeared in the last weeks, it accumulated'—leads to a state of readiness for insight (Dane 2020), in which the manager has the issue top-of-mind, searches both actively and idly for an explanation and a solution, and scans the environment for clues to clarify the matter and to spark the insight: 'It's a concern, but a reactive concern, not a proactive one, in the sense that I listen to audiobooks, I read stuff, and things jump out and help me systemize; it's a need that draws from the environment what it helps.'

Eventually, such a clarifier appears in the form of an analogy (as in the example below), an observed inconsistency, or a random piece of information. This clarifier helps the manager make sense of the situation by sparking a triple insight:

- *What was not true*—What assumption was in fact flawed and caused the failure
- *What is true instead*—A new principle which, if applied, will prevent the reoccurrence of the failure and which will be captured into a conceptual simple rule heuristic
- *What to do about it*—A way to enact this new principle through an operative simple rule heuristic

---

Vignette: Two entrepreneurs who structure their organization into autonomous teams were puzzled by an unexpected failure: counterintuitively, the more successful a team, the more its internal dynamics altered. The dissonance between this observation and their previous assumption (that success must harmonize a team's internal dynamics) initiated a state of readiness for insight, characterized by discomfort and a constant search for the root cause.

One of them describes that the insight came during a conversation with his partner, sparked by an analogy which acted as a clarifier: 'Mastermind teams must be small to function well, and we realized that business teams must have the same size, as they function similarly; we recognized the parallel with mastermind teams and we said, this is it!'

The triple insight was about (a) what was not true—success does not automatically lead to a team functioning well; (b) what is true instead—success sometimes leads to an increase in team size, which alters its internal dynamics, a principle which they captured in the conceptual simple rule heuristic, 'When small teams grow, their dynamics change'; and (c) what to do about it—enacting this new principle through an operative simple rule heuristic: 'When a team reaches ten members, it must split.'

The immediate context for insight varied for our respondents. To some managers, the insight happened when alone, 'Everything happened in my head, I never found conversations very helpful for this'; at various moments of the day, 'In the morning, as things that I probably pondered while asleep crystalize when I open my eyes'; or 'During running, which is active meditation.' To others, the insight happened during one-to-one conversations 'With people I resonate with.' Yet others have the insight during meetings, but our respondents stress that,

'The collective realization still came from an individual insight.' The personal (or life) contexts shared similarities among our interviewees, such as that intuitive realizations mostly happened during a moment of transition—change of jobs, moving cities, becoming a parent, doing an MBA, or even during a perceived identity crisis.

Articulating. Despite their strategic importance, simple rules heuristics are sometimes used tacitly, without ever being verbalized: 'For five years, we acted on it without discussing it; it was not written or acknowledged in any way'; and articulation may happen long after the initial insight: 'There certainly is a period between realizing such a principle and verbalizing it.' Tsoukas & Vladimirou (2001) define articulation as 'the dynamic process of turning an unreflective practice into a reflective one' (Tsoukas & Vladimirou 2001, as cited in Hazlett et al. 2005, 32), while Weick et al. (2005, 413) have defined articulation as the process 'by which tacit knowledge is made more explicit or usable.'

In the classic 4I model of organizational learning, Crossan et al. (2011) describe that learning begins at the individual level with intuiting, which leads to new understandings that are pre-verbal, matching our insight phase, and continues with interpreting, which stabilizes these insights through words—articulation. These perspectives may lead us to consider articulation a predominantly reflective practice.

Our respondents confirm the reflective aspect of articulating insights: 'Articulating helps me personally in clarifying the issue.' However, our data show that, for articulation, managers also appeal to intuition. In a handful of instances, our interviewing was what caused the respondent to first articulate a simple rule: 'Its verbalization came to me ten minutes ago, during this conversation; I never thought of it before in this form.' As one manager admitted, somewhat poetically: 'I knew it, but I didn't know I knew it.' In these instances, we had the opportunity to further inquire on this process, and we found that articulation not only puts pre-existing ideas into words, but also clarifies, through a second wave of insight, these ideas: 'This interview is like therapy, it helps me analyze, make sense of, and verbalize ideas that are still taking shape in my head.'

In another instance in which articulation happened during the interview, the manager showed genuine surprise by how she just formulated her simple rule, further supporting the pre-conscious, intuitive aspect of articulating: 'I was surprised I formulated it so decisively: this means that I had reached that belief without being aware of it.' Often, this second insight which leads to articulation inspires the manager to effortlessly formulate the simple rule in a proverb-like form—such as, 'The cool factor does not pay the salaries.' Therefore, although most theoretical frameworks consider articulation a purely reflective process which renders intuition explicit, our data suggest that articulation in fact lies on the border between intuition and reflection, drawing from both types of processing.

How can this initial, intuitive phase fail? And how can a manager prevent this? Our respondents mentioned that, surely, they missed turning some other past failures into valuable insights because, often, 'We are caught in buzz work and don't pay attention to higher-order themes,' and 'You need some detachment from operational tasks.' Although intuitive, the birth of a simple rule heuristic requires managers to focus their attention and time on the failure and to entertain the resulting tension and dissonance.

Some of our respondents have created personal systems to facilitate coming up with such valuable insights: 'I meditate, sometimes daily, on where I go wrong,' or, 'I take breaks from current tasks and I self-reflect,' or even, 'Every other day I sit and think about managing this company.' Yet others have scaled this intention as a system to the entire company: 'Aha moments may come in the shower, during a crisis, while running, but we also try to create here a deliberated culture, which we try to purposefully influence; so, we encourage thinking and self-reflection.' In this quote, thinking and self-reflection are not the epitomes of rational analysis, but more likely they describe the state Dane (2020) describes as 'readiness for insight.'

Other managers, after understanding that conversations with people holding different perspectives are their appropriate context for having and articulating such insights, have started to purposefully encourage similar moments: 'I spend 50 percent of my time outside of the company, talking to people outside the company; it's an active goal,' or, 'I entered circles outside the business world where discussions did not start with, "We need to decide whether we give bonuses this Christmas," but with, "How does everyone feel, why are you here, what are the expectations from this context, from this group?"'

How do managers use simple rules to test their intuition?

'Intuition comes first, and it relies on nothing, you just know; then, if you want to check your intuition, you take the numbers and analyze them, and that's how the magic gets certified.' (respondent)

After the more intuitive phase of the process, simple rules heuristics go through a predominantly reflective phase, when they are tested (and, if confirmed, reinforced), refined, and adapted. One of our respondents mentioned that this second, reflective phase, came with a sense of urgency: 'Coming up with the intuitive rule is like the sky clearing, but then you can't wait to test it and validate it.' The manager tests the new simple rule heuristic in successive feedback loops, in various situations; if confirmed, the rule is reinforced: 'It worked repeatedly, and that has made it stronger.' Then the manager analyzes these results and purposefully reshapes the simple rule in accordance with the principles of ecological rationality (Gigerenzer & Brighton 2009; Gigerenzer & Gaissmaier 2011), making it better fit for the specific context and better adapted and generalized for larger contexts: 'It's in perpetual testing, and on this new job we perfected it, it's already version 3.0 now.'

This sequence—intuition followed by reflection, which yields from our data, supports the default-interventionist hypothesis (Basel & Brühl 2013; Evans & Stanovich 2013), which states that we rely on Type 1 processing—rapid and autonomous—as the default response for a situation, and then, if required, we intervene with Type 2 processing—slow and purposeful—to validate or adjust the default response. One of our respondents perfectly described the role of reflection to certify the magic of intuition: 'Intuition comes first, and it relies on nothing, you just know; then, if you want to check your intuition, you take the numbers and analyze them, and that's how the magic gets certified.' These reflective processes overlap with the integrating phase of the 4I model of organizational learning (Crossan et al. 1999) and with the *enactment, selection,* and *retention* phases of the sensemaking model proposed by Weick et al. (2005).

However, we found that reflection is required not only for testing and refining the insight, but also for having the insight in the first place. More precisely, our respondents describe that, in order to generate an insight, they purposefully put themselves in a position of assumed responsibility for the initial failure: 'For principles to arise, a manager must look at pain points reflectively, not defensively. Because, if you look defensively, you will not look for real answers, but for answers that keep you in your comfort zone, like "the world is mean," "it cannot be done differently," "I've tried and it doesn't work."' This empirical observation concurs with the conclusion of Bingham and Haleblian (2012), who found internal attribution (assuming responsibility for the failure) to be the necessary condition to learn simple rules heuristics from failures. The role of reflection is, therefore, not only to check and refine the intuition, but also to purposefully induce a mindset that favors looking at the situation with an internal locus of control.

How can this second, more reflective phase, fail? And how can a manager prevent this? Making sense of failures cannot take place without enacting the intuitive lesson you have learned (Weick et al. 2005). Some of our respondents remembered a time when they discounted their intuition and refrained from acting on it, mainly because of social pressure: 'I fought it hard, saying to myself to stop this nonsense of listening to how I feel about things.' Only later, when similar failures happened repeatedly, did they purposefully build the courage to trust their intuition and act on it.

The opposite situation can also happen, when managers trust so deeply in their intuition and the resulting simple rule heuristic that they will never doubt, test, or discard it, even if necessary. Most managers we interviewed maintain that, 'If I see it doesn't work anymore, I will discard it,' but we also encountered the occasional manager who admitted that, even after the simple rule would not function anymore, 'Giving it up would mean giving up a part of me, of who I am, and that is complicated.' The potential stickiness of a simple rule is an issue recognized by the extant literature: 'Not only the question of how heuristic strategies are initially selected, but particularly how they are switched after they have become maladapted, largely remains a central but not yet sufficiently answered question' (Artinger et al. 2015, 45).

One potential explanation of this stickiness is the feelings which accompany the moment of insight. Clever experiments designed by Laukkonen et al. (2020, 2022) have shown that the feeling of awe associated with aha moments will make the insight appear more valid and be remembered longer, even if the aha moment is induced artificially, by solving an anagram. A potential solution for avoiding the stickiness trap is to continuously check the results of our simple rules heuristics, especially when the conditions have changed and ecological fitness (Luan et al. 2019) no longer holds. One interviewee pinpointed this attitude: 'This is something that preoccupies me—being flexible, not making up your mind for life; I wouldn't doubt it constantly, but I would pay attention if, at some point, it doesn't function anymore, and then I will be OK to change it.'

How do managers use simple rules to share their intuition?

Instead of a leadership course, I could give you a single sheet of paper with such principles. (respondent)

Simple rules heuristics, born from intuition and shaped through reflection, are often used exclusively by the individual manager (Guercini et al. 2015). However, when appropriate, they are shared to peers, teams, organization: 'Heuristics move from individual-level rules of thumb (. . .) to firm-level understandings' (Bingham et al. 2019, 121), and even to the entire industry, as described by Kazakova and Geiger (2015) and Monaghan and Tippmann (2018). According to our data, the process of sharing their simple rules begins timidly: 'I use it for myself, but I also shared it recently to my team,' and it can later become well-systemized: 'With time, I not only used it for myself, but I transmitted it, imposed it, required it from my team, and then asked them to implement it in their teams.' This phase overlaps with the institutionalizing phase of the 4I model of organizational learning (Crossan et al. 2011) and with the organizing through communication phase of the sensemaking model proposed by Weick et al. (2005).

Extant literature describes that heuristics can be shared either informally (Barberà-Mariné et al. 2019; Bingham et al. 2019; Guercini et al. 2015) or through formal communication, such as regular meetings (Bingham & Haleblian 2012). Our data support these conclusions, with managers reporting that they share their simple rules formally, during 'our first or second meeting' or in 'weekly one-to-ones'; informally, through 'open discussions'; or even tacitly, through enacting them together: 'I didn't always tell, but they all know it, we reached a common way of doing things,' or through co-creating these simple rules: 'Because we experienced these together, everyone knows them, it's a common experience that we solidified together.'

Our data show that, as some managers use their simple rules before being articulated, it is their first need to share a rule which initiates articulation: 'I learned it while being a CEO, but I articulated it during my subsequent practice as a consultant, because consultancy requires you to formalize these rules somehow.' The need to be easily shared, understood, memorized, and applied also shapes the formulation of the simple rule (Atanasiu 2021; Atanasiu et al. 2022; Bingham & Eisenhardt 2014; Katsikopoulos 2016; Eriksson & Kadefors 2017). To these aims, managers formulate their simple rules heuristics like proverbs, with proverbial markers (Mieder 2014) such as shortness—'If there are 3 "ifs," don't do it!' (Atanasiu 2017), humor—Amazon's 'Every internal team should be small enough that it can be fed with two pizzas' (Hern 2018), symmetry and contrast—'Buy on the rumour, sell on the fact' (Shapin 2001), rhyme—'Sell in May and go away' (Bouman & Jacobsen 2002), and repetition—Cisco's 'Companies to be acquired must have no more than 75 employees, 75 percent of whom are engineers' (Eisenhardt & Sull 2001).

Proverbialization is mainly done for the benefits of those to whom the simple rule is shared: 'It helps me be concise and inspirational,' but not exclusively. Sometimes, these features are for the personal benefit of the manager who created the simple rule: 'Being like a proverb brings clarity and helps me transform complex problems into simple ones, so that I can move on.' Sometimes, this manager shapes her simple rule like a proverb without even noticing: 'I didn't realize that it sounds like a proverb, but when I said it, people started writing it down, so perhaps it struck a chord.'

How can this phase fail? And how can managers deal with such obstacles? First of all, a manager may not be aware that such personal lessons might be of good use to others. Personal simple rules can prove valuable for peers who face similar situations: 'I shared it with some entrepreneurs I know'; for colleagues who are at an earlier career stage: 'The condensed form helps pass experience forward: instead of a leadership course, I could give you a single sheet of paper with such principles'; or for a team or an entire organization to align. One of our CEO respondents mentioned that: 'Heuristics are useful for yourself, but I mainly see benefits for the team. People in the organization inherently have less information or less correlated information. And, without some guidance, they either create their own narrative, which is hard to replace, or are confused and feel that there is no direction. So, heuristics are useful for communicating the strategy.' However, especially when they still apply their intuitive rule tacitly, managers might not be aware of others' similar needs. During our interviews, when asked whether they have shared their rules to others, some managers admitted that: 'I have shared it, but now I realize that I haven't shared it enough.' To overcome this, a good method would be to create context for and encourage informal communication within teams and organizations.

When sharing, some of our respondents faced either resistance: 'I tried to share this lesson with some of the managers I work with, but unfortunately, many of them are of the impression that a square can be hammered to fit into a cylindrical shape'; or limited effect: 'I shared it with my team in one of our meetings, but the effect is visible almost only in those who faced something similar.' To prevent this, we gathered from the practice of our top managers three lessons on how to share simple rules heuristics effectively:

- **Select your audience.** Some of these insights are applicable at a certain level of maturity and self-development—'If someone had come to me 10 years ago with this set of rules, it wouldn't have helped me'—so one of our interviewees admitted that he shares his insight-turned-into-simple-rule 'with as many as are ready to hear; I don't share it with people who don't hear me or are not ready, because I see myself in them years back and I wouldn't have listened either.'

- **Adapt to your audience.** When a rule can be used by people who are at different career or maturity stages, sharing must be preceded by empathically adapting the rule to the receiver: 'I share it, yes. And I make it about them.'

- **Share your narrative.** As described earlier, simple rules are distilled as intuitive lessons after a failure, and many a top manager realized that sharing their lessons is futile, as one must experience the triggering failure and the subsequent insight firsthand: 'Saying "don't play with the axe, you will cut your fingers!" doesn't work until you cut your fingers; after you cut your first finger, you realize how good the advice was.' While some managers abandon here because, 'Even if the present me would have traveled back in time 12 years to tell these rules to my former self, I wouldn't have taken them, because you need to experience things beforehand'; and others struggle with sharing: 'It's hard to transfer simple rules because they rely on intuition and I cannot transfer that, you need to develop your own intuition; I can only transmit what I've learned, my experiencing is untransmissible'; one of our respondents has devised a clever way to overcome the obstacle. He shares not only his insight (the new simple rule), but the whole story of his failure: 'When I share it, I also share its story, what I did wrong before; if shared without its story, the rule would be ignored, but if the story is there, they pay more attention and they remember better.'

How can managerial intuition be trained to produce simple rules?

If you would travel the world with this process, you could clarify a lot of things for a lot of people. (respondent)

The positive role of intuition in management has been well documented (Patterson et al. 2012), explained (Dane & Pratt 2007; Simon 1987), and even measured (Sinclair & Ashkanasy 2005). However, in practice, intuition still struggles to gain the image of a trustworthy managerial tool, and therefore, the efforts for igniting and developing managers' intuition are rather the exception (Sadler-Smith & Shefy 2007). So far in this chapter we have described how managers naturally have their intuitions and insights captured into, tested through, and shared as simple rules heuristics. This section aims to propose, based on our research, two methods for purposefully igniting and developing managerial intuition. One addresses individual managers based on dialogue, while the second addresses teams based on formal lessons-learned meetings.

Dialogue. Within the top and senior managers in our samples, very few acknowledge and purposefully work on their intuition: they tend to be those who have a strong intuition but have long fought against it, only to understand that ignoring their intuition leads to negative outcomes, especially in domains such as deciding about people (clients, employees); those who never had strong instincts and used to rely mostly on rational analysis, only to discover that colleagues who 'shoot from the hip' have better results; and those rare cases who are in constant touch with their intuitive sense, who use it and cultivate it purposefully.

This leaves a majority of managers who have never thought about the role intuition has in their decision-making and who were surprised to realize that a conversation of less than one hour—our interview—could make them discover that they had an intuitive sense all along: 'It makes me uncover things inside me that I do not access when I think alone—a discussion is more efficient,' and crystallize insights for systematic future use: 'Once you talk about it, it stays in your mind, it becomes an axiom.' The interviews helped managers acknowledge, articulate, clarify, memorize, and prepare these insights for sharing with others.

It also increased their intuitive awareness, prompting them to replicate the process. These outcomes are aggregated and illustrated in Table 6.1.

Inspired by these unexpected outcomes, we propose a dialogue technique based on our interview guide as a tool for purposefully replicating the process. By being subject to such an intervention, managers can acknowledge and clarify their insights, articulate them into simple rules heuristics, write them down in a 'personal decalogue' (as one respondent named his newly found toolbox of—not necessarily ten—simple rules heuristics), and, if appropriate, prepare them to be shared. The idea came from one of our interviewees, the head of a not-for-profit organization, who said, 'If you would travel the world with this process, you could clarify a lot of things for a lot of people.' What we propose, thus, is a one-session intervention, led by a guide—someone whom the respective

Table 6.1 Discussion Helps Managers Capture Intuitions into Simple Rules

Outcome	Exemplary quotes
Acknowledging tacit knowledge	'If we talk for another three hours, I will acknowledge 10 more rules.' 'When you talk about them, you find that you have them.'
Articulating tacit knowledge	'It crystalized some words and some thoughts that I had in the background.' 'Helped me articulate in a concrete way things that were vague in my head.'
Helping the sensemaking process	'Helped me structure my principles, as I was implementing them without them being well structured.' 'Helps me personally in clarifying the issue; because I didn't think about it until now, it didn't occur to me that there are patterns.'
Storing this knowledge for personal use	'This discussion brings rules from hard disk to RAM, makes them easily accessible.' 'Now, after being asked, I realize I have some principles, they are there, I should write them down myself.' 'This kind of discussion is good for creating a repository of lessons learned and a reminder to apply them.'
Sharing their knowledge	'The process is useful for knowledge transfer. We accumulate things as passive knowledge, then we share different things at different times with different people. It would be better to systematically structure 4–5 things to be shared consistently.'
Desire to replicate the process	'I will do this process with myself from now on.' 'It determines me to look actively for such insights.'

manager knows and trusts (e.g., an advisor, a coach, a mentor, or a senior colleague)—who proposes to the subject the following thought experiment:

> Imagine you are promoted and you have already found and trained your successor—someone who resembles you but is less experienced. After all the official transfer of knowledge and procedures, on your last day at the office, you tell your successor: "Before I go, there are three rules which I learned the hard way, rules you will not find written anywhere. They are: . . ."

The manager is then prompted to complete the phrase. Initially, they might doubt they have such rules, but, as we found from our interactions, after brief introspection, everybody found they indeed had something to say. One method for unblocking the thought process is for the guide to offer an example of one of their insights which turned into a simple rule heuristic, illustrated with the story of the trigger situation, the clarifying event, and the sensemaking process. Then, each time the subject of the intervention discovers one of their own simple rules, the guide would encourage them to write it down, as this process further structures the idea.

Lessons learned. Despite being a well-known process in project management, a process which is routinely run in organizations, lessons-learned meetings have yet to yield the expected effect (McClory et al. 2017). Love et al. (2016) argue that, to make the lessons-learned process more efficient, the lessons must be documented, communicated, and archived. We add to this that the project team must first make sense of what happened during the project, especially of the unexpected negative aspects, in order to derive lessons.

Based on our findings and, especially, on the triple insight we found as a source of simple rules heuristics, we propose a tool for the lessons-learned meeting—a simple framework to catalyze the sensemaking process and to articulate the learned lessons into pairs of simple rules heuristics. The project manager could start by leading the team to identify the unexpected negative aspects they encountered during the project, then lead the discussions based on the following three-question framework:

> *Previously, we thought that . . .*
> *But then, we realized that . . .*
> *Now, we must . . .*

This framework aims to catalyze, during discussions, the three insights: what was the false assumption that led to the respective negative situation, what is true instead, and how should we operationalize this new understanding. The following is a real example for what such a framework could yield (from Atanasiu et al. 2022):

Previously, we thought that a client's creditworthiness could be financially calculated.

But then, during the financial crisis, usual client appraisal methods failed, so we realized that you cannot assess a client from a distance by looking at numbers. We realized that the person is more important than the numbers.

Now, we don't send offers—we meet people face to face.

By adopting such a framework, a team can catalyze the triple insight and make sense of the negative situation and of what they need to learn. Moreover, the project manager should then lead the team to articulate the new understanding and its operationalization into a pair of simple rules heuristics (conceptual and operative). In our illustrative case, these are: 'The person is more important than the numbers,' and: 'We don't send offers, we meet people face to face.' Team effort should be put into proverbializing such insights if their initial form is not short and memorable from the beginning. Going back to the criteria set by Love et al. (2016), we argue that simple rules heuristics are the perfect tool to capture collective insights as lessons during formal lessons-learned meetings. Encoded into proverb-like simple rules heuristics, these lessons are perfectly documented, are adopted swiftly (as they yield from a team effort), can be easily communicated to others due to their proverbial form, and are safely but accessibly archived, not in a file cabinet, but in the team's folklore.

Conclusion

This chapter describes how managers naturally capture their intuitions and insights into simple rules heuristics. This articulated form allows for testing the intuition and for refining and adapting the new understanding. It also facilitates the easy remembering, sharing, and applying of the intuitively-learned lessons. We propose that this natural process can also be replicated by individual managers and by teams for sparking insights and for uncovering intuitions that would not surface otherwise.

References

Artinger, F., Petersen, M., Gigerenzer, G., and Weibler, J. (2015). Heuristics as adaptive decision strategies in management. *Journal of Organizational Behavior*, 36(1): 33–52.

Atanasiu, R. (2017). The use of heuristics in business decisions. *Proceedings of the 11th International Management Conference*, 2017, Bucharest, 1046–1053.

Atanasiu, R. (2021). The lifecycle of heuristics as managerial proverbs. *Management Decision*, 59(7): 1617–1641.

Atanasiu, R., Ruotsalainen, R., and Khapova, S. N. (2022). A simple rule is born: How CEOs distill heuristics. *Journal of Management Studies* (in press).

Atanasiu, R., Wickert, C., and Khapova, S. N. (2023). Steppingstones and Ulysses contracts: How managers use simple rules heuristics to unlearn and self-change (under review).

Barberà-Mariné, M. G, Cannavacciuolo, L., Ippolito, A., Ponsiglione, C., and Zollo, G. (2019). The weight of organizational factors on heuristics: Evidence from triage decision-making processes. *Management Decision*, 57(11): 2890–2910.

Basel, J. S., and Brühl, R. (2013). Rationality and dual process models of reasoning in managerial cognition and decision-making. *European Management Journal*, 31(6): 745–754.

Bingham, C. B., Eisenhardt, K. M., and Furr, N. R. (2007). What makes a process a capability? Heuristics, strategy, and effective capture of opportunities. *Strategic Entrepreneurship Journal*, 1(1/2): 27–47.

Bingham, C. B., and Eisenhardt, K. M. (2011). Rational heuristics: The 'simple rules' that strategists learn from process experience. *Strategic Management Journal*, 32(13): 1437–1464.

Bingham, C. B., and Eisenhardt, K. M. (2014). Response to Vuori and Vuori's commentary on 'Heuristics in the Strategy Context.' *Strategic Management Journal*, 35(11): 1698–1702.

Bingham, C. B., and Haleblian, J. J. (2012). How firms learn heuristics: Uncovering missing components of organizational learning. *Strategic Entrepreneurship Journal*, 6(2): 152–177.

Bingham, C. B, Howell T., and Ott, T. E. (2019). Capability creation: Heuristics as microfoundations. *Strategic Entrepreneurship Journal*, 13(2): 121–153.

Bouman, S., and Jacobsen, B. (2002). The Halloween indicator, "Sell in May and go away": Another puzzle. *American Economic Review*, 92(5): 1618–1635.

Crossan, M. M., Lane, H. W., and White, R. E. (1999). An organizational learning framework: From intuition to institution. *Academy of Management Review*, 24: 522–537.

Crossan, M. M., Maurer, C. C., and White, R. E. (2011). Reflections on the 2009 AMR decade award: Do we have a theory of organizational learning? *Academy of Management Review*, 36(3): 446-460.

Dane, E. (2020). Suddenly everything became clear: How people make sense of epiphanies surrounding their work and careers. *Academy of Management Discoveries*, 6(1): 39–60.

Dane, E., and Pratt, M. G. (2007). Exploring intuition and its role in managerial decision making. *Academy of Management Review*, 32: 33–54.

DeMiguel, V., Garlappi, L., and Uppal, R. (2009). Optimal versus naive diversification: How inefficient is the 1/N portfolio strategy? *Review of Financial Studies*, 22: 1915–1953.

Eisenhardt, K. M., and Bingham, C. B. (2017). Superior strategy in entrepreneurial settings: Thinking, doing, and the logic of opportunity. *Strategy Science*, 2(4): 246–257.

Eisenhardt, K. M., and Sull, D. N. (2001). Strategy as simple rules. *Harvard Business Review*, 79(1): 100–116.

Eriksson, T., and Kadefors, A. (2017). Organisational design and development in a large rail tunnel project—Influence of heuristics and mantras. *International Journal of Project Management*, 35(3): 492–503.

Evans, J. St. B. T., and Stanovich, K. E. (2013). Dual-process theories of higher cognition advancing the debate. *Perspectives on Psychological Science*, 8(3): 223–241.

Gigerenzer, G. (2008). Why heuristics work. *Perspectives on Psychological Science*, 3(1): 20–29.

Gigerenzer, G., and Brighton, H. (2009). Homo heuristicus: Why biased minds make better inferences. *Topics in Cognitive Science*, 1(1): 107–143.

Gigerenzer, G., and Gaissmaier, W. (2011). Heuristic decision making. *Annual Review of Psychology*, 62: 451–482.

Guercini, S., La Rocca, A., Runfola, A., and Snehota, I. (2015). Heuristics in customer-supplier interaction. *Industrial Marketing Management*, 48: 26–37.

Hazlett, S. A., McAdam, R., and Gallagher, S. (2005). Theory building in knowledge management: In search of paradigms. *Journal of Management Inquiry*, 14(1): 31–42.

Hern, A. (2018). The two-pizza rule and the secret of Amazon's success. *The Guardian*, April 24. https://www.theguardian.com/technology/2018/apr/24/the-two-pizza-rule-and-the-secret-of-amazons-success

Hodgkinson, G. P., Sadler-Smith, E., Burke, L. A., Claxton, G., and Sparrow, P. R. (2009). Intuition in organizations: Implications for strategic management. *Long Range Planning*, 42(3): 277–297.

Hogarth, R. M. (2001). *Educating Intuition*. Chicago, IL: The University of Chicago Press.

Katsikopoulos, K. V. (2016). Behavior with models: The role of psychological heuristics in operational research. In: Kunc, M., Malpass, J., and White, L. (Eds.). *Behavioral Operational Research*. London: Palgrave Macmillan.

Kazakova, T. V., and Geiger, D. (2015). The complexity of simple rules: Heuristics in strategic decision making. *Academy of Management Proceedings*, 2015(1): 17732.

Laukkonen, R. E., Kaveladze, B. T., Protzko, J., Tangen, J. M., von Hippel, W., and Schooler, J. W. (2022). Irrelevant insights make worldviews ring true. *Scientific Reports*, 12(1).

Laukkonen, R. E., Kaveladze, B. T., Tangen, J. M., and Schooler, J. W. (2020). The dark side of eureka: Artificially induced aha moments make facts feel true. *Cognition*, 196: 104122.

Love, P. E. D., Teo, P., Davidson, M., Cumming, S., and Morrison, J. (2016). Building absorptive capacity in an alliance: Process improvement through lessons learned. *International Journal of Project Management*, 34(7): 1123–1137.

Luan, S., Reb, J., and Gigerenzer, G. (2019). Ecological rationality: Fast-and-frugal heuristics for managerial decision making under uncertainty. *Academy of Management Journal*, 62: 1735–1759.

Luo, J., and Niki, K. (2003). Function of hippocampus in "insight" of problem solving. *Hippocampus*, 13: 316–323.

McClory, S., Read, M., and Labib, A. (2017). Conceptualising the lessons-learned process in project management: Towards a triple-loop learning framework. *International Journal of Project Management*, 35(7): 1322–1335.

Mieder, W. (2014). Origin of Proverbs. In: H. Hrisztova-Gotthardt and M. Aleksa Varga (Eds). *Introduction to Paremiology: A Comprehensive Guide to Proverb Studies*, 2: 28–48. Sciendo De Gruyter.

Mintzberg, H., and Waters, J. A. (1985). Of strategies, deliberate and emergent. *Strategic Management Journal*, 6(3): 257–272.

Monaghan, S., and Tippmann, E. (2018). Becoming a multinational enterprise: Using industry recipes to achieve rapid multinationalization. *Journal of International Business Studies*, 49(4): 473–495.

von Neumann, J., and Morgenstern, O. (1953). *Theory of Games and Economic Behavior*. Princeton, NJ: Princeton University Press.

Patterson, A., Quinn, L., and Baron, S. (2012). The power of intuitive thinking: A devalued heuristic of strategic marketing. *Journal of Strategic Marketing*, 20(1): 35–44.

Pieper, T. M., Smith, A. D., Kudlats, J., and Astrachan, J. H. (2015). The persistence of multifamily firms: Founder imprinting, simple rules, and monitoring processes. *Entrepreneurship Theory and Practice*, 39: 1313–1337.

Sadler-Smith, E. (2019). Intuition in management. *Oxford Research Encyclopedia of Business and Management*.

Sadler-Smith, E., and Shefy, E. (2004). The intuitive executive: Understanding and applying "gut feel" in decision making. *Academy of Management Executive*, 18: 76–91.

Sadler-Smith, E., and Shefy, E. (2007). Developing intuitive awareness in management education. *Academy of Management Learning and Education*, 6(2): 186–205.

Schildt, H., Mantere, S., and Cornelissen, J. (2020). Power in sensemaking processes. *Organization Studies*, 41(2): 241–265.

Senge, P. M. (1994). *The Fifth Discipline Fieldbook: Strategies and Tools for Building a Learning Organisation*. Boston, MA: Nicholas Brealey Publishing. ISBN: 9780385472562.

Shapin, S. (2001). Proverbial economies: How an understanding of some linguistic and social features of common sense can throw light on more prestigious bodies of knowledge, science for example. *Social Studies of Science*, 31(5): 731–769.

Simon, H. A. (1947). *Administrative Behavior; A Study of Decision-Making Processes in Administrative Organization*. New York: Macmillan Publishers.

Simon, H. A. (1987). Making management decisions: The role of intuition and emotion. *Academy of Management Executive*, 1(1): 57–64.

Sinclair, M., and Ashkanasy, N. M. (2005). Intuition: Myth or a decision-making tool? *Management Learning*, 36(3): 353–370.

Sull, D. M., and Eisenhardt, K. M. (2012). Simple rules for a complex world. *Harvard Business Review*, 9: 69–74.

Tsoukas, H., and Vladimirou, E. (2001). What is organizational knowledge? *Journal of Management Studies*, *38*(7): 973–993.

Tversky, A., and Kahneman, D. (1974). Judgment under uncertainty: Heuristics and biases. *Science*, 185(4157): 1124–1131.

Weick, K. E., Sutcliffe, K. M., and Obstfeld, D. (2005). Organizing and the process of sensemaking. *Organization Science*, 16(4): 409–421.

Chapter 7

Executive Decision Making: Logic or Intuition?

Chaudron Carter Short

Temple University Health System and Temple University Hospital Inc., Philadelphia, PA

Introduction

There has been much research on the topic of decision-making as it relates to intuition or logic under conditions of uncertainty. Making decisions requires executives to choose from a set of solutions or alternatives for action based on standards and criteria that meet the highest possibility of success in achieving the objective or goal. Each decision that an executive must make shares its own challenges, and leaders have varying methods for considering solutions to the problem (Nita & Solomon 2015; Carter Short 2021).

Intuition or logic can be the solution or alternative to foster creativity when faced with a decision. For the purposes of this discussion, intuitive decision-making processes are defined as "experimental, involving quick, complete processing of information in which the receiver is possibly uninformed, pattern recognition, non-systematic, being mindful and having an attentiveness to a hunch or gut feeling, or having a deductive approach" (Wonder & Blank 1992; Hodgkinson & Sadler-Smith 2018; Julmi 2019; Carter Short 2021). Alternatively, logic refers to "a structure, process, inductive, fixed, analytical of assumptions, synthesis of information or steps" (Wonder & Blank 1992; Julmi 2019).

Intuition

Driven by theoretical and analytical research, Weston Agor (1986) has been credited as the creator of intuitive decision-making within management. Agor's research findings, which are often cited, found that top executives rate higher in intuition than do low-level managers. During his two-phase study, Agor found intuition as one of the most dominant traits as leaders grew within their profession (Sinclair & Ashkanasy 2005; Carter Short 2021). Agor (1986) discovered that top executives use intuition when there is an elevated level of uncertainty, when there are no previous standards or guides, when variables are not scientifically predictable, or when facts are limited. These studies validated that executives used intuition while making decisions (Agor 1986, 1989).

Logic/analytical

Logical or analytical decision-making is another powerful way of making decisions. This process, coined by Daniel Kahneman, is *slow, deliberate, or needs effort* (Akinci & Sadler-Smith 2012). Kahneman brought to light System 1 and System 2, originally identified by psychologists Keith Stanovich and Richard West (Stanovich et al. 2014). Scholars have posited that the process of analytical decision-making is a model that consists of identifying and assessing decisions encoded in sequential rules (Dijkstra et al. 2013). Hallo et al. (2020) classify this process as *satisficing,* which is identified as exploring alternative options until an acceptable option is identified.

Decision-making

Executives face myriad questions that require quick and sound decision-making. These decisions are characterized by uncertainty and heightened by fear but must be made with a sound competitive edge (Sayegh et al. 2004). Followers look to their leaders to make the best decision for the most complex problems. How these decisions get made has been studied for centuries across various disciplines. According to Hallo et al. (2020), decision-making is defined as "generating alternatives and selecting one of those alternatives in order to prepare a suitable action." Even with the plethora of research, there is no clear explanation or understanding of how executives make decisions.

There is a large body of evidence that suggests intuitive decision-making is integral to the success of executives as they make decisions. On the other hand, there is equally an entire body of evidence that suggests executives' approach to decision-making is both intuitive and analytical (Liebowitz et al. 2019). People can make decisions that are purely based on intuition, purely data driven, or a combination of both (Potančok 2019).

You may ask yourself, which decision-making process is superior for the executive to guide their organization to success? Williams (2012) suggests they are complementary to one another. In general, executives use a blended approach. They blend a combination of intuitive logic and analytical decision-making approaches to their methodology of decision-making (Patton 2003; Williams 2012). This blended style has been credited by some as the "two-wing approach," and it implies that this approach allows executives to soar in their confidence regarding decision-making (Patton 2003; Williams 2012). However, intuition and analytics are independent constructs, not one and the same (Liebowitz et al. 2019).

Dual process theory

The dual process theory explains these independent constructs as System 1 (intuitive) and System 2 (analytical) (Carter Short 2021). The dual-process theory concept, built on social and cognitive theories, demonstrates how people process information (Constantiou, et al. 2019). Akinci and Sadler-Smith (2012) suggest these are two similar systems of knowing—two minds, one brain—comparing two intersections of systems and how they process information by the brain. System 1 is a gut feeling, a person's intuition, which accounts for the quick thinking during decision-making. System 2 is when an individual is more deliberate regarding their decision and slower thinking in their response to decision-making (Kahneman 2011; Akinci & Sadler-Smith 2012; Carter Short 2021). Koshy et al. (2020) suggest people have two interrelated phenomena, coined *the intuitive brain* and *the logical brain.*

There are many perspectives about how these two systems interact, from both the conscious and subconscious thinking perspectives. An example of how System 1 informs our thought processes would a person getting up and begin walking or a parent running to save a child from a dangerous situation. With humans, there is no real thought to these actions, simply an automatic response to a situation or a natural response to knowing. The reaction to the response is fast, gut-eliciting, and instinctive.

Conversely, when humans are faced with System 2 decisions, they require much more deliberation. An example of System 2 would involve going to purchase furniture for a home. This decision requires making sure the furniture will fit within the designated space and weighing the cost of the furniture or the appropriateness of color. These decisions require focus, rational thought, and deliberation. There are no mental shortcuts within System 2 to making these critical decisions.

Similarly, these two systems remind me of when I had to make a crucial decision when being promoted. As an established executive, having to change the trajectory of my career to an unfamiliar setting required the use of both Systems 1 and 2. I was quite familiar with leading individuals (System 1), something I had done for over 20 years within a healthcare setting. I was offered an executive-level position within academia. As an executive having to pivot into a new setting required me to operate under System 2 for a period, demanding thoughtful decision-making skills and slower responses to questions and actions (Kahneman 2011; Akinci & Sadler-Smith 2012; Carter Short 2021).

Even though academia was a remarkably familiar place for me, having been a professor for a few years, the transition into a leadership role was unfamiliar, requiring me to learn what are called "the 3Ps" (policy, procedure, and process). In getting to understand the characteristics of the new leadership role, I found immediate organizational decisions and changes that needed to be made. I recall frequently requesting previous analytical data and reports to help solidify my decisions, as I was unsure and needed assistance. Any executive would agree that making the wrong decision could cost the organization significant hardship, and this was not my intent or desire. The focus was solely on making the trajectory of the organization financially sound. Nevertheless, there was still hesitancy and apprehension, requiring System 2 to guide the decision-making process until I became familiar with the 3Ps.

Alternatively, executive leadership decisions came significantly easier, requiring little to no thought, using System 1. Any issues regarding human relations, budget, or leadership development were innate and effortless. The ability to succeed in that role, from my perspective, was the blend of intuition being my dominant (System 1), with logic or analytical (System 2) as the supplemental function (Williams 2012).

In my experience, an executive with years of experience requires using both System 1 and System 2 to make decisions. The question remains, which system is used most frequently? Patton (2003) asserts that this is based on expertise. He maintains that experts have the talent to decipher a situation based on past events. Both new and experienced executives agree that most decisions, even those that are intuitive in nature, require a subset of deliberation (Simon 1987). Koshy et al. (2020) recognize that intuitive decision-making and logical thinking are essential together rather than separately.

Impact of intuitive and analytical decision-making

There is an ongoing debate between intuitive decision-making and analytical decision-making, with scholars opposing both sides of the debate (Okali & Watt 2018; Bullini & Pierce 2020). Amid the debate, the real question is, what are the effects or impact of using either intuitive or analytical decision-making or both? Thanos (2022) argues that previous research suggests that leaders embrace a logical decision-making method. When leaders are charged with making important decisions, they are to collect information and rely on analytical data before making that decision.

Humans make good and bad decisions even with the best intentions. Some marry the wrong person or enter a profession they dislike and consider to be the wrong choice. Similarly, executives make large and small decisions daily, in both their personal and professional lives. Many of these decisions in the professional domain of an executive need to be strategic in nature. I could speak for most executives in that the decisions made for our respective organizations are made with the best intentions and optimism that they will positively benefit the organization. As an executive, my decisions will shape and impact the organization either favorably or unfavorably. Failure to make the optimal decision is costly to organizations, and the executive must always recognize both the impact and the outcome of that decision (Milkman, et al. 2009).

Intuitive impact

Akinci and Sadler-Smith (2012) explored more than 80 years of intuitive research and referred to intuitive decision-making as recalled patterns from the past that are retrieved to make decisions. Intuitive decision-making is said to be learned, repetitive in nature, and a customary reactive pattern demonstrated by leaders when challenged with a decision (Uzonwanne 2015). Executives draw on their skill set of past experiences, which are at times faint signs but produce great outcomes that are innovative and creative (Sadler-Smith & Shefy 2004). It has been noted that executives with experience in their respective fields rarely employ just analytical options to make decisions. Executives typically use their intuition and previous patterns of decision-making (Klein 2015; Carter Short 2021).

Carter Short (2021) conducted a study to evaluate years of experience and intuitive thinking. There were 70 nurse executive survey participants with a mean score of 14.56 years of leadership experience. The results of the simple linear regression analysis (see Table 7.1 on next page) revealed a statistically significant association between years of experience and intuitive thinking. The regression coefficient B = 1.108, 95% C.I. [.040, 2.176] associated with intuitive thinking suggests that with each additional year's experience in leadership, intuitive thinking increases by 1.108 points (Carter Short 2021).

Matlzer et al. (2007) expand on this concept and add that intuitive decision-making is a developed trait that is garnished based on years of experience. With time, the executive develops a keen sense of how and when to use their intuition. The more years of experience an executive has, the faster and more precise patterns from past experiences are recalled and used for decision-making (Sadler-Smith & Shefy 2004).

With intuitive decisions, the notion of recalled experiences or patterns to make quick decisions involves executives trusting their gut. Robert Anthony Lutz, the CEO of Exide Technologies, describes it as a *subconscious visceral feeling* (Hayashi 2001, 60). Matzler et al. (2007) refer to intuitive decision-making as a *magical sixth sense* (p. 14). Hayashi (2001) further explains that executives use this method

Table 7.1 Results of the Linear Regression Analysis
of Intuitive Thinking and Years of Experience

Residuals Statistics[a]					
	Minimum	Maximum	Mean	Std. Deviation	N
Predicted Value	10.17	20.15	14.56	1.937	70
Residual	−13.713	20.395	.000	7.716	70
Std. Predicted Value	−2.264	2.885	.000	1.000	70
Std. Residual	−1.764	2.624	.000	.993	70

[a] Dependent Variable: Years of Experience

to make decisions when logical methods are not valuable, the logical/analytical information is vague, or the information is too burdensome to understand.

So why is this important, many may ask? In my view, intuitive decision-making is essential because analytics are ever-changing. In the world of technology, data sources are evolving and are only as good as the time at which they are provided to the executive. Many times, the data requested may not be readily available to the executive. The literature suggests that intuitive decision-making is a learned behavior. The more it is used and developed, the more it becomes a natural form of decision-making, and the executive forms muscle memory from each interaction (Sadler-Smith & Shefy 2004; Evans 2010). Consider the following hypothetical vignettes of two nurse executives:

- James has been with the organization for eleven years and has moved through the ranks, first as a clinical nurse, charge nurse, supervisor, and then as a manager. James has just been promoted to AVP (Associate Vice President). He is very well respected by his peers and the go-to for many of his subordinates in his past roles. James is a leader others can rely upon because he makes quick, sound decisions that are always accurate in the face of complex decisions. His approach to decision-making is one of the reasons top executives approached him to be promoted to the AVP role.

  James' quick decision-making, or intuitiveness, did not always come easy to him. He made many mistakes in his past leadership roles, some detrimental and some non-detrimental, all due to his lack of experience. James learned valuable lessons from those mistakes. He internalized and acted on the feedback received and developed innovative approaches and paradigms for handling similar situations throughout this leadership career. Many of these approaches developed over time, and he applied them without recognizing it. In his new AVP role, he has mentored his subordinates and shared his past experiences, errors, and instincts in problem-solving. Having the ability to learn from his past mistakes gave James the confidence in his own intuitive mindset that formulated his leadership approach to decision-making. James was asked to develop a plan to decrease agency nursing usage by 30 percent, and he was able to articulate a process by which this could be a phased approach over three months. The plan was implemented and successful.

- Carol has been with the organization for a little over three years. She began her career with the organization as a clinical nurse and was then promoted to charge nurse when her immediate supervisor left the organization to care for an aging parent. Carol was next in line as it relates to years of experience and was promoted to a managerial role in her department. She is a talented and hard worker and is known to offer a helping hand with various projects but is the last to deliver on her assignment/task; however, they are completed. Since being promoted, Carol's subordinates have raised concerns over her ability to make leadership decisions.

  Carol does not deal with constructive feedback well, and it has only enhanced her self-doubt in her ability to make decisions. To delay making a sound decision, Carol requests additional data and asks her subordinates further clarifying questions. Carol explains that she must be sure she is making the best decision with the data available. The real reason Carol takes longer to deliberate is that she has not been equipped with past knowledge of decision-making, so her intuition is not as keen.

How and why executives like James and Carol use intuitive decision-making varies from one person to the next. What is evident in the vignettes is that experience and past patterns are recognized by the brain. This is done with no deliberation or thought. Arguably, becoming more intuitive depends on one's ability to trust their judgment and use it on a regular basis (Sadler-Smith & Shefy 2004).

What the research makes clear is that when executives make decisions based on their intuition, it is done rapidly (Meissner & Wulf 2014; Tabesh & Vera 2020). In addition, the literature indicates that the more experience an executive has, the more robust their ability to make intuitive decisions. Using intuitive modeling to make decisions results in a faster response time than that of the analytical approach (Sadler-Smith & Shefy 2004; Milkman et al. 2009; Meissner & Wulf 2014; Tabesh & Vera 2020). One executive explains it as intuitive decision-making in which "analytics can never trump the intuition of a thoughtful executive, wrought by years of experience and accumulated knowledge" (Matzler et al. 2007, 15).

Analytical impact

As mentioned above, the debate about the merits of the analytic and the intuitive approaches still rages (Okali & Watt 2018; Bullini & Pierce 2020). On one side, scholars support analytical decision-making, while others support intuitive decision-making (Agor 1986; Okoli & Watt 2018). Decision-making has been associated with the processing of information within an "analytical or rational" framework (Dane & Pratt 2007, 35). An analytical/rational framework permits executives time to understand ideas as they evolve and engage in data analysis. Analytical decision-making does not rely on gut feelings but reflects on a set of programmed factors relevant to the problem. As the executive uses conceptual factors to promote an outcome, these become analytical tools that offer the executive opportunities to achieve a competitive edge (Luoma & Martela 2021). In addition, the executive who functions from an analytical framework makes decisions by identifying, evaluating, and analyzing data (Maljers 1990; Morecroft 1984). However, despite the executive's best efforts, there is no guarantee that an accurate decision will be made (Fahey 2009).

It is important to note that analytics provide quantitative and statistical predictability for business performance. There are claims that both analytics and data have created a new paradigm in management and decision-making. Being skillful at utilizing both analytics and data can fundamentally improve an organization's performance (McAfee et al. 2012). Using data offers the executive the ability to make an informed decision but requires that they must gain a particular information skill set through reasoning thought. Executives who seek to foster their decision-making approaches based on this paradigm may face challenges—the data may not be the most robust, the data is ever-changing, and the organizational culture must accept a longer time for deliberation (Sadler-Smith & Shefy 2004).

The power of data analytics is that it complements the executive's intuitive knowledge. This approach makes for an effective decision-making process. It has been noted that organizations that use both data analytics and intuitive decision-making have better performance and productivity outcomes, which have a direct reflection on an organization's profit margin, value, and resources (Chang et al. 2014). Hargreaves and Ding (2014) note that organizations that use analytical decision-making have a competitive advantage over their competitors and operate in a state of pro-activeness; however, it is time-consuming for most organizations.

Some may ask if there is enough time for executives to understand big data when making decisions entirely. There is a belief that the organization's culture plays a role in effective decision-making. Organizational culture has been studied back to the early to mid-1980s. Peters and Waterman (1984) suggest that organizational culture applies pressure on value, predisposing the executive to make decisions rooted in management thinking. The cultural values within an organization that exist within a group can inhibit executives from relying on their own set of decision-making skills (Gamble & Gibson 1999).

Schein (2010) describes in his book *Organizational Culture and Leadership* that organizational culture and how it functions when specific problems arise can become obstacles and prohibit executive decisions. Organizations have a challenging time pivoting to accomplish a task because they never had to do it in the past. Relying on what was successful significantly impacts the organization's culture. For an executive to make decisions using data and analytics, there must be a degree of cultural norm that supports using such a method.

Conclusion

Executives in organizations are continually faced with the demand to make complex decisions based on an intuitive or analytical approach. According to Sadler-Smith and Shefy, (2004) executives who consider both approaches as interdependent techniques can enhance their decision-making capabilities. In the world of data overload, the most basic assumption is that data trumps the gut feeling, sense-of-knowing type decision-making. This is far from the truth. Some scholars negate intuitive decisions, claiming they are irrational. Intuition is a form of reason and does not come quickly. It takes years to sharpen intuition as a problem-solving technique (Khatri & Ng 2000). In addressing both these strategic paradigms, contingencies must be made to provide the best possible solution to the problem (Tabesh & Vera 2020). Irrespective of what paradigm one subscribes to, decision-making is complicated, and executives need to approach the decision-making process in the best interest of the organization.

References

Agor, W. H. (1986). *The Logic of Intuitive Decision Making: A Research-Based Approach for Top Management.* Quorum Books.

Agor, W. H. (1989). *Intuition in Organizations: Leading and Managing Productively.* Sage.

Akinci, C., and Sadler-Smith, E. (2012). Intuition in management research: A historical review. *International Journal of Management Reviews,* 14(1): 104–122. https://doi.org/10.1111/j.1468-2370.2011.00313.x

Bullini Orlandi, L., and Pierce, P. (2020). Analysis or intuition? Reframing the decision-making styles debate in technological settings. *Management Decision*, 58(1): 129–145. https://doi.org/10.1108/MD-10-2017-1030

Carter Short, C. (2021). "Nurse executives' intuitive decision making and leadership personality styles during organizational change." (Publication No. 28777492) (Doctoral diss., Walden University). ProQuest Dissertations Publishing.

Chang, R. M., Kauffman, R. J., and Kwon, Y. (2014). Understanding the paradigm shift to computational social science in the presence of big data. *Decision Support Systems,* 6(3): 67–80. doi:10.1016/j.dss.2013.08.008

Constantiou, I., Shollo, A., and Vendelø, M. T. (2019). Mobilizing intuitive judgement during organizational decision making: When business intelligence is not the only thing that matters. *Decision Support Systems*, 121: 51–61. https://doi.org/10.1016/j.dss.2019.04.004

Dane, E., and Pratt, M. G. (2007). Exploring intuition and its role in managerial decision making. *Academy of Management Review*, 32(1): 33–54. https://doi.org/10.5465/amr.2007.23463682

Dijkstra, K. A., van der Pligt, J., and van Kleef, G. A. (2013). Deliberation versus intuition: Decomposing the role of expertise in judgment and decision making. *Journal of Behavioral Decision Making,* 26(3): 285–294. https://doi.org/10.1002/bdm.1759

Evans, J. St. B. T. (2010). Intuition and reasoning: A dual-process perspective. *Psychological Inquiry,* 21(4): 313–326. doi:10.1080/1047840X.2010.521057

Fahey, L. (2009). Exploring "analytics" to make better decisions: The questions executives need to ask. *Strategy & Leadership,* 37(5): 12–18. doi:10.1108/10878570910986434

Gamble, P. R., and Gibson, D. A. (1999). Executive values and decision making: The relationship of culture and information flows. *Journal of Management Studies*, 36(2): 217–240. https://doi.org/10.1111/1467-6486.00134

Hallo, L., Nguyen, T., Gorod, A., and Tran, P. (2020). Effectiveness of leadership decision-making in complex systems. *Systems,* 8(1): 5. https://doi.org/10.3390/systems8010005

Hargreaves, C. A., and Ding, L. (2014). Business analytics as a framework for an evolving multi-agent system. *GFTF Journal on Computing,* 2(3). doi:10.5176/2010-3043_2.3.200

Hayashi, A. M. (2001). When to trust your gut. *Harvard Business Review,* February: 59–65.

Hodgkinson, G., and Sadler-Smith, E. (2018). The dynamics of intuition and analysis in managerial and organizational decision making. *Academy of Management Perspectives,* 32(4). doi:10.5465/amp.2016.0140

Julmi, C. (2019). When rational decision-making becomes irrational: A critical assessment and re-conceptualization of intuition effectiveness. *Business Research,* 12(1): 291–314. https://doi.org/10.1007/s40685-019-0096-4

Kahneman, D. (2011). *Thinking, Fast and Slow*. New York: Macmillan.

Khatri, N., and Ng, H. A. (2000). The role of intuition in strategic decision making. *Human Relations,* 53(1): 57–86. https://doi.org/10.1177/0018726700531004

Klein, G. (2015). A naturalistic decision making perspective on studying intuitive decision making. *Journal of Applied Research in Memory and Cognition,* 4(3): 164–168. https://doi.org/10.1016/j.jarmac.2015.07.001

Koshy, G. J., April, K. A., and Dharani, B. (2020). Intuition and decision-making: Business and sports leaders. *Effective Executive*, 23(2): 31–65.

Liebowitz, J., Chan, Y., Jenkin, T., Spicker, D., Paliszkiewicz, J., and Babiloni, F. (2019). If numbers could "feel": How well do executives trust their intuition? *VINE Journal of Information and Knowledge Management Systems,* 49(4): 531–545. https://doi.org/10.1108/VJIKMS-12-2018-0129

Luoma, J., and Martela, F. (2021). A dual-processing view of three cognitive strategies in strategic decision making: Intuition, analytic reasoning, and reframing. *Long Range Planning,* 54(3): 102065. https://doi.org/10.1016/j.lrp.2020.102065

Maljers, F. A. (1990). Strategic planning and intuition in Unilever. *Long Range Planning,* 23(2): 63–68. https://doi.org/10.1016/0024-6301(90)90200-N

Matzler, K., Bailom, F., and Mooradian, T. A. (2007). Intuitive decision making. *MIT Sloan Management Review,* 49(1): 13.

McAfee, A., Brynjolfsson, E., Davenport, T. H., Patil, D. J., and Barton, D. (2012). Big data: The management revolution. *Harvard Business Review,* 90(10): 60–68.

Meissner, P., and Wulf, T. (2014). Antecendents and effects of decision comprehensiveness: The role of decision quality and perceived uncertainty. *European Management Journal,* 32(4): 625–635. https://doi.org/10.1016/j.emj.2013.10.006

Milkman, K. L., Chugh, D., and Bazerman, M. H. (2009). How can decision making be improved? *Perspectives on Psychological Science,* 4(4): 379–383. http://dx.doi.org/10.1111/j.1745-6924.2009.01142.x

Morecroft, J. D. (1984). Strategy support models. *Strategic Management Journal,* 5(3): 215–229. https://doi.org/10.1002/smj.4250050303

Nita, A. M., and Solomon, I. G. (2015). The role of intuition and decision making in public administration. *Juridical Current,* 18(2). Retrieved from http://revcurentjur.ro/old/arhiva/attachments_201502/recjurid152_7F.pdf

Okoli, J., and Watt, J. (2018). Crisis decision-making: The overlap between intuitive and analytical strategies. *Management Decision,* 56(5): 1122–1134. https://doi.org/10.1108/MD-04-2017-0333

Patton, J. R. (2003). Intuition in decisions. *Management Decision,* 41(10): 989–996. https://doi.org/10.1108/00251740310509517

Persson, A., and Ryals, L. (2014). Making customer relationship decisions: Analytics vs rules of thumb. *Journal of Business Research,* 67(8): 1725–1732. https://doi.org/10.1016/j.jbusres.2014.02.019

Peters, T. J., and Waterman, R. H. (1982). *In Search of Excellence.* New York: Harper & Row.

Peters, T. J., and Waterman, R. H. (1984). In search of excellence. *Nursing Administration Quarterly,* 8(3): 85–86.

Potančok, M. (2019). Role of data and intuition in decision making processes. *Journal of Systems Integration,* 10(3): 31–34. doi:10.20470/jsi.v10i3.377

Sadler-Smith, E., and Shefy, E. (2004). The intuitive executive: Understanding and apply 'gut feel' in decision making, *Academy of Management Executive,* 18(4): 76–91. https://doi.org/10.5465/ame.2004.15268692

Sayegh, L., Anthony, W. P., and Perrewé, P. L. (2004). Managerial decision-making under crisis: The role of emotion in an intuitive decision process. *Human Resource Management Review,* 14(2): 179–199. doi:10.1016/j.hrmr.2004.05.002

Schein, E. H. (2010). *Organizational Culture and Leadership*, Vol. 2. John Wiley & Sons.

Simon, H. A. (1987). Making management decisions: The role of intuition and emotion. *Academy of Management Executive,* 1(1): 57–64. https://doi.org/10.5465/ame.1987.4275905

Sinclair, M., and Ashkanasy, N. M. (2005). Intuition: Myth or a decision-making tool? *Management Learning,* 36(3): 353–370. https://doi.org/10.1177/1350507605055351

Stanovich, K. E., West, R. F., and Toplak, M. E. (2014). Rationality, intelligence, and the defining features of Type 1 and Type 2 processing. In: J. W. Sherman, B. Gawronski, and Y. Trope (Eds.), *Dual-Process Theories of the Social Mind.* The Guilford Press, 80–91.

Tabesh, P., and Vera, D. M. (2020). Top managers' improvisational decision-making in crisis: A paradox perspective. *Management Decision,* 58(10): 2235–2256. https://doi.org/10.1108/MD-08-2020-1060

Thanos, I. C. (2022). The complementary effects of rationality and intuition on strategic decision quality. *European Management Journal,* 40, 1–9. https://doi.org/10.1016/j.emj.2022.03.003

Williams, K. C. (2012). Business intuition: The mortar among the bricks of analysis. *Journal of Management Policy and Practice,* 13(5): 48–65.

Wonder, J., and Blake, J. (1992). Creativity east and west: Intuition vs. logic? *The Journal of Creative Behavior,* 26(3): 172–185. https://doi.org/10.1002/j.2162-6057.1992.tb01174.x

Uzonwanne, F. (2015). Leadership styles and decision making models among corporate leaders in non-profit organizations in North America. *Journal of Public Affairs,* 15(3): 287–299. https://doi.org/10.1002/pa.1530

Chapter 8

Top Managers' Intuition and Analytics in Trusting Individuals from Inside and Outside of the Organization

Joanna Paliszkiewicz,[1] Fatih Çetin,[2] and Markus Launer[3]

[1] Warsaw University of Life Sciences, Poland

[2] Baskent University, Turkey

[3] Ostfalia University of Applied Sciences, Germany

Introduction

Managerial decision-making styles and trust are two crucial factors in management. It has been a research topic in management and other areas (Thunholm 2004; Albaum et al. 2010; Liebowitz, Paliszkiewicz, & Gołuchowski 2018; Liebowitz et al. 2019; Robinson et al. 2023; Paliszkiewicz, Chen, & Launer 2023). Trust is important in business life because it helps to build relationships, foster loyalty, enhance reputations, facilitate negotiations, and boost productivity. By focusing on building trust in their business relationships, leaders can create a culture of mutual respect and collaboration that can lead to long-term success. Making a decision based on intuition can be a powerful tool for leaders when they need to make quick decisions or when faced with complex situations requiring a high level of judgment. Analytics-based decision-making involves using data and statistical methods to analyze information and make decisions based on facts rather than emotions or biases.

This chapter will aim to contribute to the gap in the literature on the relationship between managerial decision-making styles and trust. The purpose of this chapter is to compare the intuitive, analytic, and wise decision-making styles of top managers when it comes to trusting people from both inside and outside the organization.

The chapter consists of the theoretical part related to the literature review of managerial decision-making style and trust and the empirical part, based on the research made on the sample of 911 top-level managers. In the empirical part, the method, procedure, and results are described. The conclusion, with the limitations and future directions, are presented at the end of the chapter.

Managerial decision-making style and trust—Literature review

The management style can be defined as, "a recurring set of characteristics that are associated with the decisional process of the firm" (Albaum et al. 2010, 65). Scott and Bruce (1995) attempted to consolidate previous research on decision-making styles by defining them as a learned habitual response pattern displayed by an individual in the face of decision-making situations. Scott and Bruce (1995) believe that decision-making styles are not a personality trait but rather a habitual preference for specific methods of action in certain decision-making scenarios. However, Thunholm (2004) raised doubts regarding whether individual decision-making styles rely solely on one's habits, suggesting that there are individual variations among decision-makers that encompass differences in not only habits but also essential cognitive abilities such as information processing, self-assessment, and self-regulation. These differences ultimately impact decision-making patterns in various decision-making scenarios and data.

Top managers' decision-making styles can have a significant impact on their trust in people both inside and outside of the organization (Ferrin, Bligh, & Kohles 2008). Intuition-based decision-making is typically based on gut feelings, emotions, and personal experiences. It involves focusing on details in the flow of information and is a less structured approach to seeking and processing information. Individuals who exhibit this style tend to rely on their intuition and emotions when making decisions (Henåker 2022). The intuitive style has been linked with innovative and creative behavior and a preference for solving problems rather than avoiding them (Thunholm 2004). People who possess a positive, outgoing, and open personality are more likely to use the intuitive style. Intuitive decision-making can be a powerful tool, particularly in situations where there is limited time or information available or when the decision is particularly complex or uncertain.

Analytic decision-making, on the other hand, is based on facts, data, and logical analysis (Kahneman & Klein 2009). Individuals who exhibit an analytical decision-making style are known for their thorough search for information, logical assessment of alternatives, and structured approach to time (Henåker 2022). This approach involves using various analytical tools, such as statistical modeling, data mining, and machine learning algorithms, to extract insights from large and complex data sets. The analytic style is characterized by a tendency to solve problems rather than avoid them (Thunholm 2004) and is associated with personality traits such as politeness, agreeableness, conscientiousness, and emotional stability (Alacreu-Crespo et al. 2019). Geisler and Allwood (2018) also found that time is a motivator for those with a rational decision-making style to make successful and rewarding decisions.

Developing a decision style can influence the process of trust building. Academic discourse often recognizes trust as a complex, abstract, and dynamic concept that operates on multiple levels (Costa, Fulmer, & Anderson 2018). Scholars have differing opinions regarding how to approach the study of trust. Some suggest a comprehensive, interdisciplinary approach to fully understand the nature and evolution of trust (Gillespie & Hurley 2013), while others propose narrower definitions specific to their research area (Paliszkiewicz, Gołuchowski, & Chen 2022).

Trust is a concept rooted in the conviction of one party, known as the *trustor,* that another individual or entity, known as the *trusted,* will fulfill their commitments and behave in a positive and beneficial way towards the trustor's welfare. Trust is positioned at one end of the spectrum, with distrust being situated at the opposite end (Lambert et al. 2021). It is a mechanism that arises from the fundamental reality that people often have to make decisions and take actions without complete information or certainty. In addition, the concept of trust can be defined through its attributes, which usually encompass qualities such as reliability (dependability, trustworthiness), capabilities (relevant knowledge and skills), integrity (ethics and fairness), and benevolence (kindness and generosity) (Colquitt & Salam 2009).

Trust can be built over time through consistent and predictable behavior, open and honest communication, and a track record of fulfilling promises and commitments. Trust can also be lost or damaged through dishonesty, unreliability, or a failure to fulfill commitments. Trust is essential for effective collaboration, decision-making, and innovation in a business context. It enables individuals to collaborate and share information freely without fear of judgment or retribution. Overall, trust is a critical component of healthy and productive relationships, both in personal and professional settings. It involves a willingness to be vulnerable, to rely on others, and to work together to achieve shared goals and objectives.

In terms of trust, managers who rely on intuition may be more likely to trust their instincts when it comes to people, both inside and outside the organization. They may place more emphasis on personal connections and relationships and be more willing to take risks based on their intuition. However, this approach may also lead to biases and assumptions that could negatively impact their judgment. Research has shown that intuition-based decision-making can lead to more trust in people inside the organization (Sproull & Kiesler 1991). This is because intuitive decision-making is often perceived as more authentic and personal, leading to a stronger emotional connection between the decision-maker and the recipient. Moreover, managers who use intuition may be more likely to trust people who are similar to themselves, as they may believe that people who share their values and beliefs are more likely to make good decisions (Jung & Avolio 2000).

On the other hand, managers who rely on an analytics decision-making approach may be more likely to trust people based on objective data and evidence. They may be more cautious and risk-averse and prefer to base their decisions on solid facts and figures. However, this approach could also lead to a lack of flexibility and an inability to respond to changing circumstances or unexpected events. An analytics decision-making style can be perceived as cold and impersonal, leading to a weaker emotional connection between the decision-maker and the recipient (Choi & Mai-Dalton 1998). In addition, managers who use analytics decision-making may be more likely to trust people who have a proven track record of success, as they are more likely to have objective data to support their decision (Zhang & Rajagopalan 2014).

Intuition and analytics are not mutually exclusive, and combining the two can lead to more balanced decision-making. A top manager who relies solely on intuition may make snap judgments that aren't well thought out, while one who relies solely on analytics may overlook important emotional or intuitive signals. By using a combination of the two, a manager can make decisions that are both logical and intuitive, which can lead to better outcomes and stronger supplier relationships. When top managers combine both styles, they can use their intuition to assess situations quickly and make decisions based on their experience and knowledge. At the same time, they can also apply analytic decision-making to ensure that their choices align with the organization's goals and values (Sadler-Smith & Shefy 2004).

Based on these explanations, the hypotheses are formulated as follows.

H1. Top managers who rely on a high degree of intuition are more likely to trust individuals who are directly involved in their organization's operations (employees) than those who are not directly involved (customers, suppliers, and government).

H2. Top managers who rely on a high degree of analytics are more likely to trust individuals who are not directly involved in their organization's operations (customers, suppliers, and government) than those who are directly involved (employees).

H3. Top managers who employ a balanced decision-making style, incorporating both intuition and analytics, are more likely to trust individuals who are directly and indirectly involved in their organization's operations compared to those who rely solely on intuition or analytics.

Method

A total of 911 top-level managers, including CEOs, presidents, board members, and vice presidents from various industries around the globe (more than 32 countries), participated in the study. Data were collected with an online questionnaire using snowball sampling after the original English version of the survey was translated into 12 languages. We employed a five-step translation and back translation methodology with the help of experts from each country. Gender distribution was 32.5% female, 8.4% non-binary, and 59.1% male. The professional experience of the participants ranged from less than one year (4.1%), 1–3 years (10.2%), 4–10 years (45.9%), 11–20 years (29.4%), 21–30 years (8%), 31–40 years (1.8%), to more than 40 years (0.5%).

Procedure

We used the Preference for Intuition and Deliberation Scale (PID, Betsch 2004) for measuring intuition and analytics decision-making styles. A total of 14 questions with relatively higher factor loadings were selected from the original study. The respondents were asked to rate their level of agreement with each question using a 4-point Likert scale, with 1 indicating "strongly disagree" and 4 indicating "strongly agree." First, we conducted a confirmatory factor analysis (CFA) for determining construct validity of the scale. The results indicated acceptable fit indices (X2/df = 3.45, TLI = .96, CFI = .96, RMSEA = .055).

Second, we calculated Cronbach's alpha coefficients of intuition (.81) and deliberation (.88) factors for the consistency of items. The results indicated the validity and reliability of the instrument for the research. Then, we conducted a cluster analysis using the scale to explore possible alternatives in the dual prefer-ences for decision-making style. This involved considering high or low conditions, as well as possible combinations for each style. The K-means clustering method (Hartigan-Wong algorithm) presented an optimal solution with three clusters: Cluster 1, Cluster 2, and Cluster 3 (see Figure 8.1).

Based on these results, we found that Cluster 1 represents a group with high intuition and low analytics (Intuitional), while Cluster 3 represents a group with low intuition and high analytics (Analytical). On the other hand, Clus-ter 2 is characterized by high levels of both intuition and analytics (Wise). We used the question, "What is the level of your trust with the following people who have direct or indirect access in the workplace," for measuring the level of trust. A 4-point Likert scale, with 1 indicating "not trusting at all" and 4 indi-cating "highly trusting," was used for each of the following categories: employ-ees, customers, suppliers, and government officials. Then we calculated the level of trust differences among these three groups through one-way ANOVA.

Results

The descriptive statistics presented that 25.9% of top managers predominantly use intuition-based decision-making with mean values of 3.85 for intuition and

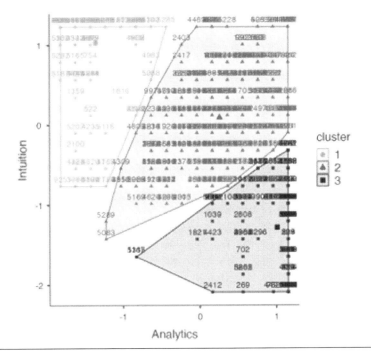

Figure 8.1 Clusters based on intuition and analytics styles

1.73 for analytics; 28.1% of top managers predominantly use analytic-based decision-making with mean values of 1.47 for intuition and 3.82 for analytics; 46% of top managers predominantly use wise decisions with mean values of 3.10 for intuition and 2.98 for analytics (see Table 8.1).

Table 8.1 Descriptive Statistics

	N	% of Total	Intuition		Analytics	
			Mean	SD	Mean	SD
Intuitional (Cluster1)	236	25.9%	3.85	.33	1.73	.43
Wise (Cluster 2)	419	46%	3.10	.50	2.98	.50
Analytical (Cluster 3)	256	28.1%	1.47	.40	3.82	.44

To test the hypotheses, we conducted one-way ANOVA to explore trust differences in employees, customers, suppliers, and government officials as perceived by top managers' decision-making styles. Results showed that top managers' decision-making styles significantly make differences for each group of people both inside and outside of the organization (F values ranged from 27.5 to 63.4, $p < .01$).

Top managers who use predominantly intuition-based decision-making placed more trust in the customers (M = 3.19, SD = .75), suppliers (M = 2.87, SD = .74), employees (M = 2.51, SD = .85), and then government officials (M = 2.08, SD = .80) in that order of priority, indicating a partial support for H1, as they trust employees more than government officials.

Top managers who use predominantly analytic-based decision-making placed more trust in the customers (M = 3.16, SD = .73), employees (M = 3.13, SD = .65), suppliers (M = 3.03, SD = .70), and then government officials (M = 2.74, SD = .78) in that order of priority, indicating partial support for H2, as they trust customers more than employees.

Top managers who use predominantly wise decisions placed more trust in the customers (M = 3.54, SD = .65), suppliers (M = 3.39, SD = .73), and employees (M = 3.32, SD = .78) in that order of priority, but not government officials (M = 2.28, SD = .69), indicating partial support for H3, as their trust levels are significantly higher for customers, suppliers, and employees (see Table 8.2 on next page).

Discussion

Results show that making wise decisions plays a significant role in building trust with people, both inside and outside of the organization. Although analytics has become increasingly important in the economy, numerous companies continue to prioritize the subjective opinion of their highest-paid personnel when it comes to making decisions with substantial consequences (McAfee & Brynjolfsson 2012).

Table 8.2 One-Way Anova Results

	Employees		Customers		Suppliers		Govern. Officials	
	Mean (SD)	F Statistic	Mean (SD)	F Statistic	Mean (SD)	F Statistic	Mean (SD)	F Statistic
Intuitional	2.51 (.85)	63.4**	3.19 (.75)	27.5**	2.87 (.74)	32.9**	2.08 (.80)	56.9**
Wise	3.32 (.78)		3.39 (.73)		2.28 (.69)			
Analytical	3.13 (.65)		3.03 (.70)		2.74 (.78)			
Mean differences (Games-Howell Post-hoc Test)								
Intuitional – Wise	-.81**		-.34**		-.52**		-.20**	
Intuitional – Analytical	-.62**		.03		-.16*		-.66**	
Wise – Analytical	.18**		.38**		.35**		-.45**	

$^*p <.05$, $^{**}p <.01$

However, studies have demonstrated that decision quality is adversely affected when subjective inputs from managers are given precedence over hard data (Henry & Venkatraman 2015). According to our research, managers should combine analytical and intuitive styles to make wise decisions that support trust-building inside and outside the organization. Alacreu-Crespo et al. (2019) believe that individuals with rational and intuitive personalities exhibit better management of repetitive, distinctive patterns and possess greater emotional stability.

Overall, making appropriate decisions can help build trust within an organization or team by creating a sense of consistency, transparency, inclusiveness, effective communication, and follow-through. By making decisions that are fair, inclusive, and communicated effectively, decision-makers can build trust and create a sense of unity and collaboration within their teams and organizations.

The research provides various theoretical implications that are significant to scholars and also offers practical recommendations to managers. Combining analytical and intuitive decision-making can lead to more balanced decision-making as a wise decision. A top manager who relies merely on intuition may make snap judgments that aren't well thought out, while one who relies merely on analytics may overlook important emotional or intuitive signals. By using a combination as a wise decision, a manager can make decisions that may lead to a better understanding of people for more trustful relationships. In addition, adopting a wise style leads to more transparency about managers' thought processes and the factors that go into their decisions. This may construct and enhance trust with people inside and outside of the organization by appreciating managers' openness and honesty. If they feel that a manager is making a decision based on hidden agendas and opaque reasoning, people are less likely to trust that manager.

And last, managers who use both intuition and analytics are more likely to consider the long-term impact of their decisions on their relationships. Adopting a holistic view by explaining both emotional and logical factors, managers make decisions that not only are good for their business in the short term but also are sustainable in the long term. This holistic view may help to construct and develop trust with people who value the partnership and are more likely to feel secure in a long-term relationship. By constructing trust through transparency and considering the long-term impact of decisions, managers may cultivate a strong relationship with outsiders and build a successful business with insiders.

There are also some limitations to the study. First, the sampling technique used in this study is the snowball method, which may limit the ability to generalize the findings. Therefore, future research could use the probabilistic sampling method to enhance the generalizability of the results. Second, this study relied solely on self-report as the source of data, which some researchers have criticized. However, this approach was necessary due to the challenges involved in measuring these constructs. Third, this study utilized a quantitative approach.

Future studies could benefit from adopting a mixed-method approach by combining both quantitative and qualitative research methods to explore the topic. Investigating the cultural and country-specific differences in this area would also be interesting.

Conclusions

In conclusion, the study highlights the importance of making wise decisions that go beyond analytical and intuitive approaches in trusting others. This indicates that building trust requires not only cognitive but also emotional abilities. When managers are able to make wise decisions that demonstrate their ability to consider all factors and perspectives, they are more likely to earn the trust and respect of those around them. This, in turn, can lead to greater success and positive outcomes for the organization as a whole. Managers who prioritize making wise decisions in their decision-making processes can enhance their credibility, inspire confidence, improve teamwork, and foster positive relationships with stakeholders both inside and outside the organization.

References

Alacreu-Crespo, A., Fuentes, M., Abad-Tortosa, D., Cano-Lopez, I., González, E., and Serrano, M. A. (2019). Spanish validation of general decision-making style scale: Sex invariance, sex differences and relationships with personality and coping styles. *Judgment and Decision Making,* 14(6): 745.

Albaum, G., Yu, J., Wiese, N., Herche, J., Evangelista, F., and Murphy, B. (2010). Culture-based values and management style of marketing decision makers in six Western Pacific Rim countries. *Journal of Global Marketing,* 23(2): 139–151.

Choi, Y., and Mai-Dalton, R. R. (1998). On the leadership function of self-sacrifice. *The Leadership Quarterly,* 9(4): 475–501.

Colquitt, J., and Salam, S. (2009). Foster trust through ability, benevolence, and integrity. In: E. A. Locke (Ed.), *Handbook of Principles of Organizational Behavior.* United Kingdom: John Wiley Publishing, 389–404.

Costa, A. C., Ashley Fulmer, C., and Anderson, N. R. (2018). Trust in work teams: An integrative review, multilevel model, and future directions. *Journal of Organizational Behavior,* 39(2): 169–184.

Ferrin, D. L., Bligh, M. C., and Kohles, J. C. (2008). It takes two to tango: An exploration of managers' social accounts in response to stakeholder trust violations. *Journal of Business Ethics,* 81(3): 645–662.

Geisler, M., and Allwood, C. (2018). Relating decision-making styles to social orientation and time approach. *Journal of Behavioral Decision Making,* 31: 427.

Gillespie, N., and Hurley, R. (2013). Trust and the global financial crisis. In: R. Bachmann and A. Zaheer (Eds.), *Handbook of Advances in Trust Research*. Cheltenham, UK: Edward Elgar Publishing, 29–55.

Henåker, L. (2022). Decision-making style and victory in battle—Is there a relation? *Comparative Strategy*, 41(4): 415–436.

Henry, R., and Venkatraman, S. (2015). Big data analytics the next big learning opportunity. *Journal of Management Information and Decision Science*, 18(2): 17–30.

Jung, D. I., and Avolio, B. J. (2000). Opening the black box: An experimental investigation of the mediating effects of trust and value congruence on transformational and transactional leadership. *Journal of Organizational Behavior*, 21(8): 949–964.

Kahneman, D., and Klein, G. (2009). Conditions for intuitive expertise: A failure to disagree. *American Psychologist*, 64(6): 515–526.

Lambert, E. G., Keena, L. D., Haynes, S. H., Ricciardelli, R., May, D., and Leone, M. (2021). The issue of trust in shaping the job involvement, job satisfaction, and organizational commitment of Southern correctional staff. *Criminal Justice Policy Review*, 32(2): 193–215.

Liebowitz, J., Chan, Y., Jenkin, T., Spicker, D., Paliszkiewicz, J., and Babiloni, F. (Eds.) (2019). *How Well Do Executives Trust Their Intuition?* Boca Raton, FL: CRC Press, Taylor & Francis Group.

Liebowitz, J., Paliszkiewicz, J., and Gołuchowski, J. (Eds.) (2018). *Intuition, Trust, and Analytics*. Boca Raton, FL: CRC Press, Taylor & Francis Group, Auerbach Publications.

Mayer, R. C., Davis, J. H., and Schoorman, F. D. (1995). An integrative model of organizational trust. *Academy of Management Review*, 20(3): 709–734.

McAfee, A., and Brynjolfsson, E. (2012). Big data: The management revolution. *Harvard Business Review*, 90(10): 4. https://hbr.org/2012/10/big-data-the-management-revolution

Paliszkiewicz, J., Chen, K., and Launer, M. (Eds.) (2023). *Trust and Digital Business: Theory and Practice*. New York, London: Taylor & Francis. https://doi.org/10.4324/9781003266525

Paliszkiewicz, J., Gołuchowski, J., and Chen, K. (2022). The meaning and interdisciplinary nature of trust in the digital economy—Future directions. In: J. Paliszkiewicz and K. Chen (Eds.), *Trust, Organizations and the Digital Economy. Theory and Practice*. New York, London: Taylor & Francis Group, 3–14.

Robinson, E., McAdams, B., Somogyi, S., and Kimberly, T. F. (2023). Managerial decision-making during the COVID-19 pandemic and its impact on the sustainability initiatives of Canadian food service businesses. *Journal of Foodservice Business Research*, 26(2): 352–380.

Sadler-Smith, E., and Shefy, E. (2004). The intuitive executive: Understanding and applying 'gut feel' in decision-making. *Academy of Management Perspectives,* 18: 76–91.

Scott, S., and Bruce, R. (1995). Decision-making style: The development and assessment of a new measure. *Educational and Psychological Measurement,* 55(5): 820.

Sproull, L., and Kiesler, S. B. (1991). *Connections: New Ways of Working in the Networked Organization.* Cambridge, MA: The MIT Press.

Thunholm, P. (2004). Decision-making style: Habit, style or both? *Personality and Individual Differences,* 36: 941–942.

Zhang, Y., and Rajagopalan, N. (2010). Once an outsider, always an outsider? CEO origin, strategic change, and firm performance. *Strategic Management Journal,* 31: 334–346.

Chapter 9

Knowledge for a World of Complexity: The Intuitive Executive and Smart Heuristics

Corresponding authors: Daniela Dumitru,[1] Gabriela Paula Florea,[2] and Mihaela Minciu[3]

[1] Bucharest University of Economic Studies, Teacher Training Department, Bucharest, Romania

[2] Doctoral School of Philosophy, University of Bucharest, Bucharest, Romania

[3] Bucharest University of Economic Studies, Teacher Training Department, Bucharest, Romania

1. Introduction

In an organizational environment in which changes occur with a high frequency, it is necessary for both employees and managers to develop new competencies and skills to effectively manage all critical events that occur. Today's world, in which most people operate, is characterized by *volatility, uncertainty, complexity,* and *ambiguity* (VUCA). In a VUCA society, the professional world expects people to be able to respond to the complexity of the world by becoming "knowledge workers" who can solve problems, finding quality solutions adapted to the continuous changes that the organization is facing (Canzittu 2020; Hasgal & Ahituv 2017). Moreover, in order to operate in VUCA environments, it is necessary to emphasize flexibility, agility, and resilience (Poteralska, Labedzka, & Brozek 2022; Millar, Groth, & Mahon 2018). To respond to situations of uncertainty and ambiguity for which employees don't have much information, the best solution is represented by *smart heuristics* (Gigerenzer & Todd 2000). Smart heuristics are particularly useful in situations where traditional methods (deductive or scientific) are not feasible, such as in complex optimization problems, or where the problem space is too large to explore exhaustively. Intuition can be seen both as a higher-order instinct that enhances creative thinking and as a tool for adaptability through finding solutions to situations where there is little or nonexistent predictability.

We claim that the *ideal intuitive executive* builds decisions on *metacognitive grounds* via a socially shared approach. Thus, we also introduce the term *mind-inclusive executive* to highlight the cooperative intuitive type of leadership which, especially in a VUCA world, is essential for successful leadership.

To endorse this claim, we will first detail and analyze each component of the VUCA world; then we will specify the working definition of metacognition and intuition and their social derivatives and explain what smart heuristics mean; and in the last part we will present "The ideal intuitive executive in the VUCA world".

2. The new world—VUCA world

The abbreviation *VUCA* was first used by the US military at the end of the Cold War to characterize a complex world of unpredictable change in which the enemy appeared out of nowhere (Deepika & Chitranshi 2020; Whiteman 1998). In time, the acronym VUCA has been adopted in all organizational sectors, including education and higher education, considering that the four components (volatility, uncertainty, complexity, and ambiguity) sometimes interact with each other in a conflicting and chaotic way (Yehezkel 2020).

The first component, *volatility,* refers to the relatively unstable changes that occur in organizations, as even if a situation is identifiable and understandable, it can be exposed to unpredictable changes (Bennett & Lemoine 2014). The concept of volatility can be encountered within the organization, being specific to "social categorization of people" situations in terms of the reactions or traits that arise when they face a certain critical situation (political instability, floods, drought, the spread of epidemics, etc.) (Patnaik 2020). Also, if we refer to the external environment, people's choices for or against a product are extremely volatile, especially since the factors influencing these decisions are numerous and sometimes even impossible to identify with certainty, even by research in the area (Canzittu 2020). As volatility refers to sudden changes from one state to another, changes that cannot be predicted in a rational way (Nowacka & Rzemieniak 2022), agility is the best way to respond to these situations, so organizations need to promote flexibility among their employees so they can successfully handle each situation (Bennett & Lemoine 2014).

The second component, *uncertainty*, refers to the unpredictability of events, especially with respect to the lack of information about the possible effects of an event that might occur (Deepika & Chitranshi 2020). Today's leaders must think innovatively (Horney, Pasmore, & O'Shea 2010; Stockton, Joseph, & Hunt 2014) because the challenges they face are in most cases unprecedented, so traditional skill sets are no longer sufficient to organize the work environment and coordinate subordinates (Deepika & Chitranshi 2020). Some of the most common factors that can create long-term uncertainty in an organization are the continuous needs of customers and therefore permanent changes in their preferences, improvements in technology, and the introduction of new business policies (Patnaik 2020). The direct effect of uncertainty is the difficulty in taking the best business decisions (Nowacka & Rzemieniak 2022).

The third component, *complexity,* is related to the multitude of information that circulates within an organization. Each network of information is interconnected with another network and influenced by several factors that can often cause turbulence and stress within the organization (Bennett & Lemoine 2014). More and more managers are using their intuition, having to trust their instincts because, in situations that are completely new, previous experiences do not give them much information (Kaivo-oja & Lauraeus 2018). Thus, managers of organizations must become true leaders (Nowacka & Rzemieniak 2022) and keep things simple, navigate through complexity, and act on key problems by communicating succinctly and rationally (Kaivo-oja & Lauraeus 2018).

The last component, *ambiguity,* is the most abstract component of the VUCA world, referring to misinterpretation, considering the multiple meanings of conditions and outcomes of an activity (Schick, Hobson, & Ibisch 2017). Considering that the cause-effect relationship is not identifiable or is very difficult to understand, it follows that anticipating the consequences is sometimes impossible in the absence of a similar event (Canzittu 2020). Ambiguity is an essential condition of nature and can be interpreted in a number of ways, leading to a series of assumptions that can indicate a variety of attractive solutions, some of which will be good and others bad (Schick, Hobson, & Ibisch 2017; Yargar 2008).

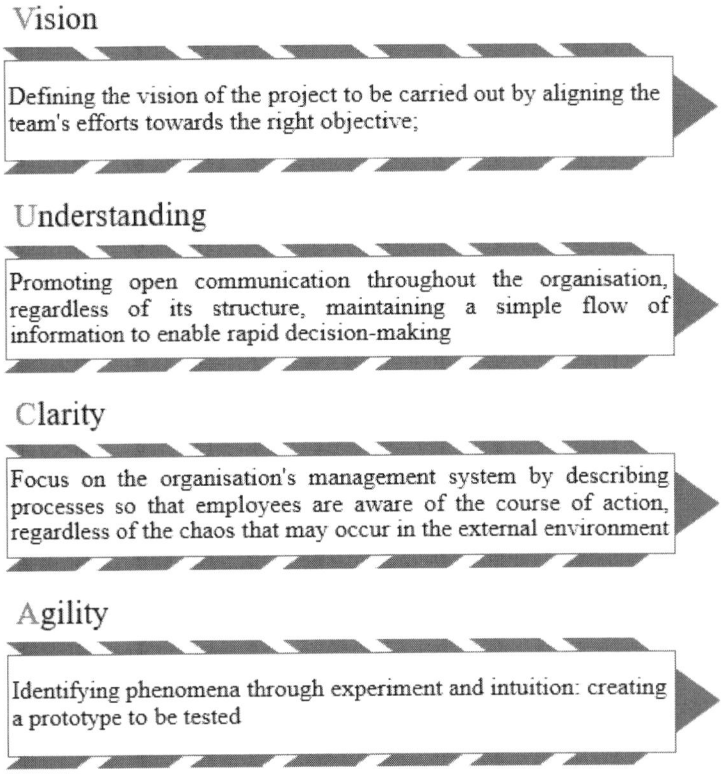

Vision

Defining the vision of the project to be carried out by aligning the team's efforts towards the right objective;

Understanding

Promoting open communication throughout the organisation, regardless of its structure, maintaining a simple flow of information to enable rapid decision-making

Clarity

Focus on the organisation's management system by describing processes so that employees are aware of the course of action, regardless of the chaos that may occur in the external environment

Agility

Identifying phenomena through experiment and intuition: creating a prototype to be tested

Figure 9.1   The transformation of the four components of the VUCA world (*Source:* Adapted from Nowacka & Rzemieniak [2022])

To respond to the four components of the VUCA world, Nowacka and Rzemieniak (2022) propose a set of skills that any manager facing unexpected situations should have (Figure 9.1).

Anticipatory thinking in terms of early identification of new factors that could have a negative impact on work and workers is increasingly becoming a requirement in organizations (Poteralska, Labedzka, & Brozek 2022; Schulte, et al. 2020). Thus, managers of organizations need to be able to hold subordinates responsible, eliminating unnecessary bureaucratic processes by developing transparent communication channels, and encouraging collaboration by enabling teams to do a great job, even in volatile and uncertain conditions (Kaivo-oja & Lauraeus 2018).

The dynamics of uncertain and complex changes in the labor market—resulting in, among other things, increasing digitization and technological development—call for a systematic approach to constantly update and verify the skills of people working in the fields of economics and research and development organizations (Poteralska, Labedzka, & Brozek 2022). Thus, in an ambiguous business environment, managers of organizations need to have *vision* (Minciu, Berar, & Dobrea 2020; Saleh & Watson 2017), show *agility*, become good decision-makers, take decisions with confidence, and adapt quickly to changing circumstances, learning from mistakes and constantly looking for new ways to improve (Kaivo-oja & Lauraeus 2018). In research on management and leadership, Krupp and Schoemaker (2014) propose a model characteristic of six disciplines—habits, attitudes, and capabilities, respectively—to meet the challenges of the VUCA world (see Table 9.1).

The VUCA world is a challenging environment full of complexity and ambiguity, so everyone should feel involved while working (Deepika & Chitranshi

Table 9.1 The Six Disciplines (Habits, Attitudes, Capabilities)

Discipline (habits, attitudes, capabilities)	Meaning
Anticipate	Maintaining close links with partners, customers and competitors, as opposed to being disconnected and inactive
Challenge	Challenging/analyzing assumptions and surrounding themselves with people who are open to new ideas and think outside the box
Interpret	Interpreting a wide variety of data versus looking only for evidence to confirm previous opinions/beliefs
Decide	Taking a decision on what to do after considering options and encouraging employees to take action, rather than hesitating or delaying the decision-making process
Align	Aligning/harmonizing stakeholder interests and motivations through understanding different points of view, as opposed to relying on their power or position
Learn	Learning from successes and failures through experimentation, learning from both good and bad results, ensuring rapid learning cycles

Source: Adapted from Krupp and Schoemaker (2014)

2020). Managers of organizations, transformed into true leaders in the VUCA world, not only act to reduce the negative impact of a risky situation, but also promote continuous, flexible learning in a participative work environment where employees are listened to and involved in the decision-making process.

3. Metacognition and intuition in the VUCA world

Intuition is the non-deliberate and non-analytical thinking felt "in the gut" as a hunch. A person perceives these gut feelings in situations where new variables or unforeseen elements appear. They may be experienced in already known or unprecedented situations as those described in the VUCA world.

Through *intuition*, one may have access to the conclusion regarding a situation and not to the hard data that may objectively justify it (Sadler-Smith & Shefy 2004). When intuition is taken together with **metacognition**, the quality of that mental processing is enhanced, since the new thought is based on implicit knowledge and experience that are brought into the conscious mind and then analyzed. Intuition is thus not an irrational mental process, although not voluntarily accessible, but rather a mental asset when validating the "hunch" or "gut feeling" through the metacognitive toolkit by bringing unconscious information through conscious reasoning (Dumitru & Florea 2023).

Accordingly, we can distinguish between two forms of intuitive thoughts: One category consists of *non-deliberate* thoughts, unprocessed, and overtly delivered as they reach the conscious mind—pertaining to the System 1 cognitive process (Kahneman 2003). The other category comprises *covert* intuitive thoughts that are first processed through conscious, deliberate thinking and metathinking processes and then overtly expressed—pertaining to the System 2 cognitive process. If the former is the "raw" form of an intuitive thought due to its subjective, biased charge, with a high rate of error, the latter is the "processed" version of the former. As such, once they have been consciously analyzed and filtered, the non-deliberate, unrefined intuitions will fall into the processed category.

The process that makes this possible is metacognition. Therefore, *metacognitive strategies* applied to intuition may be the appropriate tool that enables one to discern between a true or false intuition, where even the conclusion of its being false is a step toward progress (Wilder 1967). In this case, intuition is educated, informed, objective, and, consequently, less prone to errors in the decision-making processes. At this point, we can assert that processed intuitions are the informed, educated guess, whilst unfiltered intuitive thoughts are prone to shallow thinking and implicitly to erroneous decision-making. From this perspective, informed intuitions may be seen as the bridge between the two systems of cognitive processing. As mentioned above, we will refer to the first category of intuitions as raw intuitions and to the latter category as the processed intuitions.

Thus, metacognition is the mental capacity to *think about one's thinking* through which one can monitor, evaluate, and control one's own mental processes (Flavell 1979). It is a complex skill set relying on knowledge and experience about one's performance. This self-mental feature's effectiveness depends on the ability to regulate cognition based on past outcomes (Efklides & Misailidi 2010). In other words, metacognition is a cognitive, inherent, self-improvement mechanism that the human species developed and refined, based on evolutionary precepts. As such, it may also be linked to our capacity to adapt or resile, depending on the case.

This mental process of thinking about thinking, metacognition, requires a set of mental skills that often come with specific embodied or affective feelings determining a metacognitive experience. On the one hand, the *mental skills* on which metacognition is based are mental monitoring and evaluating the progress of one's own task performance, as well as planning and controlling future strategies to enhance task efficiency. On the other hand, *metacognitive processing* can be experienced through bodily incorporation of metalevel mental processing like the *Feeling of Knowing,* the *Feeling of Rightness* (Thompson, Prowse Turner, & Pennycook 2011), or gut feelings, where the latter is a raw intuition trademark.

Another feeling associated with metacognition is the tip-of-the-tongue feeling, or the temporary inaccessibility of a word predicated as a metacognitive experience (Schwartz 2006). Moreover, feelings with an affective load, thus perceived as mental states and not embodied, that relate to metacognition imply certain beliefs connected with the cognitive experience non-consciously and non-analytically derived. These metacognitive-related feelings are pivotal since they have an ascendant upon the process of cognition regulation through evaluation when pursuing a specific goal. They are related to the level of difficulty, satisfaction, confidence, and familiarity with the task and determine an implicit attribution of qualitative features to the process of reaching that objective. Therefore, they work on the motivational aspect of achieving the goal by measuring one's own strengths and weaknesses which predict success or failure. The decision to engage or disengage in starting, continuing, or not following the tasks is thus a result of perceiving one of these metacognitive affective feelings essential for efficient work (Efklides & Misailidi 2010).

We regularly make easy decisions, but also, we must decide over difficult situations. At the end of each decision, depending on the outcome, we ascribe a good or bad attribute to that judgment. If the outcome is positive, and the circumstances repeat themselves, we will also repeat that specific decision. If the marking is negative, we run a self-evaluation process to determine what was wrong during the process of making that decision. This exact process is metacognitive and may be reached with or without awareness. This thought-action-effect chain changes into an automatic response (reaction) that determines the easiness of deciding in already known situations (unless other unforeseen elements change the initial setting). It follows that it then turns into rapid thinking creating mental shortcuts, thus heuristics-based, bypassing the control and regulation process and leading to (automatic) behavior.

On the other hand, in unknown situations, decision-making becomes an intensive mental process with a higher cognitive load. If the person is not consciously present in the process, it is considered *implicit* metacognition. If, on the contrary, is deliberate and consciously brought, we are talking about *explicit* metacognition (Frith 2012; Koriat 2002; Koriat & Levy-Sadot 2000). Whilst implicit metacognition is spontaneous and non-analytical, the explicit form is slow and deliberate. Similar to bounded rationality theory, metacognition can pertain to System 1 if it is implicit, and to System 2 if it is explicit. Since people often try to justify the reason for their decision rather than tracing the logic of their judgment (Frith 2012), the manifestations of implicit (unconscious) and explicit (conscious) forms of metacognition prove that access to higher-order thoughts is limited. Nevertheless, a joint action of socially sharing metacognition facilitates the occurrence of explicit metacognition, as we will prove below.

So far, we have presented metacognitive processes and experiences applied to the self. To picture the ideal intuitive executive, especially in the VUCA world, we bring into discussion metacognition applied to others, also known as *mentalizing* (Frith & Frith 1999). We claim that it is a significant resource in business-environment working groups through collective intentionality. By mentalizing, we refer to a form of the implicit metacognitive process to monitor and predict others' mental states and, respectively, their behavior (Frith 2012).

The interaction between two or more people forms a social group. Like an automatic reflex, activity inside the group raises a "joint action" effect where the participants coordinate their actions and bring changes to the environment (Sebanz, Bekkering, & Knoblich 2006). If they share resources, intentions, information, and knowledge whilst discussing "perceptual and decision-making processes with others", they encourage the manifestation of explicit metacognition with the power of improving decisions (Frith 2012). This is a specific human trait that facilitates the occurrence of explicit metacognition. It is thus a play between metacognition applied to self and metacognition applied to others that enables explicit metacognition.

For joint action to lead toward high performance, mentalizing is not only inherent but also essential. In other words, mentalizing links minds that create an effect of joint action. Joint action is thus based on action prediction, predicted effects integration, and then integrating the effects of self and others' actions. This intrinsic mental process makes one understand the others' set of beliefs and adopt a *we-mode* instead of an *I-mode* attitude (Frith 2012), which can contribute to balancing intuition and rationality. Therefore, if metacognition is individual centered, then mentalizing, socially shared metacognition, and the we-mode approach represent a collectivist mental processing centered on the group rather than on the individual.

In a business environment, as well as in any other social group, shared metacognition focused on the we-mode approach has a holistic view of the decision-making process. It is the individuals who form a group and work together to achieve more than the total of each individual's work (Frith 2012). In other words, the idiom that the whole is greater than the sum of its parts is applicable also in the mental life within a business working group focused on decision-making. Along these lines, we can consider group intuition higher than the sum of each individual. Therefore, by adopting and facilitating a we-mode working group approach, those involved share intuitions and go from implicit to explicit metacognition in arguing their opinion. Likewise, executives who share their subjective, raw intuition with their followers, acknowledging their input as well as their intuitions on the same matter, will reach an elaborated decision based on objective, processed intuitions.

Joint action between executive and followers would facilitate creative thinking among all participants in the decision-making process, and those with more experience may have the chance to express their gut feelings, which could then be analyzed and validated or invalidated by the less experienced through hard data. Thus, intuitive executives would cross from an implicit metacognitive process to an explicit one, with their followers' support.

Since the basis of intuition lies in knowledge and experience, one could never be sure if the right lesson was learned (Hogarth 2001). As such, the social sharing approach will be less prone to error in deciding. Up to this point, we have indirectly built the image of the ideal intuitive executive as one who would (1) have their intuitive thought (soft data) checked by others using analysis (hard data) and thus (2) evolve from raw intuition(s) to the processed form through socially shared metacognition, implying that (3) the final decision would be the end result of a group intuition—let us say *shared intuition*—which is greater than the executive's automatic, raw, individual intuition. Therefore, the shared intuition method promotes a blend of participative and servant-style leadership resulting in a decision with a lesser probability of failure, where the quality of the executive's intuition is greater and more accurate. We, therefore, claim that this pictures the ideal intuitive executive.

The ideal intuitive executive thus adopts the we-mode, where each follower involved in the working team is encouraged to express ideas and create an exponential effect in the efficiency and quality of the decision-making process that leads to successful leadership.

If joint action in a social interaction determines a we-mode attitude which enables and enhances explicit metacognition which, in turn, improves how one makes decisions, it then follows that successful leadership in organizations must follow certain principles. These principles ought to focus on creating (social) groups in which information is being shared and in which the followers receive support and are empowered whilst their input is valued. As such, a blend of participative and servant styles is required.

Thus far we have distinguished between raw intuition—automatic, unconscious, unprocessed intuition, as intuition is commonly referred to—and processed intuition—the processed form of intuition by means of metacognitive strategies in a social group that adopts a joint action approach with shared intuition implications. It is common sense to assert that the conscious and unconscious mental processes work independently and conjointly. To set aside one in favor of another is to limit the expansion of one's mind. The complexity and creativity of thinking are provided by the power of these two systems, rational and intuitive, working together. Not allowing them to coexist is like amputating one's arm and expecting to climb a steep mountain.

Intuition is the mind's sensitive part because it "senses" solutions and outcomes, whilst objective thinking, or reasoning, complements the intuitive mind by bringing clarity to its senses, validating or invalidating them. In other words, reasoning pertains to the mind's objective response whilst intuition to its subjective response (Salk 1984). When working together, they enhance reasoning, whilst dividing them or rejecting one or the other creates delusion or paralysis by analysis (Sadler-Smith 2023).

4. The good use of intuition: Smart heuristics

As shown previously, the VUCA world is a concept largely used in the business environment today—a concept that emerged from the unstable Cold War context. The COVID-19 pandemic is another example in which people had to make rapid decisions with little to no information. But how does this differ from our everyday life? It does not, and our brain has already developed a solution to respond to situations: *smart heuristics,* or *"heuristics that make us smart"* (Gigerenzer & Todd 2000).

These are defined as *intelligent algorithms* to solve complex problems or make decisions based on incomplete or uncertain information. This involves using a set of rules or strategies that guide decision-making processes in a way that is more efficient and effective than traditional methods. We are born with an "adaptive toolbox" that includes recognition heuristics—"take-the-best" heuristic—and the wisdom of others—such as the "imitate-the-majority" heuristic. They are useful in situations where there is uncertainty or incomplete information, as they can guide decision-making processes based on the available data.

Gigerenzer believes that humans have evolved to use heuristics to simplify decision-making processes and that these heuristics can be more effective than traditional methods when used correctly (Gigerenzer & Todd 2000).

Heuristics are "ecologically rational" (Gigerenzer 2008) as a result of having been adapted to the environment. A new field of study is ahead: *naturalistic decision-making* (Klein 1998; Galotti 2002), which demonstrates that heuristics are useful tools in everyday life, and the concept is not artificial, laboratory created or validated. Heuristics are used more, and are more useful, than deductive reasoning, or in Kahneman words (2011), we are using System 1 (intuitive) more than System 2 (analytic).

Gigerenzer and Todd (2000) presented an experiment (Eysenck & Keane 2020) in which they gave an eight-item test, each item having two options. For example, this is Question 6:

Which is the larger country?
a. Benin
b. Uganda

After answering, test takers are asked to assess their knowledge about African geography, having three options: above average, average, below average. Thus, if you know nothing about Africa (below average), you'll use the recognition heuristic and choose Uganda (you've heard about it occasionally) and not Benin, which is less well known. But if you know something about African geography (average or above average), you will have to think, where is Uganda, where is Benin; represent their sizes in comparison; and, thinking this might be a trick question, will not use the obvious answer. It seems that knowledge was getting in the way, because Uganda *is* the correct answer.

The utility theory of smart heuristics says that, for the eight questions, you are more likely to answer questions correctly if you have less than average knowledge of the topic rather than better than average knowledge. Therefore, your percentage of correct answers for questions where you have above average knowledge is expected to be lower than for those questions where you have below average knowledge. But this is not the side of the story we wish to highlight. We argue that the brain has found a solution to get an adaptive answer in conditions of uncertainty.

In yet another experiment, Gigerenzer (2008) pointed to the merits of "ignorance". In 2000, a stock-picking competition was announced by *Capital,* an investment magazine. Over 10,000 participants, including the editor-in-chief, submitted portfolios. Participants used various methods to gain information and pick stocks, including high-speed computers and expert knowledge. However, the portfolio that stood out the most was based on collective ignorance, rather than expertise or software. It was submitted by economist Gigerenzer and a colleague. They surveyed a hundred pedestrians in Berlin, fifty men and fifty women, to find people who were semi-ignorant about stocks and had not even heard of many of them. The portfolio was submitted to the competition with a buy-and-hold strategy and gained 2.5 percent in a down market, while the editor-in-chief's portfolio lost 18.5 percent.

The recognition portfolio also outperformed 88 percent of all other portfolios submitted and beat various *Capital* indices. In the same work where analyzing gender differences, women recognized fewer stocks, but their recognition portfolio made more money than those based on men's recognition. These findings support earlier studies, says Gigerenzer, suggesting that women are less confident about their financial knowledge yet perform better intuitively. The studies show that partial ignorance, rather than extensive knowledge, paid off in the competition.

Herbert Simon's research (1957) was revolutionary in exploring the limits of rationality and how this relates to the idea of agents in economics having perfect knowledge. Simon's work was built on the concept of perception and vision. He proposed the recognition heuristic, which assigns a greater value to an object that is recognized when presented with a set of two objects. This habit of a sensorial process is kept to all the way to reasoning, and the cognitive system still favors the more familiar concept, to the detriment of others less well known, in making decisions based on this heuristic.

The very optimistic theory of knowledge that is still dominant in some economics works is based on what Felin, Koenderink, and Krueger (2017) name "the all-seeing eye". Some economists believe in the rational man—in the power of reasoning that can solve all problems if it has all the information, which will, of course, give the right answer—the only one—and that will be unquestionable and definitive.

In their latest book, Kahneman, Sibony, and Sunstein (2021) coin the term *noise* for a flaw in our judgment. It consists of variability in judgments that should be identical. For example, we expect decisions to be similar, even identical, when a judge sets the sentence. The authors cite an experiment from 1981, where 208 judges were involved. They had 16 hypothetical cases for which they had to set sentences. In only three out of 16 cases did the judges agree to impose a prison term. But the variations among them were staggering. In one example among many, a fraud case where the mean prison term was 8.5 years, one judge set a term of life in prison. How are these disparities even possible when there is law involved? Why could judges, persons with good educations in critical thinking and reasoning, produce this wide variety of noisy decisions? The answer, according to the authors, is that individual judgment equation, personal beliefs and personal history, biased information gathering, and faulty decision-making processes (for example, fallacies) are responsible for the wide variability of judgments.

Reality looks noisy, but we expect our thinking to perform spotlessly in every situation. The reality is that we cannot do this because our mind is not equipped with spotless reasoning. What is the solution then?

Gigerenzer (2008) stresses the importance of using smart heuristics in conjunction with data and evidence, rather than relying solely on intuition or personal experience. He believes that combining smart heuristics with empirical data can lead to more effective decision-making and better outcomes. Kahneman, Sibony, and Sunstein (2021) propose using algorithms and structured decision-making processes and suggest that organizations should pay more attention to the problem of noise in their decision-making.

This is where we propose using metacognition to help select the right sources, evidence, and empirical data. It means that we should start from intuitive thinking, but we should also continue to look for supporting evidence of our gut feelings. Or in Klein's words (1998), to use a combination of intuition and analysis to make decisions. We argue that organizational decisions have to take into consideration both intuition and reasoning because the VUCA world in particular, and the world in general, will not offer the perfect information for our imperfect mind.

5. Discussions and conclusions: The ideal intuitive executive in the VUCA world

The VUCA world is where raw and processed intuitions are challenged. This is a notable example where both fast and slow thinking processes are being confronted. It is the moment when the fittest survive in an altered reality. In the business environment, the fittest must be the executive who is able to overcome the unstable wave of uncertainties, with all its implications, for the company to survive. On the other hand, the intuitive executive has the responsibility not only to maintain the survival of the company, with an implicit responsibility to help the employees ride the same challenging wave, but also to make it thrive in turbulent times. In the VUCA world, the executive who—no matter how experienced and less prone to error (Sadler-Smith & Shefy 2004)—chooses to follow the autocratic style of decision-making, expecting subordinates to follow orders without question, instead of starting a virtuous cycle, may reach mental paralysis by too much analysis; or, on the other hand, he or she may be prone to error in decision-making due to the overwhelming load of unknown variables considered.

Research is still at an early stage regarding the leadership style most suitable to the VUCA environment: transformational leadership, transactional leadership, authentic leadership, and servant leadership (Johnson 2012). In the VUCA world, at the transformational level, leaders set high standards of performance goals, encouraging teamwork and innovative ideas (Sarkar 2016). The servant style is more and more common in organizations because the more leaders who are responsible and put the interests of their subordinates above their own (creating an open climate), the more creativity is encouraged in the workplace (Sarkar 2016)—and this is one of the most important elements ensuring successful operation in the VUCA world. Authentic style is found in leaders who work in the VUCA world, particularly in terms of the four key competences: genuineness while dealing with others, self-awareness, internalized moral perspective, and balanced processing (Avolio & Gardner 2005).

Therefore, either way, an independent cognitive approach would lead to collapse by inadequate decision-making or none at all. Consequently, we endorse the need for an open climate in an organization, where the leader(s) put the subordinates' interest above their own, ensuring a blend between participative and servant-style leadership that promotes a we-mode and shared-intuition approach for moving from implicit to explicit metacognition. In this way, decisions would be less probable to fail, and the executive's intuition would be the result of the group's intuition, greater than one person's individual, automatic, and prone-to-error intuition.

In known and routine circumstances, decisions are reached with a light cognitive load, easy and automatic, whilst in uncertain circumstances the cognitive load is far above the average. It is then when ideal intuitive executives ask for their raw intuitions to be validated, invalidated, or complemented by the group members through available hard data or through the other participants' soft data, challenged over and over until the most probable decision is reached and leads to success to be implemented further. It is then that the ideal intuitive executive has fluency and rapidity in finding the best solution for the unforeseen variables that appear in volatile, uncertain, complex, and ambiguous situations. Hence, smart heuristics come in handy for decision-making under VUCA, but a decision based on multiple experiences (the we-mode) is a solid strategy to turn Volatility into Vision, Uncertainty into Understanding, Complexity to be tackled down and turn into Clarity, and last, but not least, Ambiguity to be transformed by the inclusive intuitive executive into Agility.

If we try to best characterize the ideal intuitive executive, the syntagma should be *mind-inclusive executive.* Since it is difficult to identify biases, heuristics, and reasoning errors, intuitive executives should not let themselves be driven exclusively by intuition. We remember that Gigerenzer and Todd's (2000) experiment has shown that people get the right answer in a proportion from 80 to 100 percent. Thus, intuition is fallible, just as Kahneman, Sibony, and Sunstein demonstrated (2021). Intuition is noisy. By getting more people involved through *mind-inclusion*, the ideal executive increases the chances of making a suitable decision and conducting better metacognition process to understand their gut-feeling cognitions.

Further note on artificial intelligence (AI): Does it have intuition?

Since AI is not a person, the following section is not about an executive, but rather about intuition. We generated the graphical abstract (see Figure 9.2 on next page) using an artificial intelligence program and modified it to serve our purpose to capture the transformation of each VUCA component into positive features. AI is the new miracle of the technosphere. But this idea is not new. What changed? As of this writing, the OpenAI chatbot ChatGPT version 4 is the most fashionable of the new artificial intelligence project wave. The merit of ChatGPT is that it uses close to natural language expression in its answers. Plus, it brings plausible answers.

However, Noam Chomsky, in his latest article from *The New York Times* (Chomsky, Roberts, & Watumull 2023), says that AI functions profoundly differently from human reasoning and language usage: although ChatGPT is unlimited in what it can memorize, it is "incapable of distinguishing the possible from the impossible", says Chomsky. The creators of ChatGPT (OpenAI 2022) explain in their introduction, the limitation section, that during training it was not set a source of truth. This often leads to plausible, but untrue, answers—for example, for one question about the ten most famous Romanian football (soccer) players, ChatGPT lists Hristo Stoicikov—a Bulgarian who never played in Romania—and fabricates a story about his time at Steaua Bucharest to support its output. This happens because the creators say that "training the model to be more cautious causes it to decline questions that it can answer correctly" (OpenAI 2022).

Figure 9.2 Graphic representation of the ideal intuitive executive in a VUCA world (generated by the authors using MidJourney® artificial intelligence software)

The chatbot has biases too, according to its creators. Thus, it is less cautious and presents biased answering—resembling another famous character, System 1 from Kahneman's bounded rationality theory (2011). It can also "guess" what the client asks by making approximations from the unclear questions.

It begs the question, does ChatGPT have intuition? We answer "No." Congruent to Chomsky's opinion, we believe that AI in general functions differently from the human mind, but its output is meant to look human, using natural and fluid language, in the conditions of an algorithmic software. The achievement is remarkable. But the program is trained to follow statistically probable language patterns (not human-like) to give the most probable answer—not the *true* answer, but the most probable. This is how AI gets to impossible outputs, which for people are a barrier. We cannot claim the impossible to be true in order to support our opinions.

We ascertain that AI does not have intuition (or System 1), but the output is meant to look intuitive.

Conflicts of Interest: The authors declare no conflict of interest.
Funding: This research received no external funding.

References

Avolio, B., and Gardner, W. (2005). Authentic leadership development: Getting to the root of positive forms of leadership. *The Leadership Quarterly*, 16(3): 315–338.

Bennett, N., and Lemoine, J. (2014). What a difference a word makes: Understanding threats to performance in a VUCA world. *Business Horizons*, 57(3): 311–317.

Canzittu, D. (2020). A framework to think of school and career guidance in a VUCA world. *British Journal of Guidance & Counselling*, 1–12. https://doi.org/10.1080/03069885.2020.1825619

Chomsky, N., Roberts, I., and Watumull, J. (2023, March 8). Noam Chomsky: The false promise of ChatGPT. Retrieved March 27, 2023, from https://www.nytimes.com: https://www.nytimes.com/2023/03/08/opinion/noam-chomsky-chatgpt-ai.html

Deepika, D., and Chitranshi, J. (2020). Leader readiness of Gen Z in VUCA business environment. *Foresight*, 23(2): 154–171. https://doi.org/10.1108/FS-05-2020-0048

Dumitru, D., and Florea, G.-P. (2023). The "irrational" within rational thinking: Proofs from medical sciences and the arts. In: N. Rezaei (Ed.), *Brain, Decision Making and Mental Health*, 135–156. Springer Nature Switzerland. https://doi.org/10.1007/978-3-031-15959-6_8

Efklides, A., and Misailidi, P. (2010). *Trends and Prospects in Metacognition Research*. Springer US. https://doi.org/10.1007/978-1-4419-6546-2

Eysenck, M. W., and Keane, M. T. (2020). *Cognitive Psychology: A Student's Handbook*. 8th ed. Taylor & Francis.

Felin, T., Koenderink, J., and Krueger, J. I. (2017). Rationality, perception, and the all-seeing eye. *Psychonomic Bulletin and Review*, 24(4): 1040–1059. https://doi.org/10.3758/s13423-016-1198-z

Flavell, J. H. (1979). Metacognition and cognitive monitoring: A new area of cognitive-developmental inquiry. *American Psychologist*, 34(10): 906–911. https://doi.org/10.1037/0003-066X.34.10.906

Frith, C. D. (2012). The role of metacognition in human social interactions. *Philosophical Transactions of the Royal Society B: Biological Sciences*, 367(1599): 2213–2223. https://doi.org/10.1098/rstb.2012.0123

Frith, C. D., and Frith, U. (1999). Interacting minds: A biological basis. *American Association for the Advancement of Science*, 286(5445): 1692–1695.

Galotti, K. M. (2002). *Making Decisions That Matter: How People Face Important Life Choices.* Lawrence Erlbaum Associates Publishers.

Gigerenzer, G. (2008). *Gut Feelings: The Intelligence of the Unconscious.* Penguin Books.

Gigerenzer, G., and Todd, P. M. (2000). *Simple Heuristics That Make Us Smart.* Oxford University Press.

Hasgal, A., and Ahituv, N. (2017). The development of knowledge workers in an organization characterized as complex adaptive systems (CAS). In: E. Tsui and B. Cheung (Eds.), *14th International Conference on Intellectual Capital, Knowledge Management and Organizational Learning* (ICICKM 2017), Academic Conferences and Publishing, 97–103.

Hogarth, R. M. (2001). *Educating Intuition.* University of Chicago Press.

Horney, N., Pasmore, B., and O'Shea, T. (2010). Leadership agility: A business imperative for a VUCA world. *Human Resource Planning*, 33(4): 34–42.

Johnson, C. (2012). *Meeting the Ethical Challenges of Leadership: Casting Light or Shadow.* London: Sage Publications.

Kahneman, D. (2003). A perspective on judgment and choice: Mapping bounded rationality. *American Psychologist*, 58(9): 697–720. https://doi.org/10.1037/0003-066X.58.9.697

Kahneman, D. (2011). *Thinking, Fast and Slow.* New York: Farrar, Strauss, and Giroux.

Kahneman, D., Sibony, O., and Sunstein, C. R. (2021). *Noise: A Flaw in Human Judgment.* William Collins.

Kaivo-oja, J., and Lauraeus, I. (2018). The VUCA approach as a solution concept to corporate foresight challenges and global technological disruption. *Foresight*, 20(1): 27–49. https://doi.org/10.1108/FS-06-2017-0022

Klein, G. (1998). *Sources of Power: How People Make Decisions.* MIT Press.

Koriat, A. (2002). Metacognition research: An interim report. In: T. J. Perfect and B. L. Schwartz (Eds.), *Applied Metacognition*, 261–286, Cambridge University Press. https://doi.org/10.1017/CBO9780511489976.012

Koriat, A., and Levy-Sadot, R. (2000). Conscious and unconscious metacognition: A rejoinder. *Consciousness and Cognition*, 9(2): 193–202. https://doi.org/10.1006/ccog.2000.0436

Krupp, S., and Schoemaker, P. (2014). *Winning the Long Game: How Strategic Leaders Shape the Future.* New York: Public Affairs.

Millar, C. C., Groth, O., and Mahon, J. F. (2018). Management innovation in a VUCA world: Challenges and recommendations. *California Management Review*, 61(1): 5–14. 10.1177/0008125618805111

Minciu, M., Berar, F., and Dobrea, R. (2020). New decision systems in the VUCA world. *Management & Marketing, Challenges for the Knowledge Society*, 15(2): 236–254. 10.2478/mmcks-2020-0015

Nowacka, A., and Rzemieniak, M. (2022). The impact of the VUCA environment on the digital competences of managers in the power industry. *Energies*, 15: 185. https://doi.org/10.3390/en15010185

OpenAI. (2022, November 30). *Introducing ChatGPT*. Retrieved March 27, 2023, from https://openai.com/blog/chatgpt

Patnaik, S. (2020). Applied machine learning and management of volatility, uncertainty, complexity & ambiguity (VUCA). *Journal of Intelligent & Fuzzy Systems*, 39(2): 1–8. 10.3233/JIFS-179915

Poteralska, B., Labedzka, J., and Brozek, K. (2022). Identification and development of future-oriented competences. *12th International Scientific Conference Business and Management 2022*, 852–858. Vilnius, Lithuania. https://doi.org/10.3846/bm.2022.854)

Sadler-Smith, E. (2023). *Intuition in Business*. Oxford University Press.

Sadler-Smith, E., and Shefy, E. (2004). The intuitive executive: Understanding and applying 'gut feel' in decision-making. *Academy of Management Perspectives*, 18(4): 76–91. https://doi.org/10.5465/ame.2004.15268692

Saleh, A., and Watson, R. (2017). Business excellence in a volatile, uncertain, complex and ambiguous environment (BEVUCA). *The TQM Journal*, 29(5): 705–724.

Salk, J. (1984). *Anatomy of Reality. Merging of Intuition and Reason*. Columbia University Press.

Sarkar, A. (2016). We live in a VUCA world: The importance of responsible leadership. *Development and Learning in Organizations*, 30(3): 9–12. 10.1108/DLO-07-2015-0062

Schick, A., Hobson, P., and Ibisch, P. (2017). Conservation and sustainable development in a VUCA world: The need for a systemic and ecosystem-based approach. *Ecosystem Health and Sustainability*, 3(4): 1–12.

Schulte, P., Streit, J., Sheriff, F., Delclos, G., Felknor, S., Tamers, S., . . . Sala, R. (2020). Potential scenarios and hazards in the work of the future: A systematic review of the peer-reviewed and grey literatures. *Annals of Work Exposures and Health*, 64(8): 786–816. https://doi.org/10.1093/annweh/wxaa051

Schwartz, B. L. (2006). Tip-of-the-tongue states as metacognition. *Metacognition and Learning*, 1(2): 149–158. https://doi.org/10.1007/S11409-006-9583-Z/METRICS

Sebanz, N., Bekkering, H., and Knoblich, G. (2006). Joint action: Bodies and minds moving together. *Trends in Cognitive Sciences*, 10(2): 70–76. https://doi.org/10.1016/j.tics.2005.12.009

Simon, H. A. (1957). *Models of Man: Social and Rational.* John Wiley & Sons.

Stockton, H., Joseph, S., and Hunt, N. (2014). Expressive writing and posttraumatic growth: An internet-based study. *Traumatology: An International Journal*, 20(2): 75–83. https://doi.org/10.1037/h0099377

Thompson, V. A., Prowse Turner, J. A., and Pennycook, G. (2011). Intuition, reason, and metacognition. *Cognitive Psychology*, 63(3): 107–140. https://doi.org/10.1016/j.cogpsych.2011.06.001

Whiteman, W. (1998). *Training and Educating Army Officers for the 21st Century: Implications for the United States Military Academy.* Army War Coll Carlisle Barracks PA.

Wilder, R. L. (1967). The role of intuition. *Science*, 156(3775): 605–610. https://doi.org/10.1126/science.156.3775.605

Yargar, H. (2008). *Strategy and the National Security Professional.* Westport, CT: Praeger Security International

Yehezkel, O. (2020). Traditional organizations in a VUCA world. *Advancement in Management*, 4–22.

Chapter 10

Intuition and Competitiveness

Richard Szántó

Corvinus University of Budapest, Hungary

Introduction

It has been debated for many decades whether or not managerial intuition and "non-rational" decision-making are advantageous for firms (Ireland & Miller 2004). There are abundant business examples of when managers' gut feelings were the basis for groundbreaking decisions that resulted in huge commercial success. For example, Chrysler's decision to develop the sports car Dodge Viper® was based on the synthesis of various experiences, a novel combination of knowledge, and strong feelings that the new product would be successful (Miller & Ireland 2005). However, less rosy stories are also frequently told by those who do not favor intuitive decisions. Zapmail, Federal Express's service based on fax transmission of documents in the 1980s, was an instant failure and an illustrative negative example of the use of gut feelings of highly ranked managers (Bonabeau 2003).

Beyond these pieces of anecdotal evidence, fewer empirical studies have been carried out on how intuitive judgment and decision-making influence firm performance. Even less work was done around the relationship between intuition and firm competitiveness (see Zoltay Paprika et al. 2008 for an exception)—i.e., how, by using an intuitive approach in their managerial decision-making, companies can meet customer demand concerning quantity, quality, price, and timeliness of delivery; adjust to changes in their environment in the long run; and connect to relevant market information (Falciola et al. 2020).

In this chapter, we try to fill this gap by analyzing how an intuitive decision-making style can enhance or undermine firm-level competitiveness. At the end of the chapter, we will discuss how a combination of analytical and intuitive thinking can effectively harness the power of intuition while avoiding its weaknesses, and then we will present the results of recent survey research on the topic.

Definitions: Intuition and competitiveness

One may easily conceive that there is a lack of consensus in the literature concerning the definition of intuition. In their seminal article, Dane and Pratt (2007), for example, identified 17 different definitions in other leading studies of the field, and since then this number has been continuously growing. Intuition can be interpreted as a "form of information processing that differs from cognitive processes and is associated with gut feelings, hunches, and mystical insights" (Dayan & Elbanna 2011, 159), and it is often contrasted with rational thought. As Hodgkinson and his co-authors (2009, 280) put it, it is "a capacity for attaining direct knowledge or understanding without the apparent intrusion of rational thought or logical inference".

The widely accepted dual-processing approach differentiates System 1 and System 2 thinking modes, where the former represents a holistic, associative, and automatic information processing of the brain, while the latter can be characterized as controlled, rule-based, and analytic (Evans 2003). According to most definitions, intuition is related to System 1–type thinking processes, with no or very little involvement of conscious deliberation (Hogarth 2010).

Like intuition, the concept of competitiveness has also long been debated. Although some theorists in the field of strategic management identify firm-level competitiveness as a synonym for firm performance (Guerras-Martín et al. 2014), in this chapter we propose competitiveness as a more complex, multidimensional, and relative construct (Ajitabh & Momaya 2004). The resource-based view of the firm posits that valuable, rare, imperfectly imitable, and not sustainable resources and capabilities such as management skills, organizational processes and routines, and knowledge and information are the keys to sustained competitive advantage (Barney et al. 2001).

Beyond assets and skills, it is also critical how and where a firm competes: the former involves product strategy, positioning sourcing, pricing, and so on, while the latter concerns how the target markets are selected (Aaker 1989). Yet, in this chapter, we accept the comprehensive view of Chikán (2008: 24–25), who defines firm-level competitiveness as "a capability of a firm to sustainably fulfil its double purpose: meeting customer requirements at profit. This capability is realized through offering on the market goods and services which customers value higher than those offered by competitors. Achieving competitiveness requires the firm's continuing adaptation to changing social and economic norms and conditions."

This definition emphasizes the relationship between firm-level competitiveness and relative performance, but it stresses the importance of adaptability at the same time. While short-term profit measures are important for present success, adaptability is critical to achieving superior long-term performance.

Why does intuition boost firm-level competitiveness?

Myriad studies confirm that decision-makers in organizations might have rational intentions that are boundedly rational due to the cognitive limitations of the actors and the complex nature of the environment (Eisenhardt & Zbaracki 1992). Analytical, deliberative cognitive processes are always complemented by non-objective, unconscious processes when decision-makers cannot explain their choices. One of the founding fathers of the concept of bounded rationality, Herbert Simon, stated that the term *intuition* deserves "a high priority in the agenda of management research" (Simon 1987, 61). Most authors who tend to favor intuitive decision-making style in management highlight two important aspects that can be leveraged—namely, the expedited decision-making process and the use of tacit knowledge that cannot be replicated easily by others.

Intuition is often characterized as a fast way of information processing and a quick response to environmental stimuli (Dane & Pratt 2004). For example, Wally and Baum (1994) found evidence that using intuition in managerial decision-making resulted in a speedier decision-making process. Eisenhardt (1989), in her influential paper, confirms that fast decisions, if they follow a certain pattern of behavior, such as extensive use of real-time information, lead to superior performance in organizations. She also argues, based on her case study research, that executives who rely heavily on real-time information are often characterized as intuitive decision-makers or lateral thinkers. Time and, particularly, time pressure can strongly influence decision mode: in certain environments where available time is limited, an exhaustive search may be replaced with a reliance on intuitive decision-making and a more intensive level of trust in gut feelings (Allen 2011; Salas et al. 2010).

Intuitive decision-making relies on tacit knowledge; therefore, the insights that are fueled by intuitive information processing can be hugely valuable for the firm and are hard to replicate for competitors. It is even more critical in a multi-national environment, where local knowledge is often used in a global context (Harvey et al. 2009). Particularly in a complex environment where uncertainty and risk are high, data is plentiful and subject to interpretation—therefore, a systematic, analytic perspective could lead to "analysis paralysis" (Huang 2018), and recognition of unseen patterns is extremely valuable.

Instead of asking the overarching question of whether one should trust one's gut, more and more research asks *when* one should trust one's gut (Dane et al. 2012). Khatri and Ng (2000), for example, suggest that intuition (or as they call it, *intuitive synthesis*) should be used more often in a highly unstable environment and less frequently in stable or moderately stable environments. Nonetheless, their results suggest that we should represent an even more cautious approach towards this problem, since they experienced different results across industries, and the use of intuition was related differently to the financial and non-financial performance of the companies.

In a study that involved small and medium-sized US-based companies, using the same questionnaire used by Khatri and Ng (2000), Sadler-Smith (2004) found an unequivocal positive relationship between the intuitive cognitive style of the managers and financial and non-financial performance, where financial performance was measured with percentage sales growth over the previous 12 months, while non-financial performance scales included the efficiency of operations, public image and goodwill, and quality of products and services. It is interesting that the environment did not moderate the relationship between intuitive style and organizational performance, as the findings of Khatri and Ng (2000) earlier suggested.

In another study with similar purposes, Zoltay Paprika et al. (2008) found that Hungarian managers were rather reluctant to rely on their intuition, and in most cases, such hesitation was associated with poor financial and operational performance. They argue that this overcommitment to rational approaches may be due to some cultural biases and to the phenomenon that Haidt (2001) calls the "worship of reason". Hungarian participants, to a great extent, hold the assumption that managers are generally inherently rational decision-makers whose thinking is supposed to be untainted by feelings, unconscious mental processes, and biases (Sadler-Smith & Shefy 2004). In a different domain (US-based nonprofit university and college foundations), it was also found that executives' intuition is positively associated with some performance indicators (Ritchie et al. 2007). These findings suggest that an intuitive decision style can enhance the performance of non-profit organizations as well.

Covin et al. (2001) got more nuanced results in their study when they investigated the relationship between decision-making style and firm performance. Intuitive decision-making style was associated with higher financial performance (measured with sales growth) among firms with organic rather than mechanistic structures in high-tech environments, while in the case of other financial measures, such as return on sales, they saw opposite trends. These findings suggest that managers should align their decision-making style with the organization's structure and the characteristics of the environment to achieve different types of performance goals. The above-mentioned results demonstrate that a positive relationship between firm performance and the cognitive style of the managers may depend on many other variables, and empirical studies have produced mixed results in the previous decades.

Fewer studies have been made on the relationship between intuition and the other important element of firm competitiveness: adaptability. One would suggest that strategic adaptability needs fast reactions from managers, particularly in a hypercompetitive environment (Tejeiro Koller 2016); therefore, a less analytical and more intuitive approach seems to be more advantageous in the long run. Gallén (2006) theorizes that managers having an intuitive cognitive style usually prefer Miles and Snow's prospector or analyzer strategy as the most viable course of action for the company. A prospector strategy represents a "first-to-the-market" attitude, in contrast to the defender strategy, which competes based on value and/or cost.

Meanwhile, analyzers are in between the two groups, pursuing a second-mover strategy. Gallén's findings suggest that intuitive managers can drive and implement proactive strategies in their firms, and they will represent a confident positive attitude to market changes. Green et al. (2006) found that certain organization structure/decision-making style combinations strengthen firms' adaptability (i.e., organic structures with a more intuitive decision-making style and mechanistic structures with a more technocratic). In the event of appropriate internal alignment, firms can react to new or currently pursued business opportunities, therefore gaining some competitive advantage.

How can intuition undermine firm-level competitiveness?

Intuitive thinking processes are often described as automatic and heuristic and are therefore based on stereotypes and common beliefs. Although in many cases heuristics produce satisfactory results, they frequently lead to systematic errors or cognitive biases; hence, these quick ways of judgments usually produce far from optimal solutions. Intuition, when relying on the experience of the decision-maker, often fails to recognize the new, unseen pattern, which can be critical in business ventures. When, for example, a competitive threat is interpreted and categorized according to old managerial practices in a firm, it may trigger an imperfect or wrong strategic action (Bonabeau 2003). These categorizations may be generated as a result of the extensive use of the so-called *representativeness heuristic*, which can create a load of cognitive biases according to the behavioral decision theory (Bazerman & Moore 2012; Keller & Sadler-Smith 2019).

In a meta-analysis in which they analyzed 89 samples and a pooled sample of more than 17,000 participants, Phillips et al. (2016) found that intuition was negatively associated with decision performance. Nevertheless, they admit that the association between thinking style (i.e., analytical or intuitive) and performance is context dependent. Elbanna and Child (2007) had similar results when they found that rationality and political behavior are significant antecedents of strategic decision effectiveness; yet intuition, contrary to the findings of Khatri and Ng (2000), was not related to the variable. However, they also state that decision effectiveness is process- and context-dependent.

Hodgkinson et al. (2009) argue that strategic decision-making units, having a strong preference towards an intuitive approach to processing information, may fail to fully comprehend the business environment in which the decisions are made. In an empirical study investigating business practices of Italian small and medium-sized companies, Musso et al. (2022) found that more intuitive strategic decision-making processes usually lead to poorer performance in international markets (compared with the performance of direct competitors). The authors of the study argue that the benefits of intuitive processes, such as speed, cannot be exploited for complex decisions like internationalization.

Liberman-yaconi et al. (2010) also studied small, or even micro firms, in which circle owner/managers predominantly used intuitive approaches in their strategic decision-making. The owner/managers often reported that these decisions were based on their values and feelings and negatively influenced their firms' competitive positions, hence the researchers pointed out the need for more comprehensive analyses and more sophisticated strategic tools.

Intuition is often connected to expertise and experience (Hurteau et al. 2020), though they are not necessarily the same (Salas et al. 2010). Those who have more experience usually use their intuition more frequently (Leybourne & Sadler-Smith 2006). Intuition without expertise is sometimes called *immature intuition* (Baylor 2001). Novices usually lack domain-specific knowledge, and they may not be able to make novel insights based on their past experiences; therefore, Baylor (2001) suggests, they should rely more on their analytical understanding. The development of managers' intuition seems to be a long, effortful, and very complex process characterized by successful decisions and often painful failures (Hurteau et al. 2020).

A study by Kaufmann and his co-authors (2014) found that when team members used a highly rational approach during a supplier selection decision, supplier cost performance, as a critical decision outcome, was greater (in their study, cost performance was measured with the total cost of ownership for and the price of the purchased item). This finding suggests that intuitive reasoning may positively influence certain indicators, while some other—also critical—ones will be neglected. Leybourne and Sadler-Smith (2006) had somewhat similar findings in the project management context. Project managers deploying their intuition more intensively paid more attention to the external outcomes of the project (i.e., meeting the needs of the client), while traditional internal project outcomes like time, cost, and scope were not related to the use of intuition.

Elbanna et al. (2013) reject the idea that organizational performance is positively associated with the use of intuition. In the Egyptian context, they found that reliance on intuition increased the possibility of major negative outcomes after the decision, or as they called it, *decision disturbance.* Nonetheless, they believe that the relationship between performance and intuition is bi-directional. It is not trivial whether the use of intuition affects performance, either positively or negatively, or whether performance influences the decision-making style of managers.

One may posit that the managers of more successful companies may "afford" to be more intuitive: they have accumulated a pool of experience, and their decisions were proven successful in the past; meanwhile, less successful managers are not willing to take the risk of trusting their guts: if they fail again, they cannot justify their choices. On the other hand, it can be expected that managers relying more often on their intuition can exploit the benefits of intuitive decisions that we learned from earlier research; they may react faster to environmental changes, they more effectively exploit their expertise, and they do not need costly information for their decisions. Moreover, irrelevant pieces of information do not derail the decision-making process, as they do not distract the attention of the managers (Thanos 2022).

Combining intuition with analytical thinking

A former vice president of the leading cosmetic multinational firm L'Oreal once argued that, "Decision-making intelligence requires a fine balancing of two seemingly contradictory capabilities, intuition, and rationality: the first one allows executives to pick up on important but weak signals; the second enables executives to act on them." (Sadler-Smith & Shefy 2004: 76). This view on intuition and analysis indicates that the two approaches should be combined to exploit the potential of both. In a study by Blattberg and Hoch (1990), the authors present evidence for the effective use of the combination of database models and managerial intuition. Across five business forecasting exercises, they compared the prediction accuracy of simple quantitative models and expert judgments and the 50/50 mixture of these two. The combination of the model and the manager always outperformed these forecasts when they were made separately. Katsikopoulos et al. (2022) offer a more sophisticated model to determine the ideal proportion of intuition in these mixtures, but these proportions are usually lower than 50 percent for various forecasting tasks.

In an often-cited paper, Daniel Kahneman and Gary Klein (2009) make attempts to reconcile the differences between the two conflicting approaches towards intuition: one that emphasizes its heuristic nature and the biases it may generate, and the other that points out the remarkable judgments and decisions made by experts in risky situations where stakes are high (the latter is called the *naturalistic* decision-making approach).

Kahneman and Klein (2009) differentiate between high-validity and low-validity (or sometimes even zero-validity) task environments, depending on the degree of predictability of future events and the outcomes of possible actions based on the cues the skilled intuitive forecaster possesses. In a low- or zero-validity environment, intuitive judgments will likely be flawed, yet in a high-validity environment they may produce outstanding results.

A US-based study confirmed that investors in very risky environments rely on a decision-making process that is equally analytic and perceptually subjective. Laura Huang (2018) held interviews with 110 experienced angel investors, who often buy in early-age high-tech, high-growth start-ups that are considered enormously risky targets with high failure rates. Investors make sense of the high level of uncertainty and risk through a hybrid form of decision-making. They "call it their 'gut feel' because it is a factor that does encompass their emotions and their cognitions in a non-codifiable format, without the need for further description, calculation, or explanation" (Huang 2018: 1840).

By creating top-level decision-making teams comprising both analytical and intuitive capabilities, firms may avoid some typical dangers that characterize groups of overly analytic people, such as information overload and failing to see the big picture. Furthermore, dangers that come with a predominantly intuitive approach, such as making decisions in the absence of a sufficiently comprehensive understanding of the situation, may be avoided (Hodgkinson et al. 2009). Similarly, Kaufman et al. (2014) suggest that intuitive and rational procedures should be combined in supplier selection—inputs for the decisions may be generated by experience-based judgments, while final decisions should be guided by more analytical approaches.

There are certainly tensions between intuition and analysis (Keller & Sadler-Smith 2019). Calabretta et al. (2017), through seven case studies, analyze these tensions and identify several coping strategies. For example, they recommend that actors should be prepared for the tensions by creating emotional equanimity or should integrate divergent approaches simultaneously by structuring information. Nonetheless, some authors speculate that the more intensive use of big data and reliance on data-driven algorithms in decision-making will disrupt the above-mentioned balance between analytical and intuitive approaches (Acciarini et al. 2021). A recent study, for example, found that when an algorithm-based, data-driven decision tool of an automobile replacement parts retailer was overridden by merchants, firm profitability decreased by approximately 6 percent (Kesavan & Kushwaha 2020).

Competitiveness and decision-making style—An illustrative example

The last section of this chapter presents the major findings of recent survey research that connects decision-making style and firm-level competitiveness. The Competitiveness Research Centre of the Corvinus University of Budapest has been conducting a series of survey research since 1996 (Chikán 2008). The fifth wave of the research program took place between November 2018 and July 2019. Considered in this research were 4,295 Hungarian companies in six different sectors, and out of this pool, 2,011 firms were approached. Of this number, 237 companies responded to our questionnaire, but during data cleaning, 28 incomplete questionnaires were excluded.

Finally, 209 Hungarian firms participated in the study, and surveys were taken through in-person interviews. Small and medium-sized companies are overrepresented in the sample; hence, it is statistically not representative, and therefore findings should be interpreted with caution (Szántó 2022). During data collection, four different questionnaires were sent out to various executives of every participating firm, but in this study, we relied solely on the responses of the legal representatives of the companies, in most cases the CEO or the managing director. One must acknowledge that the responses were based on self-reports; therefore, our study may paint a more favorable picture of the firms participating than they really are.

In our study, managers' decision-making styles were measured with the same four scales, which were developed by Covin et al. (2001). Accordingly, our participants were asked to report to what extent their major decisions resulted from extensive quantitative analysis of data, and to what extent these decisions were detailed in formal reports (these were the indicators of the techno-cratic decision-making style). They also were asked to assess how often they relied on experienced-based intuition and to what degree their decisions were affected by industry experience and lessons learned (indicators of intuitive decision-making style).

A 5-point Likert scale was used to measure all four questionnaire items (1-strongly disagree, 5-strongly agree). Firm-level competitiveness was measured with the Firm Competitiveness Index (FCI) constructed by Chikán et al. (2022). FCI was built from survey-based perceptive measures of capabilities and market performance. Based on FCI, companies of our sample were sorted into two clusters labeled as (1) competitive firms, and (2) average firms. Due to missing values, 14 companies were omitted from further analysis; therefore, eventually, 110 competitive and 85 average firms were identified.

Table 10.1 elucidates that managers of competitive firms make comprehensive quantitative analyses in their major decisions just as often as their less compet-itive counterparts. However, significant differences can be observed concerning the intuitive decision-making style between the two clusters. The nonparametric Mann-Whitney test results demonstrate that differences are significant at two of the four scales. At more competitive firms, executives rely on experienced-based intuition to a greater extent ($U = 2746$, $p < 0.001$), and decisions are affected

Table 10.1 Technocratic and Intuitive Decision-Making Styles at Competitive and Average Firms

	Competitive firms (N = 110)		Average firms (N = 85)	
	mean	SD*	mean	SD*
Major decisions nearly always result from extensive quantitative analysis of data.	3.85	0.787	3.85	1.026
Major decisions are nearly always detailed in formal written reports.	3.46	0.964	3.39	1.025
We rely principally on experienced-based intuition when making major decisions.	3.53	0.904	2.84	1.163
Our major decisions are much more affected by industry experience and lessons learned.	3.78	0.935	3.15	1.170

*SD stands for standard deviation

by industry experience more (U = 2925, $p < 0.001$) than at companies with less impressive performance. It is worth noting that at firms with superior competitiveness measures, the technocratic decision-making style is as prevalent as the intuitive one (differences in the second column of Table 10.1 are not significant); however, at less competitive firms, technocratic decision-making is dominant, and executives mostly reject listening to their gut feelings when they make important choices.

As Elbanna et al. (2013) suggested, we must handle our results carefully. We can speculate that intuitive decisions may contribute to firm competitiveness in several ways, such as helping speedy decisions or recognizing non-trivial patterns in multiple forms of huge datasets. However, it is also possible that managers with good faith in their intuition may be keener to be reliant on their gut feelings because their past actions resulted in financial or non-financial success, and they are more confident in using an intuitive decision approach more intensively. It seems that executives leading less successful firms do not like to admit that they rely on their intuition some days, and they insist that they are committed to analytical decision-making most of the time. This strong commitment towards rational decision-making, and the negligence of intuition, may be for self-protection. This is due to the fact that low-performing managers can point to comprehensive analyses when they have to defend their choices, which would be much harder to do if they referred to their feelings as the basis for those major decisions.

With any reservation one might have, it can be argued that managers of competitive firms seem to use and value technocratic analyses as often as they rely on their intuition. This suggests that a more integrative approach and a mixture of cognitive styles in decision-making may be beneficial for firm-level competitiveness. Elaborating comprehensive quantitative analyses before major decisions are required but do not seem to be sufficient for business success. Furthermore, these analyses should be compared against personal and industry experience to produce financial and non-financial results in order to rapidly adapt to market changes.

Conclusion

Although there is a lack of consensus on what intuition is, researchers in this field usually agree that intuition plays an important role in human decision-making in every domain of our lives, and business decisions are certainly included. Yet, the effectiveness of intuitive decision-making style is not straightforward and is often debated—some emphasize their heuristic nature and cognitive biases that intuitive processes may generate, while others underline experts' capabilities to recognize hidden patterns and the expedited decision making that experience-fueled intuition enables. More and more researchers make attempts to investigate in what context, and under what conditions, intuitive cognitive styles may be successful. They usually agree that in complex situations where ambiguity and uncertainty are high, reliance on gut feelings is probably more efficient than comprehensive analyses. However, another group of researchers highlights the importance of using both decision-making styles: intuitive and analytic.

Similarly, mixed results can be found in the management literature when we try to assess whether or not intuitive decisions contribute to the financial and non-financial success of the firms. It is still not clear whether managers of well-performing and adaptive companies (i.e., more competitive firms) rely on their intuitive judgments more than their less successful counterparts do. Dozens of empirical studies (some of them introduced in this chapter) confirm that intuitive decision-making is more prevalent in good performers and less widespread in poor ones, but there are plenty of studies that state the opposite. Of course, there are some methodological differences across these studies, but it is rather astounding that such divergent findings can co-exist in the literature.

Some researchers believe—the author of this chapter is included in this group—that these mixed results can be explained with, beyond the methodological differences, the very complex nature of intuitive thinking. This could be due to the fact that it is very difficult to separate intuition from analysis in real life, and that managers use these processes simultaneously to achieve success. At the end of this chapter, the findings of a recent empirical study were discussed in which we saw that managers of more competitive firms use both technocratic and intuitive decision-making styles intensively, and it seems that they are both needed for being profitable in the market and being adaptive to future changes. Of course, as with all other studies, this one also had some limitations (it was made in a small emerging economy using a non-representative sample), but it certainly highlights the importance of an integrative or hybrid perspective of managerial decisions for business success.

References

Aaker, D. A. (1989). Managing assets and skills: The key to a sustainable competitive advantage. *California Management Review,* 31(2): 91–106.

Acciarini, C., Brunetta, F., & Boccardelli, P. (2021). Cognitive biases and decision-making strategies in times of change: A systematic literature review. *Management Decision,* 59(3): 638–652.

Ajitabh, A., and Momaya, K. (2004). Competitiveness of firms: Review of theory, frameworks and models. *Singapore Management Review,* 26(1): 45–61.

Allen, D. (2011). Information behavior and decision making in time-constrained practice: A dual-processing perspective. *Journal of the American Society for Information Science and Technology,* 62(11): 2165–2181.

Barney, J., Wright, M., and Ketchen, D. J., Jr. (2001). The resource-based view of the firm: Ten years after 1991. *Journal of Management,* 27(6): 625–641.

Bazerman, M. H., and Moore, D. A. (2012*). Judgment in Managerial Decision Making*. John Wiley & Sons.

Blattberg, R. C., and Hoch, S. J. (1990). Database models and managerial intuition: 50% model + 50% manager. *Management Science,* 36(8): 887–899.

Bonabeau, E. (2003). Don't trust your gut. *Harvard Business Review,* 81(5): 116–123.

Chikán, A. (2008). National and firm competitiveness: A general research model. *Competitiveness Review: An International Business Journal,* 18(1/2): 20–28.

Chikán, A., Czakó, E., Kiss-Dobronyi, B., and Losonci, D. (2022). Firm competitiveness: A general model and a manufacturing application. *International Journal of Production Economics*, 243: 108316.

Covin, J. G., Slevin, D. P., and Heeley, M. B. (2001). Strategic decision making in an intuitive vs. technocratic mode: Structural and environmental considerations. *Journal of Business Research,* 52(1): 51–67.

Dane, E., and Pratt, M. G. (2004). Intuition: Its boundaries and role in organizational decision-making. *Academy of Management Proceedings,* 1: A1–A6. New York: Briarcliff Manor.

Dane, E., and Pratt, M. G. (2007). Exploring intuition and its role in managerial decision making. *Academy of Management Review,* 32(1): 33–54.

Dane, E., Rockmann, K. W., and Pratt, M. G. (2012). When should I trust my gut? Linking domain expertise to intuitive decision-making effectiveness. *Organizational Behavior and Human Decision Processes,* 119(2): 187–194.

Dayan, M., and Elbanna, S. (2011). Antecedents of team intuition and its impact on the success of new product development projects. *Journal of Product Innovation Management*, 28(s1): 159–174.

Eisenhardt, K. M. (1989). Making fast strategic decisions in high-velocity environments. *Academy of Management Journal,* 32(3): 543–576.

Eisenhardt, K. M., and Zbaracki, M. J. (1992). Strategic decision making. *Strategic Management Journal,* 13(S2): 17–37.

Elbanna, S., and Child, J. (2007). Influences on strategic decision effectiveness: Development and test of an integrative model. *Strategic Management Journal,* 28(4): 431–453.

Elbanna, S., Child, J., and Dayan, M. (2013). A model of antecedents and consequences of intuition in strategic decision-making: Evidence from Egypt. *Long Range Planning,* 46(1–2): 149–176.

Evans, J. St. B. T. (2003). In two minds: Dual-process accounts of reasoning. *Trends in Cognitive Sciences,* 7(10): 454–459.

Falciola, J., Jansen, M., and Rollo, V. (2020). Defining firm competitiveness: A multidimensional framework. *World Development,* 129: 104857.

Gallén, T. (2006). Managers and strategic decisions: Does the cognitive style matter? *Journal of Management Development,* 25(2): 118–133.

Green, K. M., Covin, J. G., and Slevin, D. P. (2008). Exploring the relationship between strategic adaptability and entrepreneurial orientation: The role of structure-style fit. *Frontiers of Entrepreneurship Research,* 26(23): 3.

Guerras-Martín, L. Á., Madhok, A., and Montoro-Sánchez, Á. (2014). The evolution of strategic management research: Recent trends and current directions. *BRQ Business Research Quarterly,* 17(2): 69–76.

Haidt, J. (2001). The emotional dog and its rational tail: A social intuitionist approach to moral judgment. *Psychological Review,* 108(4): 814.

Harvey, M., Fisher, R., McPhail, R., and Moeller, M. (2009). Globalization and its impact on global managers' decision processes. *Human Resource Development International,* 12(4): 353–370.

Hodgkinson, G. P., Sadler-Smith, E., Burke, L. A., Claxton, G., and Sparrow, P. R. (2009). Intuition in organizations: Implications for strategic management. *Long Range Planning,* 42(3): 277–297.

Huang, L. (2018). The role of investor gut feel in managing complexity and extreme risk. *Academy of Management Journal*, 61(5): 1821–1847.

Hurteau, M., Rahmanian, J., Houle, S., and Marchand, M. P. (2020). The role of intuition in evaluative judgment and decision. *American Journal of Evaluation,* 41(3): 326–338.

Ireland, R. D., and Miller, C. C. (2004). Decision-making and firm success. *The Academy of Management Executive (1993–2005),* 18(4): 8–12.

Kahneman, D., and Klein, G. (2009). Conditions for intuitive expertise: A failure to disagree. *American Psychologist,* 64(6): 515.

Katsikopoulos, K. V., Egozcue, M., and Garcia, L. F. (2022). A simple model for mixing intuition and analysis. *European Journal of Operational Research,* 303(2): 779–789.

Kaufmann, L., Meschnig, G., and Reimann, F. (2014). Rational and intuitive decision-making in sourcing teams: Effects on decision outcomes. *Journal of Purchasing and Supply Management,* 20(2): 104–112.

Keller, J., and Sadler-Smith, E. (2019). Paradoxes and dual processes: A review and synthesis. *International Journal of Management Reviews,* 21(2): 162–184.

Kesavan, S., and Kushwaha, T. (2020). Field experiment on the profit implications of merchants' discretionary power to override data-driven decision-making tools. *Management Science,* 66(11): 5182–5190.

Khatri, N., and Ng, H. A. (2000). The role of intuition in strategic decision making. *Human Relations,* 53(1): 57–86.

Leybourne, S., and Sadler-Smith, E. (2006). The role of intuition and improvisation in project management. *International Journal of Project Management,* 24(6): 483–492.

Liberman-Yaconi, L., Hooper, T., and Hutchings, K. (2010). Toward a model of understanding strategic decision-making in micro-firms: Exploring the Australian information technology sector. *Journal of Small Business Management,* 48(1): 70–95.

Miller, C. C., and Ireland, R. D. (2005). Intuition in strategic decision making: Friend or foe in the fast-paced 21st century? *Academy of Management Perspectives,* 19(1): 19–30.

Phillips, W. J., Fletcher, J. M., Marks, A. D., and Hine, D. W. (2016). Thinking styles and decision making: A meta-analysis. *Psychological Bulletin,* 142(3): 260.

Ritchie, W. J., Kolodinsky, R. W., and Eastwood, K. (2007). Does executive intuition matter? An empirical analysis of its relationship with nonprofit organization financial performance. *Nonprofit and Voluntary Sector Quarterly,* 36(1): 140–155.

Sadler-Smith, E. (2004). Cognitive style and the management of small and medium-sized enterprises. *Organization Studies,* 25(2): 155–181.

Sadler-Smith, E., and Shefy, E. (2004). The intuitive executive: Understanding and applying 'gut feel' in decision making. *Academy of Management Executive,* 18(4): 76–91.

Salas, E., Rosen, M. A., and DiazGranados, D. (2010). Expertise-based intuition and decision making in organizations. *Journal of Management,* 36(4): 941–973.

Simon, H. A. (1987). Making management decisions: The role of intuition and emotion. *Academy of Management Executive,* 1(1): 57–64

Szántó, R. (2022). Intuitive decision-making and firm performance. *Journal of Decision Systems,* 31(supp. 1): 50–59.

Tejeiro Koller, M. R. (2016). Exploring adaptability in organizations: Where adaptive advantage comes from and what it is based upon. *Journal of Organizational Change Management,* 29(6): 837–854.

Thanos, I. C. (2022). The complementary effects of rationality and intuition on strategic decision quality. *European Management Journal.* https://doi .org/10.1016/j.emj.2022.03.003

Zoltay Paprika, Z., Wimmer, A., and Szanto, R. (2008). Managerial decision making and competitiveness: The case of Hungary. *Competitiveness Review: An International Business Journal,* 18(1/2): 154–167.

Chapter 11

Intuitive Investment Decision-Making Across Cultures

Haili Wu[1,2] and Li-Jun Ji[3]

[1] Economics Department, International Business School Suzhou, Xi'an Jiaotong-Liverpool University, China

[2] UCL Centre for the Study of Decision-Making Uncertainty, Faculty of Brain Sciences, University College London (UCL), London, UK

[3] Department of Psychology, Queen's University, Kingston, Canada

> *East is East and West is West, and never the twain shall meet*
> —Rudyard Kipling

Intuition plays an important role in all kinds of decision-making, including investment decisions. With the increasing globalization of investment, it has become more vital to understand investment from a cross-cultural perspective. Little research, however, has investigated intuitive investment decision-making across cultures. To fill this gap, the current chapter discusses intuitive decision-making across cultures. We first outline a major theoretical framework in cultural psychology that has significant implications for intuitive thinking. We then present some empirical evidence showing cultural differences in intuitive investment decision-making. Based on our findings, we offer a conceptual framework reflecting cultural and cross-cultural dimensions, which provide bases for practical recommendations and potential directions for future inquiry into this vital aspect of managerial cognition and decision-making behaviour.

What is culture?

Despite the fact that most of us think that we know what culture is, it is a rather difficult concept to define formally. Certainly, there are many aspects to culture, such as music, food, religion, child-rearing patterns, ways of thinking, values and the like. In one of the most influential and widely quoted definitions in anthropology, culture is defined as, "that complex whole which includes knowledge, belief, art, morals, law, custom, and any other capabilities and habits acquired by man as a member of society" (Tylor 1871/1924, 1). According to this definition, culture is a quality possessed by all people.

Whereas anthropologists and sociologists emphasised culture as a social construct, psychologists tend to focus on the psychological nature of culture. Hofstede (1980) and Schwartz (1999) considered culture as a set of values and ways of thinking shared by a group of people, which are communicated from one generation to the next via language or some other means of communication. For example, individualism/collectivism is one of the value dimensions discovered by Hofstede in the early 1980s. This cultural value dimension is arguably the most famous. Some have suggested that the 1990s might be characterised as "the decade of individualism/collectivism" (Kagitcibasi & Berry 1989).

Furthermore, the definition of culture we are emphasizing here also implies that culture is as much an individual construct as it is a macro construct. That is, to some extent, culture exists in each and every one of us individually as much as it exists as a global, social construct. Individual differences in culture can be observed among people to the degree by which they adopt and engage in the attitudes, values, beliefs, and behaviours.

Culture and holistic thinking

Culture shapes people's thinking styles. Cultural psychological research has presented plenty of evidence showing cultural differences in holistic vs. analytic thinking (e.g., Nisbett 2004). Specifically, Westerners (especially European North Americans) tend to think analytically, by assigning importance to focal information. Analytic thinking assumes that everything in the universe—be it an object, person, event, or abstract idea—is discrete in nature and can be understood in terms of its underlying internal attributes independent of context. To analytic thinkers, reasoning about the world is based on the attributes of the object, not the contextual factors surrounding it. In contrast, East Asians tend to think more holistically; they tend to associate focal elements with their surrounding contexts. Holistic thinking assumes that everything in the universe is fluid, complex, and interconnected in nature, and that things do not make much sense unless they are considered relative to their contexts (Nisbett et al. 2001).

Culturally specific thinking styles can be found in the attention by which people direct their focus to a specific piece of information. The way people think or feel about an issue, all the way to the judgments and decisions they make, are often based on the information captured by their attention. Over the years, psychologists have found considerable cultural differences in the extent to which people attend to the various elements in their visual fields—namely, the focal objects in the foreground or the surrounding elements embedded in the background. European-Americans tend to focus predominantly on the focal objects, whereas East Asians are more likely than Americans to pay attention to the context and objects in the context (Ji, Peng, & Nisbett 2000; Masuda & Nisbett 2001).

The differences in analytical and holistic thinking manifest themselves in a variety of social judgments and decisions. For example, holistic thinkers are more likely to attribute a behaviour to external situational factors (e.g., a person might have committed murder as a result of toxic social values instead of his own dispositions; Morris & Peng 1994). In contrast, analytical thinkers tend to assign causal responsibilities of behaviours to the internal attributes of the actors, taking few situational factors into consideration (e.g., Choi & Nisbett 1998; Cousins 1989; Hamilton & Sanders 1992; Jones & Harris 1967; Lee, Hallahan, & Herzog 1996; Morris & Peng 1994).

In sum, East Asians are more likely than Westerners to emphasize contextual information, not only in the perception of physical objects but also in judgments with social implications. All these differences have important implications for intuition in investment decision-making contexts.

Intuitive thinking and holistic thinking

Parikh and colleagues (Parikh et al. 1994) argued that analytical thinking may no longer be well suited to handling new issues. In their view, when the road ahead is foggy, intuitive thinking is essential. This section will discuss the linkage between intuitive and holistic thinking by exploring the various definitions of intuition, determinants for using intuition in decision-making and their common opposite side, analytical thinking.

The concept of intuition has been used in myriad settings and situations in which its meanings vary. For example, within philosophy, intuition is seen as an experience and a way of arriving at knowledge. In psychology, intuition is considered as a cognitive style. It was seen as an intersection between personality and cognition (Martinsen & Kaufmann 1999). Intuition has therefore been studied as a decision tool in decision-making theory and research.

As a result, when intuition is seen as a cognitive behaviour, it is often associated with holistic thinking, because the non-linear, non-sequential nature of holistic processing is generally implied in most definitions of intuition found in the literature to date. For example, Jung (1971) viewed intuition as a holistic mode of perception. Similarly, Hammond (1996, 60) described intuitions as the result of the holistic integration of multiple cues without awareness or the availability of an explicit rule.

Pretz (2011) has even coined the term *holistic intuition* to describe this type of intuition, which is holistic judgement that integrates complex information and emphasizes that the whole is greater than the sum of its parts.

There are overlaps between intuitive thinking and holistic thinking. According to a developed measure, the Types of Intuition Scale (Pretz et al. 2014), there are three types of intuition: *holistic, inferential,* and *affective.* Affective intuition is a feeling of certainty or confidence in a judgement (Bastick 1982), and inferential intuition is based on expertise that consists of well-developed schemas or mental representations of knowledge. Holistic intuition is compared with accumulative intuition in that it is theoretically based on a holistic integration of diverse cues (Pretz et al. 2014). Therefore, intuition can be holistic or emotional. In the meantime, holistic thinking can be intuitive (e.g., Norenzayan et al. 2002) or dialectic (Peng & Nisbett 1999). For example, in Norenzayan et al. (2002)'s study, in contrast to European Americans, East Asians relied on holistic thinking or intuitive strategies more, as they gave fewer rule-based responses than family resemblance responses.

On the other hand, holistic thinking can also be dialectical or moderate—for example, when dealing with seeming contradictions, Chinese tend to retain basic elements of opposing perspectives and seek a "middle way", whereas European-Americans tend to polarize contradictory perspectives in an effort to determine which fact or position is correct (Peng & Nisbett 1999). This kind of dialectic thinking is an important element of holistic thinking, yet it has rarely been measured as part of intuitive thinking (Pretz et al. 2014). Therefore, the concepts of intuitive thinking and holistic thinking share both similarities and differences.

Holistic thinking and intuitive thinking also converge in their attention to contextual information. Sensitivity to context is a key feature in holistic thinking. Intuitive decision-making may also hinge on contextual factors. Using intuition in decision-making appears to be dynamic and is contingent on a range of specific triggers (Sinclair & Ashkanasy 2005), including the contextual environment. According to Malewska (2021), there are three types of factors influencing the use of intuition in the practice of decision-making:

1. Related to the decision-maker. His or her knowledge, experience, and predispositions
2. Related to the decision problem. Its complexity, repeatability, and degree of structure
3. Related to the contextual environment. The conditions and situations in which decisions are made

Therefore, the contextual environment is another linkage here. On one hand, holistic thinkers tend to pay more attention to contextual information, as cultural psychologies have found. At the same time, the contextual information is one very important factor for determining the use of intuition. Some empirical evidence even shows that the contextual environment actually may be more influential than other factors, such as intuitive dispositions or the decision problem. For example, Elbanna and Fadol (2016) found that the characteristics specific to the firm and to the environment appear to be more significant to the use of intuition than does the nature of the decision. Likewise, Wu (2022) identified that fund managers from China and the West are very different in their use of intuition as a result of the environment of Chinese capital markets, despite the fact that differences in intuitive cognition between Chinese and Western fund managers were insignificant. Thus, it could reasonably be predicted that holistic thinkers might be more flexible in their use of intuition, as they are more sensitive to decision context when intuitive decision-making is concerned.

In addition, the linkage between intuitive and holistic thinking is via their contrast to analytical thinking. Very often analytical thinking has been treated as the opposite of holistic thinking, as well as the opposite of intuitive thinking. Perhaps for this reason these two terms, holistic and intuitive thinking, have been used interchangeably by some scholars (e.g., Hammond 1996; Jung 1971; Norenzayan et al. 2002).

For example, according to Allinson and Hayes (2012), the main differences between intuition and analysis are distinctively opposite: Intuition is unconstrained because it includes the processing of non-salient associations between elements. These associations are so weak that they are below the threshold for conscious awareness, and therefore they are inaccessible to conscious control and logical manipulation. In contrast, analysis is constrained rule based, because it is restricted to the processing of salient associations between elements.

Because learners are consciously aware of these associations, the processing of information tends to be much more rational and open to conscious manipulation. Furthermore, intuition involves synthesizing data and recognizing connections that build to provide a non-conscious understanding of the rules and principles that govern a situation. In contrast, analysis involves a search for connections that entails a conscious step-by-step application of rules or other systematic procedures and/or the formulation and testing of hypotheses. Therefore, the rules-based approach is rather typical in analytical thinking, whereas it is not a common practice for intuitive thinking.

Similarly, in much cultural psychology research, the comparison point for holistic thinking is also analytical thinking. For example, in the article entitled, Individual Differences in Analytic Versus Holistic Thinking, by Choi, Koo, and Choi (2007), the very important criterion to differentiate analytic and holistic thinking is the rule-based judgement or family resemblance-based judgement. In addition, neuroscientific evidence shows that holistic and analytic processing rely on different neural systems. Holistic and analytic cognitive systems operate independently, and activation in one system is uncorrelated (or negatively correlated) with activation in the other (Lieberman 2007).

In summary, when intuition is used as a decision-making tool, it has many linkages with holistic thinking, which has been widely examined in traditional cultural psychology research, as plenty of empirical evidence supports the notion of holistic East and analytical West. Furthermore, as the holistic thinkers tend to pay more attention to contextual information, as cultural psychologies have found, and the contextual information is one very important factor determining the use of intuition, it would help to establish some cross-cultural pattern of intuitive thinking—i.e., Chinese thinkers might be more flexible in their use of intuition, as they are more holistic and thus more sensitive to decision context when intuitive decision-making is concerned.

Likewise, as activation in a holistic system is negatively correlated with activation in an analytic system (Lieberman 2007), it may lead to the conclusion that Chinese thinkers could be more flexible in their use of analytical thinking as well. Unfortunately, there is very little empirical evidence in the existing literature about the dynamic process of intuitive/analytical decision-making. It then leads to the next section, which reveals the important evidence found by the author in supporting the theoretical prediction about cross-cultural differences in the dynamic process of intuitive/analytical decision-making in the investment domain.

Empirical evidence for the dynamic process of intuitive/analytical decision-making across cultures

The Chinese capital markets provide a unique setting for testing the dynamic process of intuitive/analytical decision-making. Embedded in the Chinese culture, the Chinese capital markets are new and are often subject to notorious bubble-crash episodes, with the most recent one being the 2015 stock market crash. According to the market data provided by Wind Ltd, a leading financial data provider in China, the positive trend in the Chinese stock markets became significantly noticeable around July 2014, reaching its peak on June 15, 2015. The markets subsequently tumbled by nearly 42% in less than three months.

In response, the Chinese government first took measures to support the markets by providing cash to large state-owned brokers with the mandate to purchase shares, and then subsequently imposed a heavy regulatory clampdown, the so-called "yanda 严打". As of 30 August 2015, the Chinese government arrested 197 people—including Wang Xiaolu, a journalist at the "influential financial magazine *Caijing*", as well as stock market officials—for "spreading rumours" about the market crash. On 1 November, 2015, billionaire hedge fund manager Xu Xiang—known as China's Warren Buffett or China's Carl Icahn—was arrested for allegedly manipulating the stock market during the 2015 Chinese stock market turbulence.

Because of the ontology of state power, this kind of political campaign can transform the financial decision context drastically. With such a campaign, the structure of capital markets in China is not transformed gradually through the workings of structures and incentives on individuals, but abruptly through the more severe or sterner enforcement of regulations or laws for a certain period and through the mobilization of a monolithically conceived society for immediate action (Hertz 1998).

Set against this epic time in the history of Chinese capital markets, the first author took two field trips to China's financial center and talked to many Chinese professional fund managers prior to and after the market crash. Within the same time period, the first author also interviewed Western fund managers with similar questions for comparison purposes. Thus, the data collection has covered the entire crisis period and was undoubtedly able to reflect the dynamic process of investors' intuitive/analytic decision-making during this epic time.

It is of interest that the comparison between fund managers from these two cultural groups changed following the dramatic changes in the Chinese capital markets. Furthermore, empirical evidence has revealed that the behaviour of Chinese fund managers has changed significantly in the wake of the crisis and subsequent regulatory changes. It thus led to the speculation that, in contrast to Western fund managers, the shift of Chinese fund managers' behaviour between these two periods may reflect their greater sensitivity to decision-making context. In the following section, we will share the results based on data collected before and after the Chinese market crash.

Before the 2015 stock market crash

We interviewed 14 Western and 28 Chinese fund managers who dealt with the Chinese stock markets. According to the analysis based on our data collection prior to the stock crash (Wu 2022), we found that, again in contrast to Western fund managers, Chinese managers had a less strict or less precise investment process, and they were also less consistent in following through with any pre-defined rules. This suggests that Chinese fund managers adopted a less analytical decision-making style and likely used a more intuitive decision-making style. For example, a Chinese manager drew an interesting analogy between fund managers and musicians,

> Investment decision-making is more like an art rather than a science. It is like playing musical instruments. The master musicians can tell the nuance by their ears, rather than by scientific measurements. (Chinese 2*)

Similarly, another Chinese manager compared fund managers to dentists:

> I have tried to reflect and build a system; however, rules are very difficult to be summed up. Investment is not a science, but more like an art. Western fund managers have strict rules, but investment decision-making is different from a dentist's check-up menu. Dentists have a checklist for the process, but investment decision-making cannot: it is very fluid and changing all the time. (Chinese 25)

Chinese 14 made an even more extreme analogy between investment and arcane martial arts; he emphasised factors such as intuition or emotion over scientific reasoning:

> Investment is not something that can be described properly. It is like some arcane martial arts. It can only be taught by experience and meditation, rather than by words. Sometimes it was difficult to tell why I had confidence in this stock, and why I thought it would make money. It is not about more information or not. (Chinese 14)

Some Chinese managers touched upon examples related to investment indicators. For example, Chinese 31 spoke about stock prices:

> As a fund manager, you don't need to make everything so precise, because the precision of the model or the precise prediction of future revenue cannot be definitely translated into positive stock prices. (Chinese 31)

---

* In the illustrative quotes numbers in parentheses refer to participants based on the sequence in which they were interviewed. Names have been removed for the purpose of confidentiality.

Similarly, although Chinese 5 repeatedly emphasised that market or sector trends are very important, he did not have a clearly defined set of indicators to assess them. He said he relied on "a mixture of many things" to gauge its direction. It seemed unlikely that there was a strict set of steps to follow during his investment process.

In contrast, the Western fund managers described a far more analytical and rule-based approach in their decision-making. Western 7 divided his investment process into five stages: screening, discussion, investigation, a full workup, and decision. During his screening process, he would carefully examine 18 factors, including liquidity, profitability, price-to-book ratio, debt-to-equity ratio and working capital. In the discussion stage, he would consider sectorial or macro information. In the investigation stage, visiting companies was an important method to find out further information. A full workup and decision may proceed at the same time.

In addition to their thorough and rigorous reasoning process, it appears that Western fund managers also tended to consistently follow a set of defined rules, even though those rules were sometimes rather strange or, in some instances, could lead to regret or losses. For example, Western 37 spoke about local rules he had generated, which appeared to have been successful:

> Over many years, I have generated a rule of thumb that there are certain people I will not deal with. Managers who have long fingernails, or a beard, or who have the top of their little finger cut off (he later explained that it meant the person might be a gangster) or whose spokeswomen are too beautiful. (Western 37)

In another example, Western 15 reported that, based on his investment experiences and philosophy, he had established a rule that whenever there was a problem related to the corporate governance standard of a company, he would sell its stocks immediately. He then dealt with a Chinese company which was reported to have a corporate governance problem, as "the founding family looted the company and hurt minority shareholders". Because this situation fit his rule, he sold the stocks immediately. However, the price of stocks then went up. He blamed the losses on the market, rather than his rule or his action of following the rule, but admitted that although following the rules did not always deliver the best result, he was glad that he had stuck to his process:

> I adhered to my basic strategy, so I am fundamentally glad about it. However, since the stock has gone up, I am also a bit frustrated. The market can be very strange sometimes. (Western 15)

As this shows, in contrast to Western fund managers, Chinese managers did not like to be constrained by existing rules, and their decision-making process was less likely to involve step-by-step application of procedures, thus is less analytical and more intuitive.

After the 2015 stock market crash

In contrast, according to the analysis based on our data collection after the stock crash (2017–2018), we have found that Chinese and Western fund managers were not significantly different in their attention to rules and precision during the decision-making process. Similarly, other empirical evidence (Luo et al. 2022) has also pointed out that Chinese fund managers have adjusted their investment behaviours in the wake of the social and regulatory changes post the 2015 stock market crash.

The data in our study is collected via a self-designed survey. The complete data set comprised 187 fund managers from two cultural groups: mainland China (N = 102) and the West including the UK, the US, and Western Europe (N = 85). The precise level of investment procedure was measured in three aspects in the questionnaire: (i) the number of stages in the investment process, (ii) the percentage of decisions that were made following the defined process, and (iii) five statements describing the importance of factors in the investment process, such as complex mathematical models. These factors are shown to be very important aspects of the preciseness of investment procedure during the earlier interview study, which are a very important dimension of analytical decision-making and, by definition, the opposite side of intuitive thinking (Lieberman 2007).

In contrast to the earlier interview study, Chinese investors after the 2015 stock market crash were not significantly different from Western investors in preciseness and rules adherence during their decision-making. And this was true when controlling for (i) personal demographic variables such as ethnic origin, age, gender, education, professional qualification, cross-cultural experiences, and investment tenure; and (ii) fund characteristics such as fund size, division size, frequency of performance evaluation, criteria of performance evaluation, and type of fund.

General discussion

Therefore, it seems that social and regulatory changes brought about by the market crash have put limits on Chinese fund managers' deployment of intuitive judgement. The conclusion that intuitive judgement is embedded in the social context resonates with the views expressed by Huff et al. (2006), who noted that strategic decision-makers require an abundance of tacit knowledge, intuitive judgement, and social competences, as well as a deep understanding of the local context. This view also strongly echoes that of many Chinese fund managers—for example, according to a senior Chinese fund manager we interviewed after the market crash, "2015 was a turning point for China's asset management industry". He stated that, "The market crash and subsequent regulatory tightening has transformed the Chinese mutual fund industry, and the investment procedure of many fund managers has really changed from 'art' to 'science', becoming more standardised and more structured".

Similarly, another study by Luo et al. (2022), which covers the same time period, found that Chinese managers who experienced a stock market crash were more value-oriented in their portfolios. Value investors typically buy and hold assets for a long time and have low portfolio turnover. Thus, it suggests that the bubble-crash experience has led to changes in investment behaviours. However, due to the quantitative nature of Luo et al. (2022)'s study, their data is static and retrospective, which does not allow for any investigations of the process of such dynamic changes in investment decision-making.

Admittedly, the finding that shocks can alter thinking is not something new. In household and corporate finance literature, there is mounting evidence that exposure to natural disasters or macro financial shocks deeply affects agents' belief formation and attitudes toward risk and thus investment style (Malmendier & Nagel 2011; Custódio & Metzger 2014; Cronqvist et al. 2015; Bernile et al. 2017; Dessaint & Matray 2017; Knüpfer et al. 2017; Schoar & Zuo 2017; Chen et al. 2021b). However, the current research has utilised the Western counterparts as a comparison point and has revealed the dynamic process of intuitive/analytical decision-making by the Chinese fund managers using both interviews and survey method. For example, although Western fund managers might not have to face a similar domestic regulatory clampdown as Chinese fund managers did during the same time period, Western fund managers should naturally be aware of the possibility of a spill-over effect from the crisis (Mensi et al. 2016).

Furthermore, because global financial markets are so connected, as the second largest capital markets in the world, Chinese capital markets should constitute a very important decision-making context for Western fund managers. Given the dramatic changes happening in Chinese capital markets, Western fund managers could have taken a more cautious approach, which would impede fast and intuitive decision-making, the same changes Chinese fund managers have adopted. However, since empirical evidence has pointed out the shift of Chinese fund managers in their analytical decision-making in contrast to Western fund managers before and after the 2015 stock crash, it may reflect Chinese fund managers' greater sensitivity to the decision-making context in contrast to Western fund managers, and thus their greater flexibility in using intuition in decision-making process.

Final thoughts

This chapter reviews influential frameworks of cultural psychology, with a particular focus on the differences between East and West in their cognitive thinking—that is, holistic and analytic thinking styles. By establishing theoretical linkage between holistic and intuitive thinking, it leads to the prediction about cross-cultural differences in using intuition during the decision-making process. Subsequently, such prediction was supported in the data collected by the author prior and post the dramatic changes of China's 2015 stock market crash.

The cultural differences discussed so far may have profound impacts on how Western (or Asian) investment managers can effectively utilise their intuitive decision-making. For example, in a multi-cultural investment team, different preferences in decision-making context may compound coaching or training for intuitive decision-making skills. For Chinese fund managers, in order to foster a greater extent to which an individual employs intuitive decision-making, it may be effective in creating a conducive decision-making context. In contrast, for Western fund managers, experience and intuitive self-efficacy, defined as a person's self-belief in their ability to make effective intuitive judgement calls (Hensman & Sadler-Smith 2011), may play a more important role in determining the use of intuition than contextual factors.

As a result, building on and interpolating from the results of our empirical study, it is possible to update the conceptual framework of intuitive decision-making in the financial industry proposed by Hensman and Sadler-Smith (2011) (Figure 11.1) from a cultural and cross cultural perspective (see Figures 11.2 and 11.3). According to their original conceptual framework (Figure 11.1), three

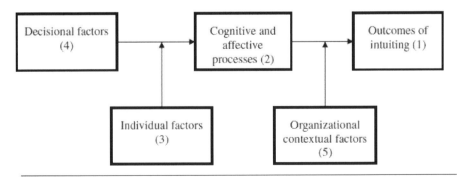

Figure 11.1   Conceptual framework of intuitive decision-making (*Source:* Hensman & Sadler-Smith 2011) *Note:* Figures in parentheses are arbitrary and refer only to the categorization scheme used in the content analysis.

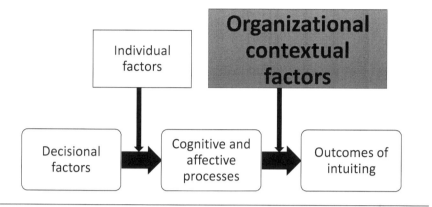

Figure 11.2   Conceptual framework of intuitive decision-making for Chinese

factors (decisional factors, individual factors, and organizational contextual factors) affect the use of intuition in decision-making. These factors were listed in an arbitrary order and thus did not convey any information regarding superiority among those factors. However, by adding a cultural dimension, the original model could be transformed into two sub-models for Chinese and Western decision-makers, respectively, based on the current research. For Chinese decision-makers, organizational contextual factors would be highlighted as more influential than individual factors, whereas individual factors would be highlighted as more influential than individual factors for Western decision-makers.

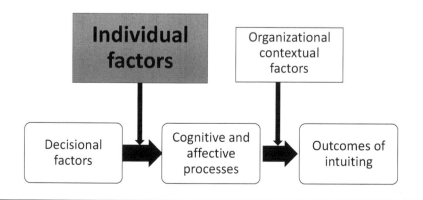

Figure 11.3   Conceptual framework of intuitive decision-making for Westerners

Some caveats

Before closing, it is important to make a few clarifications to prevent misinterpretation.

First, as discussed in the definition of culture, culture is as much an individual construct as it is a macro construct. Although we have discussed East and West differences, this chapter by no means suggests that all Westerners or Easterners think, feel, or act the same way. Most empirical studies, reviewed in this chapter or not, have pitched their analyses at the group level, meaning that results are representative of the group. For example, we expect an average American citizen to think analytically and an average Chinese citizen to think holistically, as past research has shown (e.g., Nisbett & Masuda 2003). These findings can sometimes invoke views of dichotomy that remove individual variability within a cultural group.

Such views are overly simplistic. Recognizing the variability within a cultural group, however, does not dilute the importance of studying differences around the world (Geertz 1973). In fact, numerous research programs have struck a delicate balance between the two (e.g., Leung & Cohen 2011; Schug, Yuki, & Maddux 2010). Executives, leaders, and supervisors are encouraged to go beyond the "one-size-fits-all" assumption in their managerial practices.

Second, the empirical evidence was mainly derived from two cultural groups, with study participants representing China and the West. Although this work of comparison is richly informative and important, the generalizability of these findings to other cultural groups may be limited. A potential direction for future research might be to explore a more diverse set of national cultures, as well as differences within regional boundaries.

Last but not least, stronger sensitivity to the context does not necessarily lead to superior returns. Empirical research has shown that the link between intuition and performance depends on the nature of the problem, the prior experiences of the decision-makers, and situational factors (Pretz 2011). Thus, paying more attention to context alone does not necessarily lead to higher returns.

References

Allinson, C. W., and Hayes, J. (2012). *The Cognitive Style Index: Technical Manual and User Guide.* UK: Pearson Education Ltd.

Bastick, T. (1982). *Intuition: How We Think and Act.* New York: Wiley.

Bernile, G., Bhagwat, V., and Rau, P. R. (2017). What doesn't kill you will only make you more risk-loving: Early-life disasters and CEO behavior. *The Journal of Finance,* 72(1): 167–206.

Chen, Y., Fan, Q., Yang, X., and Zolotoy, L. (2021). CEO early-life disaster experience and stock price crash risk. *Journal of Corporate Finance,* 68: 101928.

Choi, I., and Nisbett, R. E. (1998). Situational salience and cultural differences in the correspondence bias and actor-observer bias. *Personality and Social Psychology Bulletin,* 24(9): 949–960.

Choi, I., Koo, M., and Choi, J. A. (2007). Individual differences in analytic versus holistic thinking. *Personality and Social Psychology Bulletin,* 33(5): 691–705.

Cousins, S. D. (1989). Culture and self-perception in Japan and the United States. *Journal of Personality and Social Psychology,* 56(1): 124.

Cronqvist, H., Siegel, S., and Yu, F. (2015). Value versus growth investing: Why do different investors have different styles? *Journal of Financial Economics,* 117(2): 333–349.

Custódio, C., and Metzger, D. (2014). Financial expert CEOs: CEO's work experience and firm's financial policies. *Journal of Financial Economics,* 114(1): 125–154.

Dessaint, O., and Matray, A. (2017). Do managers overreact to salient risks? Evidence from hurricane strikes. *Journal of Financial Economics,* 126(1): 97–121.

Elbanna, S., and Fadol, Y. (2016). The role of context in intuitive decision-making. *Journal of Management & Organization,* 22(5): 642–661.

Geertz, C. (1973). Chapter 1/Thick description: Toward an interpretive theory of culture. *The Interpretation of Cultures: Selected Essays,* 3–30.

Hamilton, V. L., and Sanders, J. (1992). *Everyday Justice: Responsibility and the Individual in Japan and the United States.* Princeton, NJ: Yale University Press.

Hammond, K. R. (1996). *Human Judgment and Social Policy.* New York: Oxford University Press.

Hensman, A., and Sadler-Smith, E. (2011). Intuitive decision making in banking and finance. *European Management Journal,* 29(1): 51–66.

Hertz, E. (1998). *The Trading Crowd: An Ethnography of the Shanghai Stock Market.* Cambridge University Press.

Hofstede, G. (1980). Culture and organizations. *International Studies of Management & Organization,* 10(4): 15–41.

Huff, A., Tranfield, D., and van Aken, J. E. (2006). Management as a design science mindful of art and surprise: A conversation between Anne Huff, David Tranfield, and Joan Ernst van Aken. *Journal of Management Inquiry,* 15(4): 413–424.

Ji, L. J., Peng, K., and Nisbett, R. E. (2000). Culture, control, and perception of relationships in the environment. *Journal of Personality and Social Psychology,* 78(5): 943.

Jones, E. E., and Harris, V. A. (1967). The attribution of attitudes. *Journal of Experimental Social Psychology,* 3(1): 1–24.

Jung, C. G. (1971). Psychological types. In: H. Read, M. Fordham, G. Adler, and W. McGuire (Eds.), *Collected Works of C. G. Jung.* Vol. 6. Princeton, NJ: Princeton University Press.

Kagitcibasi, C., and Berry, J. W. (1989). Cross-cultural psychology: Current research and trends. *Annual Review of Psychology,* 40(1): 493–531.

Knüpfer, S., Rantapuska, E., and Sarvimäki, M. (2017). Formative experiences and portfolio choice: Evidence from the Finnish great depression. *The Journal of Finance,* 72(1): 133–166.

Lee, F., Hallahan, M., and Herzog, T. (1996). Explaining real-life events: How culture and domain shape attributions. *Personality and Social Psychology Bulletin,* 22(7): 732–741.

Leonard, N. H., Scholl, R. W., and Kowalski, K. B. (1999). Information processing style and decision making. *Journal of Organizational Behavior: The International Journal of Industrial, Occupational and Organizational Psychology and Behavior,* 20(3): 407–420.

Leung, A. K.-Y., and Cohen, D. (2011). Within- and between-culture variation: Individual differences and the cultural logics of honor, face, and dignity cultures. *Journal of Personality and Social Psychology,* 100(3): 507.

Lieberman, M. D. (2007). The X- and C-Systems: The neural basis of automatic and controlled social cognition. In: E. Harmon-Jones and P. Winkielman (Eds.), *Social Neuroscience: Integrating Biological and Psychological Explanations of Social Behavior,* 290–315. The Guilford Press.

Luo, D., Yao, Z., and Zhu, Y. (2022). Bubble-crash experience and investment styles of mutual fund managers. *Journal of Corporate Finance,* 76: 102262.

Malewska, K. (2021). Determinants for using intuition in top management decisions. *Organization Review,* 12(983): 2021.

Malmendier, U., and Nagel, S. (2011). Depression babies: Do macroeconomic experiences affect risk taking? *The Quarterly Journal of Economics,* 126(1): 373–416.

Martinsen, Ø., and Kaufmann, G. (1999). Cognitive style and creativity. *Encyclopedia of Creativity.* SR Pritzker.

Masuda, T., and Nisbett, R. E. (2001). Attending holistically versus analytically: Comparing the context sensitivity of Japanese and Americans. *Journal of Personality and Social Psychology,* 81(5): 922.

Mensi, W., Hammoudeh, S., Nguyen, D. K., and Kang, S. H. (2016). Global financial crisis and spillover effects among the US and BRICS stock markets. *International Review of Economics & Finance*, 42: 257–276.

Morris, M. W., and Peng, K. (1994). Culture and cause: American and Chinese attributions for social and physical events. *Journal of Personality and Social Psychology*, 67(6): 949.

Nisbett, R. (2004). *The Geography of Thought: How Asians and Westerners Think Differently and Why*. Simon and Schuster.

Nisbett, R. E., and Masuda, T. (2003). Culture and point of view. *Proceedings of the National Academy of Sciences*, 100(19): 11163–11170.

Nisbett, R. E., Peng, K., Choi, I., and Norenzayan, A. (2001). Culture and systems of thought: Holistic versus analytic cognition. *Psychological Review*, 108(2): 291.

Norenzayan, A., Smith, E. E., Kim, B. J., and Nisbett, R. E. (2002). Cultural preferences for formal versus intuitive reasoning. *Cognitive Science*, 26(5): 653–684.

Parikh, J., Lank, A., and Neubauer, F. (1994). *Intuition: The New Frontier of Management*. John Wiley & Sons.

Peng, K., and Nisbett, R. E. (1999). Culture, dialectics, and reasoning about contradiction. *American Psychologist*, 54(9): 741.

Pretz, J. E. (2011). Types of intuition: Inferential and holistic. In: M. Sinclair (Ed.), *Handbook of Intuition Research*. Cheltenham, UK: Edward Elgar Publishing.

Pretz, J. E., Brookings, J. B., Carlson, L. A., Humbert, T. K., Roy, M., Jones, M., and Memmert, D. (2014). Development and validation of a new measure of intuition: The types of intuition scale. *Journal of Behavioral Decision Making*, 27(5): 454–467.

Schoar, A., and Zuo, L. (2017). Shaped by booms and busts: How the economy impacts CEO careers and management styles. *The Review of Financial Studies*, 30(5): 1425–1456.

Schug, J., Yuki, M., and Maddux, W. (2010). Relational mobility explains between- and within-culture differences in self-disclosure to close friends. *Psychological Science*, 21(10): 1471–1478.

Schwartz, S. H. (1999). A theory of cultural values and some implications for work. *Applied Psychology*, 48(1): 23–47.

Shepherd, N. G., and Rudd, J. M. (2014). The influence of context on the strategic decision-making process: A review of the literature. *International Journal of Management Reviews*, 16(3): 340–364.

Sinclair, M., and Ashkanasy, N. M. (2005). Intuition: Myth or a decision-making tool? *Management Learning*, 36(3): 353–370.

Tylor, E. B. (1924). The development of culture. In: *Primitive Culture: Researches into the Development of Mythology, Philosophy, Religion, Language, Art, and Custom,* Vol. 1, 7th ed., 26–69. London: Murray. https://doi.org/10.1037/13484-002

Wu, H. (2022). Intuition in investment decision-making across cultures. *Journal of Behavioral Finance,* 23(1): 106–122.

Chapter 12

Intuition, Analysis and Sensemaking: How to Select Ideas for Innovation

Antti Sihvonen,[1] Alexandre Sukhov,[2,3] Johan Netz,[2,3] Lars E. Olsson,[2,4] and Peter R. Magnusson[2,3]

[1] Jyväskylä University School of Business and Economics, Finland

[2] CTF—Service Research Center, Karlstad University, Sweden

[3] Karlstad Business School, Karlstad University, Sweden

[4] Department of Social and Psychological Studies, Karlstad University, Sweden

The fuzzy front end of innovation

All innovations start with an idea. A simple way to describe ideas for new product and service innovations is that they consist of two parts: a problem and a solution. Viewing ideas in this way helps to define them, focus the innovation process on addressing specific challenges, identify relevant needs, assess the idea's potential value, and allow for more structured iterative improvements (Sukhov, Magnusson, & Netz 2019). Often, the problem emerges first, and subsequent activities focus on developing a solution to that problem (e.g., Sihvonen, Luoma, & Falk 2021).

However, sometimes finding a solution can be the starting point. The solution can refer to a technological opportunity or even an existing technology. In these cases, the subsequent activities are directed towards finding an application for the technology—that is, finding a problem that the new technology can address.

The early part of the innovation process is typically referred to as the *fuzzy front end*, or FFE for short. The FFE precedes the formal new product development (NPD) process and focuses on organizing the search for innovative ideas that can range from breakthrough innovations to subtle improvements of current products and services. Other names for this stage in the innovation process include the "discovery stage" or the "idea stage", among others. The word *fuzzy* was initially used as a result of the lack of clarity around what, how, and when activities take place in the early phases. However, recent research has uncovered several important processes and mechanisms at play, which has made the fuzziness somewhat less pronounced (Eling & Herstatt 2017).

The three main activities of the FFE are *generating*, *improving*, and *screening* ideas for innovations. The FFE is often described as experimental, chaotic, difficult to plan, and yielding unpredictable results, in contrast to the NPD process, which is structured, disciplined, and has clear goals (Koen et al. 2001). Therefore, it is essential for organizations to understand that the management of the two processes should be different.

There is a vast amount of research on how to manage the very first phase of the FFE, which involves generating ideas. Some studies have focused on in-house or expert ideation, while others have explored customer or user-generated ideas. In practice, using various online platforms to crowdsource ideas from customers or employees has become a highly popular method for generating new ideas for innovation. However, generating ideas is rarely a problem since companies often end up with (too) many different ideas for new products and services. This creates a need to reduce the sheer number of ideas by selecting the ones that demonstrate the highest potential and are suitable for further development and implementation.

Idea improvement is perhaps the least understood activity in the FFE. Idea improvement involves activities that help to further elaborate, develop, and refine the initial raw idea. The primary objective of this activity is to reduce decision uncertainty in the subsequent stages (Florén & Frishammar 2012). Typically, improvement focuses on enhancing the solution part of the idea, but the problem part is also often improved to make it easier to understand and better articulate how the solution can create value. While improvement is often viewed as an integral part of idea creation or even idea screening, it has recently gained more attention as a separate research area. Therefore, we can broadly define that all activities that focus on the purposeful development of ideas towards specific goals during the FFE fall under the umbrella of idea improvement.

The role of idea screening is to identify promising ideas and select the most qualified ones to proceed into the NPD process. However, it is also important to understand which ideas are not yet ready and require further improvement and which ones need to be discarded. Existing research has shown that identifying high-quality ideas can increase the chances of future success. Equally important is understanding which ideas should be avoided to prevent potential failures and avoid unnecessary expenditure of resources. Therefore, understanding the screening process, also referred to as *idea evaluation, idea judgment,* or *idea assessment,* is crucial for managers to make better decisions on idea quality and steer the innovation process effectively.

In the next section, we will take a closer look at how existing research has examined idea screening and the key activities that take place during the process of deciding whether an idea should be advanced towards becoming an innovation project.

Overview of the existing research on idea screening

Idea screening is a critical part of the FFE because it acts as a gate for deciding which ideas will be developed into new projects and which will not. This step can be challenging because evaluators must make decisions while facing high uncertainty about the ideas' potential future (Van de Ven 1986). To reduce this uncertainty and establish a trustworthy screening process, organizations often use a decision-making committee or review board. These committees consist of executives, senior management, or experts who possess knowledge of the organization's technological capabilities and an understanding of the implications that these ideas can have for users or the market. Using a group of people in idea screening also helps to distribute responsibility and account for individual preferences by favoring a collective vote with an opportunity to discuss potential differences of opinion.

When it comes to screening ideas, decision-making experts adopt different approaches to idea evaluation. Traditionally, the two main approaches are to either rely on reflective analytical thinking or follow a gut feeling by trusting intuition. These two approaches are commonly described on the basis of the dual-process theory. According to Evans (2003), this theory can be summarized as "two minds in one brain" (p. 458). Dual-process theorists have argued that humans rely on two underlying cognitive thinking styles during judgment and decision-making. These approaches are also widely referred to as System 1 and System 2. System 1 refers to the intuitive, unconscious system, while System 2 is the rational conscious thinking system.

Our own research has shown that, in addition to intuitive and analytical thinking styles, *sensemaking* also plays an important role in forming decisions to accept or reject ideas (Sukhov, Sihvonen, Olsson, & Magnusson 2018; Sukhov, Sihvonen, Netz, Magnusson, & Olsson 2021). Sensemaking comes into play when people are faced with decision-making situations that involve a high degree of ambiguity and discrepancy. In these kinds of situations, sensemaking is a process that helps decision-makers interpret what the idea means and envision what the ideas could become in the future.

Although all three approaches are relevant in decision-making situations such as idea screening, existing research often treats them in isolation from each other or sees them as alternative approaches to forming a decision. However, empirical studies suggest that intuition, analysis, and sensemaking are interrelated and act in a co-productive manner when making decisions in real life. Before discussing how these three approaches interrelate, it is important to develop a deeper understanding of each approach and to contextualize these approaches in idea screening. We will start by explaining the intuitive System 1 approach, followed by the analytical System 2 approach, and finally focus on sensemaking.

Intuitive idea screening

Intuitive idea screening can be described as an automatic, rapid, holistic, and associative judgmental response to an idea (Sukhov et al. 2021). Intuition is related to an individual's unconscious thinking (System 1) and does not rely on the individual's working memory (Evans 2008). This means that intuition is not based on rules or explicit criteria that the evaluator meticulously applies but rather on the decision-makers' own experience and expertise that subconsciously informs their rapid holistic impressions, resulting in a judgment on the quality of the idea (Dörfler & Ackermann 2012).

The intuitive approach has proven to be useful when screening ideas since it enables making quick holistic decisions that save time and effort in comparison to the slower analytical approach. However, it is of great importance that decision-making experts have relevant prior knowledge acquired over time from the specific field in which the decision or screening is made, since intuition is based on past experiences. If this is not the case, there is a risk that the decision-maker will generate undesirable outcomes without even realizing it. Nobel Prize winner Daniel Kahneman explains this with the argument that intuition is a form of heuristics that does not rely on conscious reasoning.

During intuitive decision-making, experts may favor the familiar over the new and may factor personal affection into the decision. Thus, in the context of screening ideas for innovative products, relying entirely on intuition may be risky since the task might require decision-makers to identify radical innovations and look outside of their own comfort zone. Furthermore, the risk may increase when the ideas have a high degree of ambiguity and discrepancy or have low communication quality since the decision-maker could easily misinterpret the intended meaning or simply react to their own lack of understanding of what the idea entails (Sukhov 2018).

Analytical idea screening

Analytical idea screening is a rational approach that helps decision-makers to approach ideas systematically. During analytical thinking, the decision-maker is conscious of their actions, and their thoughts are deliberative, slow, and effortful (System 2) (Evans 2008). To stimulate this approach in idea screening, explicit evaluation criteria, scoring models, or checklists can be utilized. In practice, the most common approach is to use a form of rational criteria assessment portrayed as a funnel, wherein different dimensions of an idea are assessed before a conclusive decision is made on keeping or rejecting it.

In the context of innovation management, some of the most common criteria used for evaluating ideas include originality, predicted value for the user, feasibility, and strategic fit of the idea. However, there is no best practice for what criteria to use or how to weight them effectively. Therefore, the criteria listed above are generic and can be adapted differently by different organizations based on their internal goals. Thus, before deciding on which criteria to use, it is worthwhile to consider what the use of certain criteria will give and what kind of ideas will be chosen for further development.

Although analytical decision-making is argued to increase the objectivity of idea evaluations, it is time-consuming and requires significant effort. This is because it requires people to consciously apply their domain knowledge and working memory to break down an idea into different components, identify important parameters, evaluate the idea according to criteria, and reach a decision. Therefore, the analytical decision-making approach in idea screening is more effective when the number of ideas is low and the potential benefits of these ideas outweigh the costs of conducting such a process.

The use of analytical thinking in idea screening can help decision-makers to be more thorough and methodical in their actions. However, relying solely on analytical thinking may cause decision-makers to overlook certain aspects of an idea that cannot be easily quantified or evaluated based on explicit criteria. Therefore, in combination with intuitive and sensemaking approaches, analytical thinking can be a valuable tool in the decision-making process.

Sensemaking in idea screening

Sensemaking is a process that enables people to develop plausible meanings and take actions based on that meaning making (Weick, Sutcliffe, & Obstfeld 2005). In idea screening, sensemaking can occur when a person struggles to understand an idea or how to proceed with screening, and it ends when that person arrives at a plausible interpretation that enables them to take further action. Sensemaking involves the "ongoing retrospective development of plausible images that rationalize what people are doing" (Weick et al. 2005). During this process, people can draw on past experiences, personal identity, and social context to extract and interpret cues from the environment.

Not only does sensemaking help people to interpret the meaning of ideas and understand how to proceed during idea screening, but it also has generative properties that enable individuals to generate new ideas or reframe existing ones in new ways (Sukhov et al. 2021). Therefore, screening can become a creative event when people engage with ideas and recognize their potential. Sensemaking can help people to understand what an idea currently is and what it could become, making it an important complement to the decision-making approaches discussed earlier.

While sensemaking can be beneficial in the screening process, it can also be time-consuming and lead to cognitive overload when dealing with a large number of ideas. In addition, sensemaking can be influenced by cognitive biases and individual differences, which may affect how an idea is interpreted. Therefore, it is important to strike a balance between sensemaking and other decision-making approaches to ensure that the screening process is efficient and effective.

The interplay of intuition, analysis, and sensemaking

In theoretical discussions, intuition, analysis, and sensemaking are often treated in isolation from each other or seen as alternative approaches for decision-making. In practice, we know that intuition, analysis, and sensemaking are interrelated (see Dziallas 2020; Hodgkinson & Sadler-Smith 2018; Magnusson, Netz, & Wästlund 2014; Sukhov et al. 2021). For instance, studies have found that intuition and analysis co-occur during complex decision-making situations (Hodgkinson & Sadler-Smith 2018) and that experts frequently rely on intuitive judgments, even during analytically structured idea evaluation situations (Dziallas 2020). Researchers have also shown that intuition can capture something that is beyond analytical idea screening criteria (Magnusson et al. 2014) and that rapid intuitive responses can act as cues for sensemaking, as sensemaking can help make these cues meaningful (Dörfler & Ackermann 2012; Stierand & Dörfler 2016). Some research has even suggested that an expert's sense of identity, such as their basic human values, can influence how they weight different analytical approaches (Sukhov et al. 2018).

In the context of idea screening for product and service innovations, ideas usually take the form of short narratives that communicate how a certain problem could be solved. Given the idea's relatively early stage of development and inherent uncertainty regarding its future, we can expect that there will be an interplay between intuition, analysis, and sensemaking, as shown in Figure 12.1. In the next section we will present *how* intuition, analysis, and sensemaking are combined during idea screening to reach decisions on idea quality.

What does idea screening look like in practice

To exemplify how intuition, analysis, and sensemaking are used during idea screening situations, we build upon our own research on expert idea evaluators (Sukhov et al. 2021). In this study, we analyzed the idea screening process of 14 experts from two technology companies. These experts reviewed between 7 and 33 ideas each and evaluated whether the ideas should be developed further or discarded, based on their short- and long-term potential for the organization.

Our analysis revealed seven key activities that experts use to make decisions on idea quality (see Table 12.1 on next page). Of these activities, intuition and analysis are relatively straightforward, while sensemaking can take on various

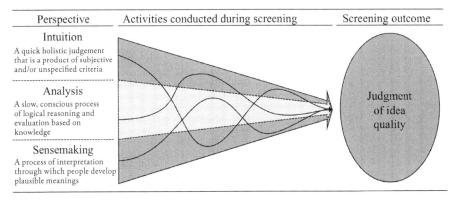

Figure 12.1 The interplay of intuition, analysis, and sensemaking during idea screening (*Source:* Illustration of the idea screening process by Sukhov, A., Sihvonen, A., Netz, J., Magnusson, P., Olsson, L.E., retrieved from https://doi.org/10.1111/jpim.12559. Used under Creative Commons Attribution License (CC BY 4.0) (https://creativecommons.org/licenses/by/4.0/)

Table 12.1 What Intuition, Analysis, and Sensemaking Look Like in Practice

Theorized activity	Activities in practice	Empirical examples
Intuition	Intuitive response	"Absolutely! Yes, absolutely, yes, yes, this is wonderful! This is fantastic!" "Wow. The basic idea is, I would say . . . the feeling I get, first feeling I get, is that the basic idea is pretty good."
Analysis	Analysis of the idea	"And I would say incremental quite high, because we have . . . yes, we have the means inside." "Yeah. I don't see it very hard to do. And we should do it, it's not that radical."
Sensemaking	Interpreting the meaning of an idea	"Well, the idea here for us, I feel like . . . it's like open innovation, and some of our adverts to companies are doing that."
	Drawing on past experiences	"I think we have . . . the market has the . . . We have the technology to do that, the customer would reward it because we are already selling anti-theft accessories, but not that sophisticated."
	Generative action	"And in order really to improve the supply chain upstream, to be more demand driven, instead of the guy saying, 'I need to make a maintenance'. And to be more proactive and so on."
	Interpreting the task	"Yes, if you think that this is good, it could be good, or maybe good in long term . . . Perhaps it is hard to get in . . . It could be perhaps lower in short term. If it is challenging, for example."
	Justification of actions	". . . this feels close to my heart!" "I think that everyone is conscious about this and it is our new boss, our new boss he has painfully made aware that many [employees] out there cannot sell customer support."

Adapted from Sukhov et al. 2021

forms. In practical decision-making situations, intuitive responses often manifest as rapid judgments that may be emotionally charged and may seem like sudden flashes of insight, such as, "No, this is . . . No, absolutely not." On the other hand, analysis is a more controlled process in which experts scrutinize ideas from both the company and customer perspectives to reach a decision. This can be done by recognizing aspects such as "anything that saves time and simplifies processes is good for us." These two modes of decision-making therefore represent opposite ends of the spectrum in terms of speed and the degree to which the evaluator can articulate why the decision was made.

In addition to these decision-making activities, experts also engage in a range of sensemaking activities. Sensemaking can relate to the ideas themselves, as well as to the task at hand. With regard to the ideas, expert evaluators often interpret their meaning to gain a better understanding of what is being evaluated. They also draw on their own past experiences to make the ideas more relatable and can generate new ideas when they encounter opportunities to improve the existing ones. Moreover, expert evaluators may interpret the task they are given to make sense of what they are supposed to do and may justify their actions by referring to their personal values or the broader social context. Overall, these sensemaking activities support the intuitive and analytical decision-making processes.

With a clear understanding of what intuition, analysis, and sensemaking entail in practice, we can now explore how these activities are used to identify good ideas. Generally, there are six primary methods for identifying high-quality ideas based on whether they are deemed good in the short term, long term, or both. Each of these prototypical approaches involves a unique combination of intuition, analysis, and sensemaking and follows a particular logic. Notably, none of these methods relies solely on a single activity, but rather, the perception of high quality results from the interplay of multiple activities. In Table 12.2 (on next page), we present these different strategies for identifying good ideas in greater detail.

Finding ideas that are good in the short term always involves both intuition and analysis, which are then combined with some form of sensemaking. The combination of these activities leads experts to recognize that the idea is either "easy to implement" or "implementable and can be improved" (Sukhov et al. 2021). In doing so, implementability drives the perception of high idea quality in the short term. For example, consider the following sequence of activities (activity type presented in italics within brackets):

> Yes, this is again a 3PP-question [*drawing on past experiences*]. This one I still think is worth to work with, so I'm putting it high on both [*intuitive response*]. We need to take a . . . some form of serious grip about the . . . invoices for 3PP. Currently there is no follow up, no central follow up, no real control of things

Table 12.2 Prototypical Ways to Identify Good Ideas

Decision-making outcome	Activities used to make a decision	Logic behind the decision
Good idea in the short term	Intuitive response Analysis of the idea Interpreting the meaning of an idea Drawing on past experiences	*Combination of intuition and analysis with idea-related sensemaking to recognize the idea as something that can easily be implemented.*
	Intuitive response Analysis of the idea Generative action	*Combination of intuition and analysis to find that the idea is implementable and identification of ways to develop it further.*
Good idea in the long term	Intuitive response Analysis of the idea Drawing on past experiences Interpreting the task	*The evaluator intuitively finds the idea good but, upon reflection and analysis, finds that there are challenges connected with it.*
	Analysis of the idea Drawing on past experiences Generative action Justification of actions	*The evaluator analyzes the idea as having potential but recognizes that it needs to be developed further to be viable.*
Good idea in both short and long term	Intuitive response Drawing on past experiences Justification of actions	*The evaluator intuitively finds the idea good since it reminds them of something that is known to have worked before.*
	Intuitive response Interpreting the meaning of an idea	*The evaluator intuitively finds the idea good since it can be associated with an important category.*

Adapted from Sukhov et al. (2021)

and events [*interpreting the meaning of an idea*]. So, if it becomes possible to shed light on who is coming in and have some people to take a look on this, perhaps there is a lot of money to be made here [*analysis of the idea*].

Here we see how a combination of activities led the expert to judge that the idea is easy to implement.

In contrast, ideas that are found to be good only in the long term are seen as challenging to implement but still hold great potential. In this way, ideas that are good in the long term are judged to be good because they are either "good but complex" or "promising but need improvement" (Sukhov et al. 2021). Consider the following decision-making situation in this light:

> This is completely right [*intuitive response*]. Solution documentation . . . We have worked with this for a hundred years [*drawing on past experiences*]. Why is it so difficult . . . [reads] Yes, this is good [pause] . . . This is good, but not that easy. Since a number of customers would absolutely not want [the company] to know how their network looks like [*analysis of the idea*]. Yes, if you think that this is good, it could be good, or maybe good in long term . . . Perhaps it is hard to get in . . . It could be perhaps lower in short term. If it is challenging, for example [*interpreting the task*].

Here we see how the expert primarily relies on intuition, analysis, and their past experiences to make a decision that the idea is good but complex.

Finally, ideas that are good on both the short and long term are good either because the idea "has worked before" or it "matches a category" (Sukhov et al. 2021). These decisions are heavily laden with intuition since intuition drives these decision-making situations, and sensemaking is used to translate these intuitive impulses into meaningful reasons. For instance:

> I will start with radical. For me it's clearly radical. [. . .] I think it's incremental also . . . [*intuitive response*]. Yes. If we only have for instance propose a complete solution just for trucks, truck plus trailer, I will decrease the score of incremental. [. . .] But here we have the fuel consumption, we have other vehicles, we have buses, construction equipment, etc. It is more the business of the group [*interpreting the meaning of an idea*].

Here, we can observe how the initial intuitive response becomes more sensible as the expert interprets the meaning behind the idea. This example exemplifies how overall good ideas are identified.

These different approaches to identifying good ideas show us that intuition is a central tool for finding high-quality ideas since most methods involve intuition. In addition, decision-making on ideas that are good for both the short and long term is primarily driven by intuition. However, intuition alone is not sufficient for complex decision-making situations and needs to be complemented with other activities.

There are also clear indicators when an idea is of poor quality. Just as we can identify patterns that lead to a judgment of high-quality ideas, we can identify several patterns that indicate low idea quality (see Table 12.3). Across these different patterns, we can see that the perception of low idea quality is primarily driven by challenges in understanding what an idea means or the fact that the ideas are too underdeveloped to be taken forward. Hence, before subjecting ideas

Table 12.3 Prototypical Ways to Identify Low-Quality Ideas

Decision-making outcome	Activities used to make a decision	Logic behind the decision
Bad idea in short term	Interpreting the meaning of an idea	*Interpreting the idea but realizing a lack of knowledge to fully understand it and assess its quality.*
	Intuitive response Analysis of the idea Interpreting the meaning of an idea	*Combining intuition and analysis with an interpretation of the idea's meaning to realize that the idea is not ready and needs further development.*
	Intuitive response Analysis of the idea Interpreting the meaning of an idea Drawing on past experiences Justification of actions	*Cycling between intuition, analysis, and different sensemaking activities to realize that the idea is highly complex and difficult to implement.*
	Intuitive response Analysis of the idea Drawing on past experiences Generative action Justification of actions	*Shifting between intuition, analysis, justification, and generative activities to conclude that the idea is not directly profitable.*
Bad idea in long term	Analysis of the idea Interpreting the meaning of an idea Generative action Justification of actions	*Searching for a plausible meaning, analyzing the idea, and generating other ideas, but realizing that what is being presented does not qualify as an idea.*
Bad idea in both short and long term	Justification of actions	*Dismissing the idea because it does not fit with beliefs or values.*
	Analysis of the idea Interpreting the meaning of an idea Drawing on past experiences Generative action	*The evaluator makes sense of the idea, analyses it, tries to develop it further, but realizes that the solution needs more elaboration.*

Adapted from Sukhov et al. (2021)

for evaluation, it's crucial to consider whether the ideas are well-articulated and well-developed enough to be taken further in the development process. Otherwise, one risks proposing ideas that never get through the finish line simply because they were underdeveloped to begin with.

Overall, this section has shown that idea screening is a complex task that consists of a combination of intuition, analysis, and sensemaking. Each mode of thinking plays a unique role in decision-making and can complement each other by addressing their respective shortcomings. Perhaps the best example of this complementarity is how sensemaking helps to give meaning to intuition, as it enables experts to delve deeper into why they made a certain decision based on their intuition. Next, we will present the key takeaways from this chapter.

Conclusion

This chapter has provided an overview of idea screening, which is a crucial activity in the fuzzy front end of innovation. As shown in this chapter, decision-making in the context of idea evaluation is a complex process where different modes of thinking are intertwined to reach a decision on whether an idea is good or bad. However, there is structure to this process. When experts evaluate ideas, they identify what the idea is good for. Hence, the experts who search for ideas with the highest potential are not simply recognizing the golden nuggets, they are also imbuing ideas with meaning and envisioning what these ideas could become. This means that in the eyes of experts, ideas are not simply good or bad, but rather they are good for particular reasons that experts can identify during screening.

By making the expert's reasoning and knowledge more explicit, in what we refer to as a *generative screening* approach, it is possible to develop ideas during screening, which could save time and resources in the following stages of the innovation process. This can also improve decision quality and transparency since experts can clearly motivate their decisions and make the logic behind the decision an additional source of valuable information.

Of course, this type of generative idea screening approach has limitations. It is time-consuming, effortful, and requires additional support for experts to engage with ideas and tools for capturing new insights that are created by the expert. Thus, this approach is not suitable for screening large quantities of ideas at a time. Instead, generative screening can be used by organizations when the intent is to explore new opportunities, use raw ideas as triggers for inspiration, and shift the role of decision-makers to co-creators and designers.

Table 12.4 summarizes the main strengths and weaknesses of the *intuitive, analytical, sensemaking*, and *generative* approaches to idea screening. Based on

Table 12.4 Strengths and Weaknesses of
Different Approaches to Idea Screening

Approach to screening	Strengths	Weaknesses
Intuition	Rapid way to make decisions on idea quality	Past experiences influence decisions which can lead to favoring familiar ideas.
Analysis	Systematic way to analyze ideas	Time consuming and requires significant effort.
	Criteria can be tailored to meet specific needs	
Sensemaking	Helps to reduce ambiguity and make ideas more understandable	Mainly feeds into decision making.
	Can help to find creative ways to improve ideas	
Generative	Provides additional information that helps to categorize ideas, stimulates creativity and idea improvement	Time consuming, effortful, and requires additional support for capturing new insights.
	Increases idea screening transparency	

this, each approach to decision-making can be used based on the organization's contextual requirements. When deciding on how to organize idea screening, it is worthwhile to consider whether screening is done just to weed out bad ideas or whether it could be used for selecting and developing ideas further before they are turned into innovation projects.

References

Dziallas, M. (2020). How to evaluate innovative ideas and concepts at the front-end: A front-end perspective of the automotive innovation process. *Journal of Business Research*, 110: 502–518. https://doi.org/10.1016/j.jbusres.2018.05.008

Dörfler, V., and Ackermann, F. (2012). Understanding intuition: The case for two forms of intuition. *Management Learning*, 43(5): 545–564. https://doi.org/10.1177/1350507611434686

Eling, K., and Herstatt, C. (2017). Managing the front end of innovation—Less fuzzy, yet still not fully understood. *Journal of Product Innovation Management*, 34(6): 864–874. https://doi.org/10.1111/jpim.12415

Evans, J. St. B. T. (2003). In two minds: Dual-process accounts of reasoning. *Trends in Cognitive Sciences*, 7(10): 454–459. https://doi.org/10.1016/j.tics.2003.08.012

Evans, J. St. B. T. (2008). Dual-processing accounts of reasoning, judgment, and social cognition. *Annual Review of Psychology,* 59: 255–78. https://doi.org/10.1146/annurev.psych. 59.103006.093629

Florén, H., and Frishammar, J. (2012). From preliminary ideas to corroborated product definitions: Managing the front end of new product development. *California Management Review*, 54(4): 20–43. https://doi.org/10.1525/cmr.2012.54.4.20

Hodgkinson, G. P., and Sadler-Smith, E. (2018). The dynamics of intuition and analysis in managerial and organizational decision making. *Academy of Management Perspectives*, 32(4): 473–492. https://doi.org/10.5465/amp.2016.0140

Koen, P., Ajamian, G., Burkart, R., Clamen, A., Davidson, J., . . . Wagner, K. (2001). Providing clarity and a common language to the "Fuzzy Front End". *Research-Technology Management,* 44(2): 46–55. https://doi.org/10.1080/08956308.2001.11671418

Magnusson, P. R., Netz, J., and Wästlund, E. (2014). Exploring holistic intuitive idea screening in the light of formal criteria. *Technovation,* 34(5-6): 315–326. https://doi.org/10.1016/j.technovation.2014.03.003

Sihvonen, A., Luoma, J., and Falk, T. (2021). How customer knowledge affects exploration: Generating, guiding, and gatekeeping. *Industrial Marketing Management*, 94: 90–105. https://doi.org/10.1016/j.indmarman2021.02.005

Stierand, M., and Dörfler, V. (2016). The role of intuition in the creative process of expert chefs. *Journal of Creative Behavior*, 50(3): 178–185. https://doi.org/10.1002/jocb.100

Sukhov, A. (2018). The role of perceived comprehension in idea evaluation. *Creativity and Innovation Management*, 27(2): 183–195. https://doi.org/10.1111/caim.12262

Sukhov, A., Magnusson, P. R., and Netz, J. (2019). What is an idea for innovation? In: *Service Innovation for Sustainable Business: Stimulating, Realizing and Capturing the Value from Service Innovation,* 29–47. https://doi.org/10.1142/9789813273382_0003

Sukhov, A., Sihvonen, A., Netz, J., Magnusson, P. R., and Olsson, L. E. (2021). How experts screen ideas: The complex interplay of intuition, analysis and sensemaking. *Journal of Product Innovation Management*, 38(2): 248–270. https://doi.org/10.1111/jpim.12559

Sukhov, A., Sihvonen, A., Olsson, L. E., and Magnusson, P. R. (2018). That makes sense to me: Openness to change and sensemaking in idea screening. *International Journal of Innovation Management*, 22(8): 1–15. https://doi .org/10.1142/S1363919618400091

Van de Ven, A. H. (1986). Central problems in the management of innovation. *Management Science*, 32(5): 590–607. https://doi.org/10.1287/mnsc.32.5.590

Weick, K. E., Sutcliffe, K. M., and Obstfeld, D. (2005). Organizing and the process of sensemaking. *Organization Science*, 16(4): 409–421. https://doi .org/10.1287/orsc.1050.0133

Chapter 13

A Literature Review of Intuition in Strategic Decision-Making

Ioannis C. Thanos

Athens University of Economics and Business, Greece

1. Introduction

The purpose of this chapter is to review the academic literature on the topic of intuition in strategic decision-making (SDM). A search was carried out in 19 well-known management and strategy journals using the following keywords: *intuition, intuitive synthesis,* and *intuitive decision-making.* To collect additional papers, other literature reviews on SDM were considered. This process resulted in 22 studies with unique samples, which formed the basis of the literature review. These 22 studies were then categorised based on the type of their research, their research design, their data collection methods and the geographic location of the sample.

The results suggested that literature on intuition in SDM is still in its early stages but has been growing over the years. Also, most of the papers have adopted quantitative methods (i.e., survey research) to collect data. Finally, most of the papers have attempted to explore whether intuition leads to positive decision and organization outcomes. The chapter concludes with suggestions for future research.

Barnand (1938), in his influential book titled *The Functions of the Executive*, was probably the first to suggest in the literature that managers might not rely on a comprehensive or logical process when making important (a.k.a. strategic) decisions and might embrace an alternative, non-logical process, called *intuition*.

The first descriptive studies on intuition appeared in the 1980s and 1990s. Both academics and practitioners, based on the preliminary findings of Barnand (1938) and Mintzberg et al. (1976), attempted to offer advice on what intuition is, how it is described by managers and if and how it is used in the real world by decision-makers. In 2000, a highly influential paper was published by Khatri and Ng in the journal *Human Relations*. The authors noted a paucity of empirical studies in academic journals on the role of intuition. They created a three-item scale to measure intuition, which assessed whether managers rely on past experience and use their gut feelings and judgment when confronted with strategic decisions. Since then, several studies have used Khatri and Ng's (2000) scale to assess intuition in SDM and have linked it to other important constructs.

This chapter aims to review the stream of research which has assessed the role of intuition in SDM. The literature review is organized as follows. The next section describes the process followed to create the list of studies on intuition in SDM to include in the review. Section 3 describes the major findings of the review. Section 4 provides five suggestions for future research.

2. Literature review methodology

Three steps were followed to review the literature on the role of intuition in SDM (see Thanos and Papadakis 2012a and 2012b for similar literature review approaches on other topics). The focus was only on papers which included empirical data measuring intuition in SDM. Conceptual (e.g., Tabesh and Vara 2020), theoretical (e.g., Dane and Pratt 2007) and/or papers examining operational and not strategic decisions were excluded from the analysis.

Second, only on papers published in well-known refereed management and strategic management academic journals were considered, because these have gone through blind reviews and multiple rounds of revisions, and their results tend to be robust and reliable. Specifically, the journals included in the search process were (presented in alphabetical order): *Academy of Management Annals, Academy of Management Journal, Administrative Science Quarterly, British Journal of Management, Decision Sciences, European Management Journal, European Management Review, Human Relations, Journal of Business Research, Journal of International Business Studies, Journal of Management, Journal of Management Studies, Journal of Product Innovation Management, Leadership Quarterly, Long Range Planning, Management Decision, Organization Science, Strategic Management*

Journal, and *Strategic Organization.* In this list of journals, a manual search was conducted using three keywords: *intuition, intuitive synthesis,* and *intuitive decision-making.* This process resulted in several papers which were screened one-by-one to ensure that only empirical papers focusing on intuition in SDM would be included in the literature review.

Third, to identify additional papers on intuition, a snowball approach was used from previous literature reviews on SDM (e.g., Elbanna et al. 2020; Elbanna 2006; Papadakis, Thanos and Barwise 2010; Shepherd and Rudd 2014), strategy process (e.g., Hutzschenreuter & Kleindienst 2006) and meta-analyses or conceptual papers (e.g., Forbes 2007; Miller 2008; Samba et al. 2021). The above-mentioned three-step process resulted in 25 papers. Three papers (Elbanna and Child 2007; Elbanna and Younis 2009; and Elbanna et al. 2015) were excluded from the literature review because their sample was used in two other studies included in the review. Thus, 22 studies with unique samples were included in our review.

Table 13.1 (on next pages) reports these studies and their basic characteristics (type of research, research design, data collection methods, location of sample, relationships explored).

3. Literature review findings

3.1 Research methods used in intuition papers

A few preliminary conclusions can be extracted from Table 13.1. For instance, with respect to the time period, the first empirical paper on intuition in SDM was published almost three decades ago, by Wally and Baum (1994). This paper, together with one more by Brouthers et al. (1998), are the only ones published prior to 2000. The remaining 20 out of 22 papers were published after 2000. This suggests that the stream of research on intuition in SDM is in its early stages but has grown after 2000 at a fast pace. This is due to two reasons: First, often-cited reviews of the SDM literature recognized intuition as an important, yet ignored, dimension (see Elbanna 2006; Papadakis et al. 2010). Second, Khatri and Ng's seminal work, which offered for the first time a scale for measuring intuition in the context of SDM.

Also, 5 out of 22 (approximately 23%) papers and 12 out of 22 (approximately 55%) have been published in the past five and ten years, respectively. Even more interesting, 4 out of 22 (approximately 18%) have been published in the last three years. This demonstrates that the role of intuition has recently received increasing empirical attention by researchers in the literature.

With respect to the type of research, quantitative and qualitative studies are indicated in Table 13.1. Most researchers, in their efforts to study intuition, have adopted *quantitative* research designs (19 out of 22 studies, approximately 86%).

Table 13.1 Empirical Research on Intuition in Strategic Decision-Making

Study	Type of Research	Research Design	Data collection Methods	Location of sample	Relationship explored
Al-Hashimi et al. (2022)	Quantitative	Cross-sectional	Survey	Qatar	Intuition-Outcomes
Baldacchino et al. (in press)	Quantitative	Cross-sectional	Protocol analyses Survey	Malta	Antecedents of Intuition and Intuition-Outcomes
Brouthers et al. (1998)	Quantitative	Cross-sectional	Survey	Netherlands	Antecedents of Intuition
Covin et al. (2001)	Quantitative	Cross-sectional	Survey	USA	Intuition-Outcomes
Calabretta et al. (2017)	Qualitative	Cross-sectional	Interviews	Netherlands	Intuition-Outcomes
Dayan and Elbanna (2011)	Quantitative	Cross-sectional	Survey	Turkey	Antecedents of Intuition and Intuition-Outcomes
Elbanna et al. (2013)	Quantitative	Cross-sectional	Survey	Egypt	Antecedents of Intuition and Intuition-Outcomes
Elbanna and Fadol (2016)	Quantitative	Cross-sectional	Survey Interviews	Egypt	Antecedents of Intuition
Elbanna (2015)	Quantitative	Cross-sectional	Survey	United Arab Emirates	Antecedents of Intuition and Intuition-Outcomes
Elbanna et al. (2015)	Quantitative	Cross-sectional	Survey	Tunisia	Intuition-Outcomes
Hensman and Sadler-Smith (2011)	Qualitative	Cross-sectional	Interviews	UK	Antecedents of Intuition
Kaufmann et al. (2014)	Quantitative	Cross-sectional	Survey	Germany	Intuition-Outcomes

Kaufmann et al. (2017)	Quantitative	Cross-sectional	Survey	Germany	Intuition-Outcomes
Khatri and Ng (2000)	Quantitative	Cross-sectional	Survey	USA	Intuition-Outcomes
Kolbe et al. (2020)	Qualitative	Longitudinal	Interviews Meeting Observations	Netherlands	Intuition-Outcomes
Ritchie, Kolodinsky, and Eastwood (2007)	Quantitative	Cross-sectional	Survey	USA	Intuition-Outcomes
Sadler-Smith (2004)	Quantitative	Cross-sectional	Survey	UK	Intuition-Outcomes
Shepherd et al. (2021)	Quantitative	Cross-sectional	Survey Interviews	UK	Intuition-Outcomes
Thanos (in press)	Quantitative	Cross-sectional	Survey Interviews	Greece	Intuition-Outcomes
Wally and Baum (1994)	Quantitative	Cross-sectional	Survey	USA	Intuition-Outcomes
Woiceshyn (2009)	Qualitative	Cross-sectional	Scenarios	Canada	Intuition-Outcomes
Zacca et al (2017)	Quantitative	Cross-sectional	Survey	United Arab Emirates	Antecedents of Intuition and Intuition-Outcomes

The first *qualitative* study on intuition in SDM (Woiceshyn 2009) appeared in the literature in 2009. This was followed by two more qualitative studies in 2017 and 2020 (Calabretta et al. 2017; Kobe et al. 2020). On a related note, only one study adopted a longitudinal research design and collected data in different points in time. The remaining 21 studies collected data based on a cross-sectional research design.

We also observe from Table 13.1 that prior studies used the following data collection methods: survey research, interviews with key participants in the SDM process, protocol analyses, and a combination of two methods (e.g., surveys and interviews or interviews and observations). It is interesting, though, that survey research has dominated the empirical literature on intuition to date, as it has been used in 18 out of 22 studies (approximately 81%).

Notable conclusions can be derived by reporting the location of the sample of prior empirical studies. Researchers studying intuition have collected data from various countries and continents. Specifically, 12 countries (Canada, Egypt, Germany, Greece, Malta, Netherlands, Qatar, Tunisia, Turkey, United Arab Emirates, United Kingdom, United States of America) are represented in Table 13.1. Three studies have been carried out in the USA and the UK, and two studies have been carried out in Egypt, Germany, Netherlands and the United Arab Emirates. The rest of the countries are represented only once in Table 13.1.

Prior literature reviews (e.g., Elbanna et al. 2020; Papadakis et al. 2010) concluded that with very few exceptions, most empirical studies on SDM have used data either from firms located in the USA or the UK. These literature reviews have welcomed research outside the US and the UK context. Table 13.1 suggests that researchers studying intuition have followed this suggestion. USA and UK institutions are represented only in 6 out of 22 studies (approximately 27%). Also, more than 50% of the studies (12 out of 22) have collected data from the European continent. Three more continents are represented in Table 13.1—the United States with four studies, and Africa and Asia with three studies each.

3.2 Empirical findings of Intuition papers

Three streams of research can be identified based on the relationships explored in these papers. Studies in the first stream of research explore whether the use of intuition when making strategic decisions is positively related to organization or decision outcomes (intuition-outcomes studies). Studies in the second stream of research explore how aspects of the broader context influence intuition in SDM. We can call this stream of research *antecedents of intuition*. Finally, studies in the third stream of research examine simultaneously how context shapes intuition and whether intuition leads to positive outcomes. We can call these studies *intuition-outcomes* and *antecedents-outcomes* studies.

3.2.1 Intuition-outcomes studies

The performance implications of intuition have been explored in 14 out of 22 studies. Studies in this stream of research have followed two distinct approaches with respect to the unit of analysis that they have employed. On the one hand, researchers have used the strategic decision as their unit of analysis (e.g., Kaufmann et al. 2014). In these studies, scholars evaluate the extent to which senior executives rely on their intuition. They then link intuition to strategic decision outcomes. On the other hand, researchers have used the organization as their unit of analysis (e.g., Kaufmann et al. 2017; Khatri and Ng 2000; Ritchie et al. 2007). In such studies, scholars evaluate the extent to which managers use intuition in strategy making. They then link intuition to overall firm performance or organizational outcomes. Both approaches of research are reviewed in the following paragraphs.

3.2.1.1 Intuition-decision outcomes studies

Studies using the strategic decision as their unit of analysis have evaluated the following outcomes: new product performance (Dayan and Elbanna 2011), strategic decision effectiveness (Elbanna et al. 2013), strategic decision success (Elbanna 2015; Elbanna et al. 2015), strategic decision pace (Wally and Baum 1994), successful decision implementation (Al-Hashimi et al. 2022), successful implementation of ideas (e.g., Kolbe et al. 2020), strategic decision quality (Shepherd et al. 2021; Thanos, in press). All these outcomes have been evaluated with perceptual data coming from survey research.

Wally and Baum (1994) developed an integrative framework which included industry effects, firm structural characteristics (e.g., centralization, formalization) and managerial characteristics (tolerance for risk, cognitive ability and intuitive style) to explore the determinants of SDM pace. With respect to intuition, the authors found that the greater its use, the faster an executive will evaluate an acquisition candidate.

Two other studies (Elbanna et al. 2015; Shepherd et al. 2021) report data about the relationship between intuition and strategic decision success/quality: In the first, Elbanna et al. (2015), by drawing on a sample of 131 Tunisian firms, conclude that these two constructs are negatively related. In the second, Shepherd et al. (2021) collected data from 117 firms in the UK and reached the exact opposite conclusion: intuition and strategic decision quality are positively related. Support for a positive relationship between intuition and decision outcomes can be traced in the German setting too (Kaufmann et al. 2014). In the more recent study on the intuition-decision outcomes linkage, Al-Hashimi et al. (2022) used data from 170 strategic decisions made by public firms in Qatar to examine whether intuition is related to implementation success. Their results suggest that there is an insignificant negative effect between these two constructs.

Finally, four studies (three qualitative and one quantitative) have explored how intuition can be combined with rationality to lead to successful decisions. Woiceshyn (2009), in the first qualitative study on intuition in SDM, argued that what distinguishes effective CEOs from ineffective ones is their ability to complement analysis with intuition. Based on a qualitative study of 19 CEOs from the oil industry, they explain that this can be achieved through two processes: *integration by essentials* and *spiraling*. Calabretta et al. (2017) drew on paradox theory and offered a framework which can be used to explain in detail how intuition and rationality interact and coexist in SDM. Their empirical focus was on innovation projects. More recently, again in the innovation context, Kolbe et al. (2020) drew on a high-tech company and investigated how intuition interacts with rationality and politics to shape the successful implementation of innovative ideas. All three qualitative studies called for more research on the topic with larger samples from different national settings.

Thanos (in press) followed the recommendations provided by Calabretta et al. (2017) and Kolbe (2020) and attempted to add new insights with respect to the effects of the joint interaction of intuition and rationality on strategic decision quality. Thanos (in press) collected data from 103 strategic decisions made by Greek services firms and hypothesized that decision-making teams which simultaneously used rationality and intuition make better decisions than those which use either one alone. Moderated regression analyses provided support to this argument. In an additional analysis, the author explored whether the relationship between rationality, intuition and decision quality is contingent upon the environmental dynamism. Results suggested that it is positive in dynamic rather than in stable environments.

3.2.1.2 Intuition-firm outcomes studies

Studies using the firm as their unit of analysis have evaluated as an outcome either a firm's financial performance (e.g., Covin et al. 2001), or a firm's financial and non-financial performance (e.g., Sadler-Smith 2004). Some studies use objective data to capture firm performance (e.g., Covin et al. 2001), whereas others use perceptual data coming from the survey research (e.g., Kaufmann et al. 2017).

With respect to firm performance, the first systematic effort to uncover the effects of intuition was a study conducted by Khatri and Ng (2000). The authors surveyed top managers from three industries—computer, banking and utility—and separated their samples into unstable and stable environments. Next, with the help of ANOVA and multiple regression analysis, they reached two major conclusions: First, managers use intuition when making strategic decisions. Second, there is a positive relationship between intuition and firm performance in unstable environments. This relationship turns negative in stable environments. The authors explained this finding based on the three characteristics of unstable environments: (1) need to gather great quantities of data and information to deal with instability, (2) constraints over the amount of data that can be gathered and (3) relative lack of reliable data to collect and analyze to make choices. To this we should add that in unstable settings decision-makers cannot always identify which data are relevant (Forbes 2007). Hence, in such environments analysis might not be helpful, while intuition might be beneficial (Khatri and Ng 2000).

Sadler-Smith (2004) examined cognitive style (analytical, intuitive) and performance in 141 British small and medium enterprises (SMEs). His results indicated that intuitive decision style is positive related to firm financial and non-financial performance. Also, this relationship was not contingent upon environmental dynamism. In other words, intuitive decision-making style leads to positive outcomes in both dynamic and stable settings. This finding casts doubts on the results of Khatri and Ng (2000).

Three years later, Ritchie et al. (2007) extended these findings in a study of non-profit organizations. The authors surveyed 144 CEOs of such organizations and examined the association between intuitive decision style and six measures of performance. After controlling for the effects of size, munificence, tenure and education level, the authors concluded that intuitive decision style is positively related to three measures of performance (i.e., revenue/expenses, contribution/expenses, public support/expenses).

3.2.2 Antecedents-outcomes studies

Studies in this stream of research explore how aspects of the broader context influence the use of intuition. According to Elbanna et al. (2020) and Papadakis et al. (2010), the broader context refers to the characteristics of the external environment, the characteristics of the organization, the strategic decision-specific characteristics and the demographic or psychological characteristics of the top management team.

Only 3 out of 22 studies have investigated the antecedents of intuition. In one of the earliest studies on the topic, Brouthers et al. (1998) collected data from 233 SMEs located around Amsterdam and made a substantial contribution to the field of SDM. Their descriptive results suggested that SME managers cannot afford to use rational approaches when making decisions and tend to rely mostly on their intuition. Hensman and Sadler-Smith (2011) restricted their sample to the banking sector in the UK, adopted a qualitative research design, interviewed 15 senior executives and examined how aspects of the context might influence the use of intuition. Their results are rather interesting. They concluded that the use of intuition is influenced by multiple layers of context related to individual factors (confidence, experience), decisional factors (uncertainty, time) and organizational factors (culture, accountability, hierarchy).

More recently, Elbanna and Fadol (2016) conducted a multi-method study which combined interviews and questionnaires referring to 117 strategic decisions made by Egyptian manufacturing firms. Their study suggested that firm characteristics (e.g., size, past performance) and the external environment (e.g., environmental uncertainty, environmental hostility) influence more the use of intuition than the characteristics of the strategic decisions (e.g., decision uncertainty, importance, decision motive). Collectively, the findings of the three mentioned studies indicate that intuition is influenced by multiple layers of context.

3.2.3 Intuition-outcomes and antecedents-outcomes

Five out 22 studies have adopted integrative frameworks and have explored simultaneously the antecedents and consequences of intuition in SDM. These papers are fairly recent in the literature, as the first one exploring such relationships was published in 2011 by Dayan and Elbanna. The authors based their study on a sample of 155 new product development projects in Turkey, found that team (team member experience, transactive memory systems, team empowerment) and the nature of the decision (i.e., decision importance, decision motive) influence the use of intuition. At the same time, intuition is positively related to product performance. The authors further suggested that the effects of intuition on outcomes does not differ between turbulent and non-turbulent environments.

Two years later, Elbanna et al. (2013) collected data from 169 strategic decisions and found several interesting results. Intuition is positively related to decision uncertainty and negatively to firm size, and it is not related to decision motive and overall firm performance. Also, intuition leads to strategic decision disturbance. This relationship becomes stronger in hostile environments. Similar results were published in a subsequent study by Elbanna (2015) which used data from 450 decision-making teams located in the United Arab Emirates. Two aspects of the external environment (competition uncertainty and complexity) increase the use of intuition, which in turn positively influences reflexivity.

In a similar vein with the results of the three studies by Elbanna and colleagues, Zacca et al. (2017) offered empirical support to the argument that intuition is shaped by multiple contextual variables and negatively influences the performance of SMEs in the United Arab Emirates. Finally, Baldacchino et al. (in press) concluded that entrepreneurial experience influences intuition, which in turn shapes new venture ideation.

4. Conclusions and suggestions for future researchers

This literature review noted substantial progress in the area of intuition in SDM over the past three decades. Published papers included in this chapter have offered several interesting insights and contributions. The literature review also identified a few weaknesses and limitations which need to be addressed by future scholars. Five priorities for future research are noted below.

First, unlike research in rationality and politics in SDM, the literature on intuition is not dominated by US or UK studies. We have data about intuition from 12 countries, which has enhanced to some extent our understanding about the effects of national culture on intuition in SDM. However, few if any studies have been conducted in some of the largest economies (in terms of GDP): China, Japan, India, Italy, etc. Future studies would enhance our knowledge by bringing in data from such countries.

Second, except for very few studies (e.g., Brouthers et al. 1998; Hensman and Sadler-Smith 2011; Thanos, in press), all the others have focused on manufacturing firms. This finding echoes conclusions from prior SDM literature reviews (e.g., Papadakis et al. 2010). Services firms are very important in the modern world, and the processes through which they make strategic decisions should be studied further.

Third, as stressed in the findings section of this chapter, 21 out of 22 studies have used a cross-sectional research design. In other words, they have collected data about their dependent and independent variables at one point in time. This represents a notable limitation of the field, confirms the results of prior SDM literature reviews (e.g., Elbanna 2006) and suggests that prior research cannot make any causal inferences among dependent and independent variables. One way to address this limitation of previous studies is to use a longitudinal research design. The latter would allow researchers to establish causal connections between intuition and outcomes.

Fourth, most studies on intuition are quantitative in nature. This is not to suggest that they have not offered us important insights and interesting findings. However, we need more qualitative studies in the future to explore how intuition is related to other SDM process characteristics and outcomes.

Fifth, the literature review highlighted that past studies have published contradictory results regarding the effects of intuition on performance. Some studies suggest that the use of intuition results in successful decisions, while some others find the opposite. Inconclusive findings have also been published regarding the impact of intuition on outcomes in dynamic settings. One way to resolve this would be to conduct a quantitative synthesis (meta-analysis) of prior empirical studies. Another way would include conducting more studies in other national and industry contexts.

References

Al-Hashimi, K., Weerakkody, V., Elbanna, S., and Schwarz, G. (2022). Strategic decision-making and implementation in public organizations in the Gulf Cooperation Council: The role of procedural rationality. *Public Administration Review*, 82(5): 905–919.

Barnand, C. I. (1938). *The Functions of the Executive.* Cambridge, MA: Harvard University Press.

Brouthers, K. D., Andriessen, F., and Nicolaes, I. (1998). Driving blind: Strategic decision making in small companies. *Long Range Planning*, 31(1): 130–138.

Calabretta, G., Gemser, G., and Wijnberg, N. M. (2017). The interplay between intuition and rationality in strategic decision making: A paradox perspective. *Organization Studies,* 38(3–4): 365–401.

Covin, J. G., Slevin, D. P., and Heeley, M. B. (2001). Strategic decision making in an intuitive vs. technocratic mode: Structural and environmental considerations. *Journal of Business Research,* 52(1): 51–67.

Dane, E., and Pratt, M. G. (2007). Exploring intuition and its role in managerial decision making. *Academy of Management Review,* 32(1): 33–54.

Dayan, M., and Elbanna, S. (2011). Antecedents of team intuition and its impact on the success of new product development projects. *Journal of Product Innovation Management,* 28(s1): 159–174.

Elbanna, S. (2006). Strategic decision-making: Process perspectives. *International Journal of Management Reviews,* 8(1): 1–20.

Elbanna, S. (2015). Intuition in project management and missing links: Analyzing the predicating effects of environment and the mediating role of reflexivity. *International Journal of Project Management*, 33: 1236–1248.

Elbanna, S, and Child, J. (2007a). Influences on strategic decision effectiveness: Development and test of an integrative model. *Strategic Management Journal,* 28(4): 431–453.

Elbanna, S., Child, J., and Dayan, M. (2013). A model of antecedents and consequences of intuition in strategic decision-making: Evidence from Egypt. *Long Range Planning,* 46(1–2): 149–176.

Elbanna, S., Di Benedetto, C. A., and Gherib, J. (2015). Do environment and intuition matter in the relationship between decision politics and success? *Journal of Management and Organization,* 21(1): 60–81.

Elbanna, S., and Fadol, Y. (2016). The role of context in intuitive decision-making. *Journal of Management & Organization,* 22(5): 642–661.

Elbanna, S., and Naguib, R. (2009). How much does performance matter in strategic decision making? *International Journal of Productivity and Performance Management*, 58(2): 437–459.

Elbanna, S., Thanos, I. C., and Jansen, R. J. (2020). A literature review of the strategic decision-making context: A synthesis of previous mixed findings and an agenda for the way forward. *M@n@gement,* 23(2): 42–60.

Forbes, D. P. (2007). Reconsidering the strategic implications of decision comprehensiveness. *Academy of Management Review,* 32(2): 361–376.

Hensman, A., and Sadler-Smith, E. (2011). Intuitive decision making in banking and finance. *European Management Journal,* 29(1): 51–66.

Hutzschenreuter, T., and Kleindienst, I. (2006). Strategy-process research: What have we learned and what is still to be explored. *Journal of Management,* 32(5): 673–720.

Kaufmann, L., Meschnig, G., and Reimann, F. (2014). Rational and intuitive decision-making in sourcing teams: Effects on decision outcomes. *Journal of Purchasing and Supply Management,* 20(2): 104–112.

Kaufmann, L., Wagner, C., and Carter, C. R. (2017). Individual modes and patterns of rational and intuitive decision-making by purchasing managers. *Journal of Purchasing and Supply Management,* 23(2): 82–93.

Khatri, N., and Ng, H. (2000). The role of intuition in strategic decision making. *Human Relations,* 53(1): 57–86.

Kolbe, L. M., Bossink, B., and De Man, A. P. (2020). Contingent use of rational, intuitive and political decision-making in R&D. *Management Decision,* 58(6): 997–1020.

Miller, C. C. (2008). Decisional comprehensiveness and firm performance: Towards a more complete understanding. *Journal of Behavioral Decision Making,* 21(5): 598–620.

Mintzberg, H., Raisinghani, D., and Theoret, A. (1976). The structure of 'unstructured' decision processes. *Administrative Science Quarterly,* 21(2): 246–275.

Papadakis, V. M., Thanos, I. C, and Barwise, P. (2010). Research on strategic decisions: Taking stock and looking ahead. In: P. Nutt and D. Wilson (Eds.), *Handbook of Decision Making,* 31–70. John Wiley & Sons, Ltd.

Ritchie, W. J., Kolodinsky, R. W., and Eastwood, K. (2007). Does executive intuition matter? An empirical analysis of its relationship with nonprofit organization financial performance. *Nonprofit and Voluntary Sector Quarterly,* 36(1): 140–155.

Sadler-Smith, E. (2004). Cognitive style and the management of small and medium-sized enterprises. *Organization Studies,* 25(2): 155–181.

Sadler-Smith, E., and Shefy, E. (2007). Developing intuitive awareness in management education. *Academy of Management Learning & Education,* 6(2): 186–205.

Samba, C., Tabesh, P., Thanos, I. C., and Papadakis, V. M. (2021). Method in the madness? A meta-analysis on the strategic implications of decision comprehensiveness. *Strategic Organization,* 19(3): 414–440.

Samba, C., Williams, D. W., and Fuller, R. M. (2022). The forms and use of intuition in top management teams. *The Leadership Quarterly,* 33(3): 101349.

Shepherd, N. G., and Rudd, J. M. (2014). The influence of context on the strategic decision-making process: A review of the literature. *International Journal of Management Reviews,* 16(3): 340–364.

Shepherd, N. G., Hodgkinson, G. P., Mooi, E. A., Elbanna, S., and Rudd, J. M. (2020). Political behavior does not (always) undermine strategic decision making: Theory and evidence. *Long Range Planning,* 53(5): 101943.

Shepherd, N. G., Mooi, E. A., Elbanna, S., and Rudd, J. M. (2021). Deciding fast: Examining the relationship between strategic decision speed and decision quality across multiple environmental contexts. *European Management Review,* 18(2): 119–140.

Tabesh, P., and Vera, D. M. (2020). Top managers' improvisational decision-making in crisis: A paradox perspective. *Management Decision,* 58(10): 2235–2256.

Thanos, I. C., and Papadakis, V. (2012a). The use of accounting-based measures in measuring M&A performance: A review of five decades of research. In: *Advances in Mergers and Acquisitions,* Vol. 10: 103–120.

Thanos, I. C., and Papadakis, V. (2012b). Unbundling acquisition performance: How do they perform and how can this be measured? In: D. Faulkner, S. Teerikangas, and R. J. Joseph (Eds.), *Handbook of Mergers and Acquisitions.* Oxford University Press. ISBN 9780199601462.

Thanos, I. C. (in press). The complementary effects of rationality and intuition on strategic decision quality. *European Management Journal.* https://doi.org/10.1016/j.emj.2022.03.003

Wally, S., and Baum, J. R. (1994). Personal and structural determinants of the pace of strategic decision making. *Academy of Management Journal,* 37(4): 932–956.

Woiceshyn, J. (2009). Lessons from "Good Minds": How CEOs use intuition, analysis and guiding principles to make strategic decisions. *Long Range Planning,* 42(3): 298–319.

Zacca, R., Dayan, M., and Elbanna, S. (2017). The influence of conflict and intuition on explorative new products and performance in SMEs. *Journal of Small Business and Enterprise Development,* 24(4): 950–970.

Index